EVOLUTION AND IMAGINAT
CHILDREN'S LITERA...

Evolutionary theory sparked numerous speculations about human development, and one of the most ardently embraced was the idea that children are animals recapitulating the ascent of the species. After Darwin's *Origin of Species*, scientific, pedagogical, and literary works featuring beastly babes and wild children interrogated how our ancestors evolved and what children must do in order to repeat this course to humanity. Exploring fictions by Rudyard Kipling, Lewis Carroll, Frances Hodgson Burnett, Charles Kingsley, and Margaret Gatty, Jessica Straley argues that Victorian children's literature not only adopted this new taxonomy of the animal child, but also suggested ways to complete the child's evolution. In the midst of debates about elementary education and the rising dominance of the sciences, children's authors plotted miniaturized evolutions for their protagonists and readers and, more pointedly, proposed that the decisive evolutionary leap for both our ancestors and ourselves is the advent of the literary imagination.

JESSICA STRALEY is Assistant Professor of English at the University of Utah. She has published articles on evolutionary theory, vivisection, and Victorian literature in *Victorian Studies* and *Nineteenth-Century Literature* and has contributed a chapter to the forthcoming collection *Drawing on the Victorians: The Palimpsest of Victorian and Neo-Victorian Graphic Texts*, edited by Anna Maria Jones and Rebecca N. Mitchell.

CAMBRIDGE STUDIES IN NINETEENTH-CENTURY
LITERATURE AND CULTURE

GENERAL EDITOR
Gillian Beer, *University of Cambridge*

Editorial board
Isobel Armstrong, *Birkbeck, University of London*
Kate Flint, *University of Southern California*
Catherine Gallagher, *University of California, Berkeley*
D. A. Miller, *University of California, Berkeley*
J. Hillis Miller, *University of California, Irvine*
Daniel Pick, *Birkbeck, University of London*
Mary Poovey, *New York University*
Sally Shuttleworth, *University of Oxford*
Herbert Tucker, *University of Virginia*

Nineteenth-century British literature and culture have been rich fields for interdisciplinary studies. Since the turn of the twentieth century, scholars and critics have tracked the intersections and tensions between Victorian literature and the visual arts, politics, social organization, economic life, technical innovations, and scientific thought – in short, culture in its broadest sense. In recent years, theoretical challenges and historiographical shifts have unsettled the assumptions of previous scholarly synthesis and called into question the terms of older debates. Whereas the tendency in much past literary critical interpretation was to use the metaphor of culture as 'background', feminist, Foucauldian, and other analyses have employed more dynamic models that raise questions of power and of circulation. Such developments have reanimated the field. This series aims to accommodate and promote the most interesting work being undertaken on the frontiers of the field of nineteenth-century literary studies: work that intersects fruitfully with other fields of study such as history, literary theory, or the history of science. Comparative, as well as interdisciplinary, approaches are welcome.

A complete list of titles published will be found at the end of the book.

EVOLUTION AND IMAGINATION IN VICTORIAN CHILDREN'S LITERATURE

JESSICA STRALEY

CAMBRIDGE
UNIVERSITY PRESS

CAMBRIDGE
UNIVERSITY PRESS

University Printing House, Cambridge CB2 8BS, United Kingdom

One Liberty Plaza, 20th Floor, New York, NY 10006, USA

477 Williamstown Road, Port Melbourne, VIC 3207, Australia

314-321, 3rd Floor, Plot 3, Splendor Forum, Jasola District Centre, New Delhi - 110025, India

79 Anson Road, #06-04/06, Singapore 079906

Cambridge University Press is part of the University of Cambridge.

It furthers the University's mission by disseminating knowledge in the pursuit of education, learning and research at the highest international levels of excellence.

www.cambridge.org
Information on this title: www.cambridge.org/9781107566811

© Jessica Straley 2016

This publication is in copyright. Subject to statutory exception and to the provisions of relevant collective licensing agreements, no reproduction of any part may take place without the written permission of Cambridge University Press.

First published 2016
First paperback edition 2018

A catalogue record for this publication is available from the British Library

Library of Congress Cataloging in Publication data
Straley, Jessica L., author.
Evolution and imagination in Victorian children's literature / Jessica Straley.
Cambridge, England : Cambridge University Press, 2016. | Series: Cambridge studies in nineteenth-century literature and culture ; 103 | Includes bibliographical references and index.
LCCN 2015041411 | ISBN 9781107127524 (hardback)
LCSH: Children's literature, English – History and criticism. | Evolution (Biology) in literature. | Imagination in literature. | BISAC: LITERARY CRITICISM / European / English, Irish, Scottish, Welsh.
LCC PR990 .S77 2016 | DDC 820.9/9282–dc23
LC record available at
http://lccn.loc.gov/2015041411

ISBN 978-1-107-12752-4 Hardback
ISBN 978-1-107-56681-1 Paperback

Cambridge University Press has no responsibility for the persistence or accuracy of URLs for external or third-party internet websites referred to in this publication, and does not guarantee that any content on such websites is, or will remain, accurate or appropriate.

For Richard,
Elliott, and Julian

Contents

Figures

Acknowledgements

This project began as a dissertation at Stanford University and matured into a book at the University of Utah. I am indebted to my reading committee in Stanford's English Department, especially to Franco Moretti for his wisdom, generosity, and enthusiasm. My other committee members and teachers at Stanford, Robert Polhemus, Seth Lerer, and Brett Bourbon, taught me to ask the right questions and to trust my instincts. My dissertation and the early stages of this book received support from Stanford's English Department, the Stanford Humanities Center, the Theodore H. and Frances K. Geballe Dissertation Fellowship, a Graduate Research Opportunities Fellowship for archival work in the British Library, and a Short-Term Fellowship at the Newberry Library in Chicago.

At the University of Utah, I have found unparalleled encouragement and invaluable readers. I would like to thank, in particular, Matthew Basso, Scott Black, Nadja Durbach, Andrew Franta, Lela Graybill, Howard Horwitz, Anne Jamison, Stacey Margolis, Ella Myers, Joy Pierce, Matthew Potolsky, Paisley Rekdal, Angela Smith, Kathryn Stockton, and Barry Weller. The completion of this book was made possible by the University of Utah's English Department and the University Research Council, which generously granted me a Faculty Fellowship Award at the most crucial time in this book's development. My Victorianist colleagues at other institutions, especially Marah Gubar, Marty Gould, Tamara Ketabgian, Rebecca Mitchell, Monique Morgan, and Virginia Zimmerman, have been unflagging sounding boards and honest critics throughout this process. Cannon Schmitt offered me generous and detailed notes on the first half of the manuscript and opened up new avenues of thought for the second half. Boundless thanks goes to Criscillia Benford, who read innumerable pages of multiple versions of this project, from dissertation to book, and always provided the perfect combination of advice, consolation, and friendship.

An earlier, shorter version of the second chapter appeared as "Of Beasts and Boys: Kingsley, Spencer, and the Theory of Recapitulation" in *Victorian Studies* 49.4 (2007); I appreciate the confidence in the project and the advice offered by Andrew Miller, Ivan Kreilkamp, and *VS* reviewers. I am deeply grateful to my editor at Cambridge University Press, Linda Bree, for navigating the book's course to publication, to Gillian Beer for supporting the project, and to anonymous reviewers, whose thoughtful critiques gave the manuscript the final pushes it needed. Luise Poulton, Alison Conner, and Matthew Brunsvik, at the Marriott Library, University of Utah, helped with some finishing touches. A special acknowledgment goes to Ethan Hollander for finding the perfect cover image for this book.

I cannot thank my parents, Tina H. Straley and William Straley, enough for their tireless love and support. I am especially grateful to my mother not only for her faith in me but also for incalculable hours of unpaid childcare while I finished this book. My extended and figurative family, Jolan and George Preiss, Meg Straley, Patricia Roylance, and Karen Gross, have encouraged me and boosted my spirits along the way. And finally, I would like to thank Richard Preiss, whose insight, humor, reassurance, and willingness to hear me talk about this project (even when talking about it was the last thing I wanted to do) made writing this book possible, and with whom I now share the privilege of experiencing the evolutions and imaginations of our two wonderful sons.

Introduction
How the child lost its tail

"Come away, children," said the otter in disgust, "it is not worth eating, after all. It is only a nasty eft, which nothing eats, not even those vulgar pike in the pond."

"I am not an eft!" said Tom; "Efts have tails."

"You are an eft," said the otter, very positively; "I see your two hands quite plain, and I know you have a tail."

"I tell you I have not," said Tom. "Look here!" and he turned his pretty little self quite round; and, sure enough, he had no more tail than you.[1]

Only three years after Charles Darwin's *On the Origin of Species* (1859) brought the theory of evolution by natural selection to the British reading public, Charles Kingsley converted it into a child's tale. In *The Water-Babies: A Fairy Tale for a Land-Baby* (1863), an orphaned chimney sweep named Tom falls into a river and is suddenly metamorphosed into an newtlike "water-baby." From this new animalized starting point, he must re-evolve back into a human boy, but just how bestial Tom's new body is remains ambiguous. The narrator tells us that Tom is now "3.87902 inches long, and having round the parotid region of his fauces a set of external gills (I hope you understand all the big words) just like those of a sucking eft."[2] Though Tom has the anatomical features of an eft and is not sure what other species he might be, he draws the line at the otter's assertion that he has a tail. Kingsley's narrator concurs, saying, "sure enough, he had no more tail than you."[3] Rather than resolve the issue, however, this phrasing only transforms the question about whether or not Tom has a tail into an inquiry about whether or not the implied child reader has one. Evolutionary theory provided no clear answer. Lord Monboddo, an eighteenth-century Scottish judge and philosopher, was famously convinced that all humans are born with tails and that midwives, doctors, and nurses conspiratorily clip them off after birth.[4] Less dramatically, Darwin confirmed in *The Descent of Man, and Selection in*

Figure 1 From Charles Kingsley, *The Water-Babies*, 1863, illustrated by W. Heath
Robinson (Boston, MA and New York: Houghton Mifflin, 1915), Title page.

Relation to Sex (1871) that the human coccyx bone, "though functionless as
a tail, plainly represents this part in other vertebrate animals."[5] Kingsley's
illustrators came to no consensus either. In a 1915 edition of *The Water-
Babies*, W. Heath Robinson offers both possibilities: on the title page, an
anatomically human Tom sits astride a tailed fish [Figure 1], but following
the table of contents, he is pictured as a baby merman with a back fin,
webbed hands, and a tail [Figure 2].[6] *The Water-Babies*, thus, foregrounds
the bizarre but intensely critical question at the intersection of Victorian
evolutionary theory and child study: to what extent are children animals?

The Victorians did not invent the notion that children are closer to
nature than are adults. Cicero referred to animals and children as *specula
naturae*, and more recently, Jean-Jacques Rousseau linked the child and the
primitive.[7] But after the incursion of evolutionary ideas into the popular
imagination, the bestial conception of childhood dictated the way children
were to be treated, cared for, and educated. In England and the United
States, child advocates borrowed legal and moral arguments from animal
protection societies; in 1885, for instance, MP Samuel Smith modeled the
Liverpool Society for the Prevention of Cruelty to Children on what he
had seen at the Royal Society for the Prevention of Cruelty to Animals
(RSPCA) meetings.[8] By the last decade of the century, the animal child was
a staple in pediatrics and child psychology. Physician Louis Robinson's

Figure 2 From Charles Kingsley, *The Water-Babies*, 1863, illustrated by W. Heath Robinson (Boston, MA and New York: Houghton Mifflin, 1915), Table of contents.

"Darwinism in the Nursery" (1891) argues that the intensity of the infant's grip, the muscularity of his arms, and his smaller lower limbs present "a striking resemblance to a well-known picture of the celebrated chimpanzee 'Sally' at the Zoological Gardens."[9] In "Babies and Monkeys" (1894), S. S. Buckman claims that "the scar which the loss of the tail has still left on children's bodies" links babies to a particular class of primates.[10] Child psychologist Milicent Shinn's *Biography of a Baby* (1900) points to the "curious resemblances between babies and monkeys, between boys and barbaric tribes" that help explain behavior as much as anatomy.[11] Likewise, James Sully's *Studies in Childhood* (1896) begins with the founding idea that for the infant "life is outward and visible, forming a part of nature's spectacle; reason and will, the noble prerogatives of humanity, are scarce discernible; sense, appetite, instinct, these animal functions seem to sum up the first year of human life."[12] Between the publication of *Origin of Species* and the beginning of the twentieth century, the association between babies and monkeys, children and animals, and boys and barbarians ceased to be a mere metaphorical formulation and became a morphological "fact" with vital psychological, moral, pedagogical, and literary consequences.

Louis Robinson, Buckman, Shinn, and Sully ground their arguments about infant and child life by extrapolating the "law of recapitulation": a corollary of evolutionary theory contending that, during gestation, the human embryo rehearses the evolution of the species, passing through all the lower animal stages from amoeba to man. This thesis about embryological development was shared, to varying degrees, by most evolutionists in the Victorian period. In his Notebook B (1837–1838), Darwin maintains that "every step of progressive increase of organization being imitated in the womb" replicates that "which has been passed through to form that species."[13] By *Origin*, he may have no longer endorsed the literal equation between individual and species – though to what extent he did is disputed – but his theory of modification counted embryological recapitulation among its foundational pieces of evidence.[14] *Descent of Man* includes sketches of dog and human embryos to show their remarkable similarity; both, by the way, have noticeable tails [Figure 3]. Herbert Spencer first applied the word "evolution," which previously referred to individual growth, to the collective adaptations of a species and in 1852 claimed that ontogenic growth suggests that phylogenic transformation is possible.[15] Just as vital to Victorian conceptions of evolution was Robert Chambers's bestseller *Vestiges of the Natural History of Creation* (1844), which employs recapitulation to show that man preserves his supreme position in nature even without special creation: if he has risen through the entirety of the animal world to arrive at its pinnacle, "man, then, considered zoologically, and without regard to the distinct character assigned to him by theology, simply takes his place as the type of all types of the animal kingdom, the true and unmistakable head of animal nature upon this earth."[16]

The scientific importance and popular appeal of recapitulation cannot be overstated. In *Ontogeny and Phylogeny* (1977), Stephen Jay Gould maintains that it "provided an argument second to none in the arsenal of evolutionists during the second half of the nineteenth century."[17] Gillian Beer's landmark work *Darwin's Plots: Evolutionary Narrative in Darwin, George Eliot and Nineteenth-Century Fiction* (1983) argues that "the blurring of the distinction between ontogeny – individual development – and phylogeny – species development – in the single term 'evolution' proved to be one of the most fruitful disturbances of meaning in the literature of the ensuing hundred years."[18] Subsequent intellectual histories of evolution – Dov Ospovat's *The Development of Darwin's Theory: Natural History, Natural Theology, and Natural Selection, 1838–1859* (1981), Peter Bowler's *Evolution: The History of an Idea* (1983), Adrian Desmond's *Archetypes and Ancestors: Palaeontology in Victorian London, 1850–1875* (1982) and *The Politics of Evolution: Morphology, Medicine, and Reform in Radical London* (1989), and Robert J. Richards's *The Meaning of Evolution: The Morphological Construction*

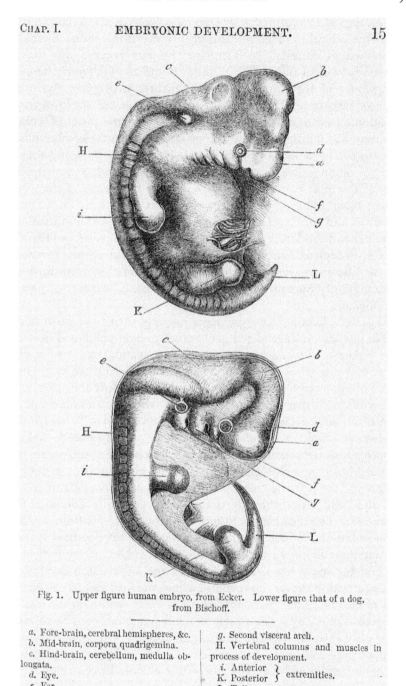

EMBRYONIC DEVELOPMENT.

CHAP. I.   15

Fig. 1. Upper figure human embryo, from Ecker. Lower figure that of a dog, from Bischoff.

a. Fore-brain, cerebral hemispheres, &c.
b. Mid-brain, corpora quadrigemina.
c. Hind-brain, cerebellum, medulla oblongata.
d. Eye.
e. Ear.
f. First visceral arch.

g. Second visceral arch.
H. Vertebral columns and muscles in process of development.
i. Anterior ⎱ extremities.
K. Posterior ⎰
L. Tail or os coccyx.

Figure 3 From Charles Darwin, *The Descent of Man, and Selection in Relation to Sex* (London: J. Murray, 1871), 15.

and Ideological Reconstruction of Darwin's Theory (1992) – continue to affirm the centrality of recapitulation in nineteenth-century biology.[19] Recapitulation appealed to Victorians in part because the analogy between individual and species promised solutions to the most damning disruptions and deficiencies in Darwin's theory. In *Origin of Species*, for instance, Darwin apologizes for the want of intermediate fossil forms transitioning from animal to man that obscured the proof of human evolution. But if ontogeny rehearses phylogeny, then the embryo fills in these lamentable lapses. "The phylogenic [record] is a worn and ancient volume," Shinn writes, "mutilated in many places, and often illegible," lacking "the most interesting chapter," but "a fresh copy of the whole history, from alpha to omega, is written out every time an infant is conceived, and born, and grows to manhood."[20] Perhaps recapitulation's greatest charm was less its scientific use-value than its palliative elegance. Darwinism depicted humans as an accident of random natural processes, but, as Chambers's enthusiasm attests, recapitulation reaffirmed the distinction of humanity and the teleological nature of man's development.

While recapitulation assuaged some concerns about our place in the organic universe, it engendered new anxieties about childhood development. Though, in its rigorously scientific formulation, the "law" applies only to embryos, it was quickly extrapolated into a description of children. Louis Robinson claims that "an animal until independent of parental care, and even beyond that point, until the bodily structure and functions are those of an adult, is still, strictly speaking, an embryo."[21] In *The Boy Problem: A Study in Social Pedagogy* (1901), the Reverend William Forbush allows the infant a postembryonic existence, but still argues that the individual's route through the stages of the species' history extends into childhood: "the prenatal child passes up through every grade of animal life," and then "after birth this 'candidate for humanity' continues this evolution ... by repeating the history of his own race-life from savagery unto civilization."[22] Such speculations about child development sparked new questions about the meaning of evolution applied to the individual life: Did the individual's rehearsal of the species' evolutionary history culminate with birth, or did it continue into the first five, ten, or fifteen years of the child's life? Was childhood but a way station on the road to fully realized humanity, a living relic of a still prehuman, even bestial past? If our early ancestors became human only through a series of fortuitous morphological and intellectual accidents, is the child's path to humanity likewise uncertain and indeterminate? Or if it could be controlled, what early childhood or formalized educational experiences are necessary to secure humanity for the individual child and thus for the future of the species? Embryology may have offered to fill the gaps in human history, but reversing the formula from speculative evolutionary history back to a prescriptive narrative of individual growth generated a crisis about childhood.

Concerns about what evolution meant for childhood development were exacerbated by contemporary debates about elementary education. After the first Parliamentary grant for education in 1833, the government began inserting itself into the school system, which had been primarily controlled by the Church of England and buttressed by charitable societies like the British and Foreign School Society.[23] Demands for cheaper, nonsectarian, and mandatory education ultimately led to the passing of the Elementary Education Act in 1870, which framed a compulsory school system for children five to twelve years of age in England and Wales.[24] In the intervening period, from the 1830s to 1870, politicians, educators, and social activists were actively seeking a standard curriculum that could suit both the upper- and middle-class pupils already enrolled as well as the working-class children just entering the system. At the center of the conversation was the vital question: what branch of knowledge was the most valuable to the greatest number of pupils? With Dissenters and nonsectarians challenging the Church of England's stranglehold over education, religion was no longer the easy answer.[25] Instead, scientific men like Richard Dawes, John Stevens Henslow, and Henry Moseley were arguing for the moral and intellectual benefits of their own disciplines.[26] But this advocacy of scientific education received its most urgent and influential cry only once it was combined with a theory of recapitulation. The year after the publication of Darwin's *Origin of Species*, Spencer wrote an influential pedagogical treatise entitled *Education: Intellectual, Moral, and Physical* (1860), which asks, "What Knowledge Is Of Most Worth?", and answers: Science.[27] Spencer's reason for this pronouncement was recapitulation. Because the growing child is repeating the evolution of the species, Spencer insists, the child must imitate the gradual advancement of our ancestors' primitive mentation, which involved careful observation, determined experimentation, patient trial and error, and thoughtful deduction and inference. Particularly persuasive among his contemporary pedagogues was Spencer's argument that elementary education must prioritize opportunities to employ the scientific method, because it was through this distinctly scientific mode of thinking that man first raised himself above the lower animals.

Fundamental to Spencer's pedagogy is not simply an argument for increased attention to science but a complementary devaluation of literature. What our ancestors all share, according to Spencer, is their common use of the rudiments of the scientific method; even the lower animals exhibit this impulse to maneuver in and to master the elements of their physical environment. What they do not share is access to written texts. Because reading and writing were late inventions in human evolution – indeed, arising only after human societies could rest from the more pressing demands of immediate survival – Spencer claims that they have no place in early education, but rather they must be postponed to occupy only the advanced students' leisure hours. Comparing human evolution to the cultivation of a flowering plant, he makes the root and the leaves analogous to scientific knowledge, while art and literature are the flowers that blossom only at the end of the growth cycle. "The root and leaves are intrinsically of greater importance," he tells us, "because on them the evolution of the flower depends"; meanwhile, "the fine arts, *belles-lettres*, and all those things which, as we say, constitute the efflorescence of civilization, should be wholly subordinate to that knowledge and discipline in which civilization rests."[28] Spencer's analogy seems to ignore that the flower is essential to the plant's reproduction, ensuring the survival of the species rather than merely decorating the life of the individual. Nevertheless, his argument waged a crucial challenge to the pedagogical power of literature: if children were indeed recapitulating the ascent of the species, then, for Spencer, reading books – performing an act neither beast nor early homonid ever did – is irrelevant (at best) and perverting (at worst) to their proper, evolutionarily prescribed course of development.

Spencer's advancement of science as a universally essential skill-set resonated with policy makers in the decade leading up to the 1870 Elementary Education Act. But beyond the walls of the Victorian school, the so-called Golden Age of children's literature began to flourish. Many canonical children's texts reveal a surprising investment in the theory of recapitulation as well as a critical stance on the Victorian school. *The Water-Babies* invokes evolutionary theory in Tom's inability to determine whether or not he has a tail, just before launching into parodies of Victorian schoolmarms and students, crammed so full of useless facts that their brains literally burst and ooze out of them. Likewise, Lewis Carroll's *Alice's Adventures in Wonderland* (1865) subjects its heroine to morphological metamorphoses and species confusion while mocking pedagogical commonplaces like rote memorization and final exams, and Rudyard Kipling's *The Jungle Book* (1894) imagines the feral child within a school story as Mowgli is tutored in geography, history, and comparative linguistics by a bear and a panther. The core texts of children's literature, during the genre's defining era, do not simply adopt the theory of the child's bestiality because it was in vogue. Rather, these works confront the maze of questions incited by recapitulation: about the bestial nature of the child, about the incapacity of the current school system to meet the challenge of humanizing him, and, not at all insignificantly, about the value of literature itself within the child's miniaturized evolution in which books might have no part.

Scholarly work on Victorian and Edwardian children's literature describes the genre's Golden Age as its retreat from reality into fantasy, its divestment of a previous commitment to pedagogy, its new allegiance to play, and its whole-hearted adoption of the Romantic celebration of childhood purity and innocence.[29] In *Evolution and Imagination in Victorian Children's Literature*, I argue that this all-too-accepted version of literary history is incomplete; in particular, it eclipses the genre's fascinating encounter with evolutionary science's relocation of the human – and in particular the child – as well as the genre's distinct defense of literature's role within our evolution. Though the writers examined here entertained the recapitulative theory of childhood, their works do not favor scientific education, or even realistic modes of exposition. They invent, elaborate, and celebrate their uniquely literary elements. If bestial children require humanization, these texts suggest, then it is by reading fantastical, non-sensical, parodic, atemporal, and palimpsestic books and engaging in activities and modes of thought available only within literature that they perfect their natures. Imaginative literature, thus, provides singular opportunities for the reader to evolve. Children's literature from 1860 to 1920, now taken for granted as the genre at its strongest, is in fact a wildly successful reaction to cultural pressures placing the genre at its most vulnerable. In this sixty-year period, the genre deftly pushed aside its former devotion to referentiality and verisimilitude and instead crystallized around a set of antirealist literary modes and techniques that are, I will demonstrate, its authors' ingenious transformation of a scientific construction of the child into the era's most eloquent defense of literature.

How the child got its tail

The theory of recapitulation gained such popularity in the second half of the nineteenth century because it provided an alternative evidentiary source for evolution besides the flawed geologic record and because it promised to restore man's preeminence in the natural world. The idea that the child repeats human evolution also appealed to the Victorians' preferences for historiography and literary genre. According to science historian Peter J. Bowler, evolutionary morphology and, in particular, recapitulation "helped to sustain the progressivist assumptions of the Victorian era, and to deflect attention away from the complexity of real life evolution."[30] Human history, understood to be moving toward ever-advancing goals, elevated Victorians as the latest, and finest, stage. In literature, the nineteenth century saw the dominance of the *Bildungsroman* – a genre that condensed narratives of national and social progress into stories about individual men and women – and, thus, it is hardly surprising that evolution was granted an individual form. The theory of recapitulation provided the nineteenth century with its most grandiose *Bildungsroman*. For recapitulation to take hold of the Victorian popular imagination, it may not have required very solid biological footing, but the controversies and conflicts that surrounded its scientific origination, as we see throughout this book, affected the ways it was adopted into other cultural arenas. The story that this study tells, then, begins with the early-nineteenth-century development of recapitulation and its influence on pedagogical practices.

Though Chambers gave recapitulation a teleological twist in the middle of the century, the first evolutionists to point out the similarities between human embryos and "lower" animals sought to explain the animal kingdom without recourse to a divine plan. At the beginning of the nineteenth century, Jean-Baptiste Lamarck's theory of transmutation challenged the divinely ordained world of natural theology. Instead of God's omnipotent hand molding each organism at Creation, the natural world now appeared to be the result of organisms' individual powers to transform themselves. Richard Owen, renowned and respected anatomist and later curator and director of London's Natural History Museum, was consistently vocal about his distaste for the tenets of Lamarckian evolution, disparaging the scheme for depending on the "self-developing energies" of organisms operating without any need for divine intervention.[31] Strangely, it was a Lamarckian eager to remove God from the picture even more definitively who offered teleology its greatest comeback by paving the way for the analogy between ontogeny and phylogeny. Étienne Geoffroy Saint-Hilaire, Lamarck's colleague at the Muséum d'Histoire Naturelle, sought to disprove George Cuvier's theory that God intermittently interceded in an ongoing creation.[32] Saint-Hilaire instead focused on the "unity of plan," holding that the anatomical similarities among the members of a particular phylum – the bird's wing, dolphin's fin, and human's hand, for instance – suggested a limited design, and he hoped, therefore, the absence of a designer.

Soon the idea of the "unity of plan" joined with embryology, on the one hand, and a scheme of developmental sequencing, on the other, to solidify the theory of recapitulation. Saint-Hilaire's student, Étienne Serres, looked to embryology for evidence of unities among seemingly separate species. In the 1820s and 1830s, he showed that, though anatomical homologies are obscured as organisms mature, vertebrate embryos resemble each other, and he notoriously pointed out that humans early on display visible gills, as if passing through a fish stage.[33] Saint-Hilaire's "unity of plan" combined with Serres's sequencing of embryological forms to suggest a developmental course from lower-order similarity through advancing differentiation and multiplicity of forms. Early proponents of recapitulation maintained that all vertebrates begin their embryological growth as the simplest backboned animal (cartilaginous fish) and have the potential to advance into the most complex (human beings); what determines species is where along this sequence gestation stops. According to Serres in 1860, "the entire animal kingdom can, in some measure, be considered ideally as a single animal which, in the course of formation and metamorphosis of its diverse organisms, stops in its development, here earlier and there later."[34] Recapitulation, in its early articulation, sought to displace theology with a purely material explanation for biodiversity. But it was taken for granted that the end of this evolutionary process (ontogenic and phylogenic) was man. The idea that humans repeat the evolution of all life on earth reestablished us comfortably as the telos of creation: the "single animal" of which all others are only a part.

The literalized analogy between individual and species was not without its challengers, though recapitulation was ultimately able to absorb even its detractors into itself. John Fletcher, a lecturer in comparative anatomy and physiology at Edinburgh, argued that though individual organs develop along a linear sequence from simpler to more complex forms, the entire embryo never perfectly resembles any adult form; "the fetus collectively," he wrote in the 1830s, "is never formed upon any model but its own."[35] The most comprehensive refutation came from a professor of zoology and comparative anatomy at Königsberg University, Karl Ernst von Baer. Von Baer denied any correspondence between the developing embryo and the adult forms of less complex animals, citing particularities of embryos (dependence on placental fluid, for instance) that did not replicate the adult stage of any organism. An embryo, in other words, is always an embryo, with its own special adaptations to survive within its immediate embryological environment. Embryological development, according to von Baer, does not progress through the adult forms of lower species, but sequentially diverges from a purely germinal similarity to a unique complexity that determines species. The human embryo, for instance, is first an undifferentiated vertebrate, then a generalized mammal, specialized primate, and finally an unmistakable unique human. In 1828, von Baer maintained that "the more homogeneous [*gleichmässiger*] the entire mass of the body, the lower the stage of development. We have reached a higher stage if nerve and muscle, blood, and cell-material [*Zellstoff*] are sharply differentiated. The more different they are, the more developed the animal."[36] Without repeating lower animal forms, the embryo develops from the general to the special: from homogeneity to heterogeneity.

Such objections were technical, and though they may have swayed embryologists, the idea that individual development encompasses the entire animal kingdom had a popular appeal that they did little to dampen. Chambers, for instance, was familiar with von Baer's disputation of recapitulation, claiming to have read William Carpenter's 1839 digest of von Baer's work, and *Vestiges of the Natural History of Creation* defers to the German anatomist: "it has been seen that, in the reproduction of the higher animals, the new being passes through stages in which it is successively fish-like and reptile-like. But the resemblance is not to the adult fish or the adult reptile, but to the fish and reptile at a certain point in their fœtal progress."[37] Despite this admission, however, Chambers immediately asserts a contrary theory of recapitulation in which a pregnant mother can volitionally extend gestation and, thus, advance her offspring one rung up the evolutionary ladder. Though historians of science debate how much of Darwin's thought relied on recapitulation, Darwin wrote in his *Autobiography* (1892) that "hardly any point gave me so much satisfaction" while working on *Origin of Species* as the embryological similarities among organisms of the same class.[38] He expresses disappointment that credit for this notion had gone to German evolutionists Fritz Müller and Ernst Haeckel who, he says, "undoubtedly have worked it out much more fully, and in some respects more correctly than I did."[39] For his part, Haeckel, a professor of zoology and anatomy at the University of Jena, thought that his codification of the recapitulative hypothesis as a "biogenetic law" was the crucial step in proving Darwinism. In *The Evolution of Man: A Popular Exposition of the Principal Points of Human Ontogeny and Phylogeny* (1874), Haeckel asserts:

This fundamental law ... on the recognition of which depends the thorough understanding of the history of evolution, is briefly expressed in the proposition: that the History of the Germ is an epitome of the History of Descent; or, in other words: that Ontogeny is a recapitulation of Phylogeny ... [T]he series of forms through which the Individual Organism passes during its progress from the egg cell to its fully developed state, is a brief, compressed reproduction of the long series of forms through which the animal ancestors of that organism (or the ancestral forms of its species) have passed from the earliest periods of so-called organic creation down to the present time.[40]

To demonstrate the evidence for recapitulation, Haeckel produced sketches of vertebrate embryos, showing their remarkable similarities, and though he pictorially "exaggerated" these likenesses, according to Edward Larson's recent history of evolution, they were "widely reprinted" and "served as a powerful argument for evolution."[41] Not only did Haeckel assert morphological correspondences, but he also used them to postulate ancestral forms of the higher animals, to construct genealogical lineages, and thus to fill in the gaps of the fossil record, though with generous creative license.[42] But despite his fantastic family trees casting embryological stages back into evolutionary time, he gives us the official formulation of the theory and the familiar phrasing: "Ontogeny is a recapitulation of Phylogeny." By the last third of the century, then, Saint-Hilaire's "unity of plan" had matured into a post-Darwinian narrative with Lamarckian inflections: each organism passes through the lower stages of its ancestors, adding one extra stage at the end of its growth to advance individual and species in tandem. Development seems law-driven, progressive, and, for humans, self-aggrandizing.

Vestiges of the Natural History of Creation, Chambers's pre-Darwinian evolutionary manifesto, popularized the analogy between individual and species, but recapitulation most effectively entered culture when it was revised to suggest that it is not only the embryo but more compellingly the child who, after birth, repeats human history. The principal figure in the extrapolation of recapitulation into childhood was none other than Spencer. Spencer had read Carpenter's digest of von Baer, but the latter's refutation of the recapitulation thesis only led Spencer to amplify the theory. He writes in *An Autobiography* (1904), "I came across von Baer's formula expressing the course of development through which every plant and animal passes – the change from homogeneity to heterogeneity," and he explains that he saw in this formulation a description of the universal progress of organisms, species, civilizations, and even solar systems.[43]

In "Progress: Its Law and Cause" (1857), Spencer says that "in its primary stage, every germ consists of a substance that is uniform throughout," and through a series of "differentiated divisions ... there is finally produced that complex combination of tissues and organs constituting the adult animal or plant."[44] "It is settled beyond dispute," he concludes, "that organic progress consists in a change from the homogenous to the heterogeneous." Here he takes von Baer's thesis that development moves from generality to specificity, but adds to it the idea of evolutionary advancement across viable lower stages; in other words, lower organisms, lower states of mind, and lower societies are simple and undifferentiated, while their advanced counterparts have differentiated limbs and organs, mental abilities, gender roles, classes, and labor forces.

Within three years of reincorporating von Baer's theory of differentiation back into the very theory of recapitulation that it was meant to refute, Spencer invented his incontrovertibly influential pedagogical philosophy, *Education*. Here he argues that science must rule the elementary curriculum because "the development of children in mind and body rigorously obeys certain laws," passed down through the evolution of the species.[45] Like every organism and social system, children begin simplistically and uniformly, their mental abilities directed only at the universal need for survival, but as they develop differentially, their education too should expand its scope. Acknowledging a quasi-Lamarckian notion of progress, Spencer is clear that there is a specific order to how this widening unfolds: "education," he writes, "must conform to the natural process of mental evolution ... a certain sequence in which the faculties spontaneously develop."[46] The child is not John Locke's blank slate upon which any text can be written at any time, nor is he Rousseau's simple naïf whose innocence should be preserved. Rather, the child carries with him the script of the entire history of organic evolution, and parents and educators must follow this evolutionarily inscribed text line by line lest they pervert the development of the child. *Education* summarizes the social duty to understand and to preserve this inviolate developmental program with the following pedagogical dictum: "if there be an order in which the human race has mastered its various kinds of knowledge, there will arise in every child an aptitude to acquire these kinds of knowledge in the same order ... and hence the fundamental reason why education should be a repetition of civilization in little."[47]

Pedagogies based on the individual's reprisal of human civilization precede both Spencer and Darwin. In the 1840s, German professor of pedagogy Tuiskon Ziller applied a Hegelian model of self-perfecting world spirit to education and proposed a curriculum based on an "epoch theory" of European religious progress; pupils first read Greek myths and then Old Testament legends and New Testament parables, culminating in the story of the Reformation.[48] In England, the analogy between individual development and human history defined not the school's coursework but its social structure. Rugby's reformist headmaster Thomas Arnold considered pupils still heathens in "the boyhood of the human race."[49] To fashion them into Christians, Arnold divided their social development into Old and New Testament phases: for the younger boys, he played the role of the remote disciplinarian, while in their final year, he befriended the pupils, forgave their rule-breaking, and taught them the power of mercy. Following this paradigm, Thomas Hughes's tribute to Arnold, *Tom Brown's Schooldays* (1857), describes its lads as "young Ishmaelites, their hands against every one, and every one's hand against them," until "the solemn prohibitions of the Doctor" bestow upon them the sequential gifts of law and grace in the order of man's religious development.[50] Ziller's epochal curriculum and Arnold's conversionary culture of school governance might seem to have presciently fulfilled Spencer's directive that "education should be a repetition of civilization in little." But the ideal course of instruction that Spencer advocated did not so much reprise particular civilizations, an ascending hierarchy of individuated past societies, as it strove to reenact civilization itself, the prior process of becoming human in the first place.

The civilizing power of science, for Spencer, lay in its methodology. Advocates for scientific instruction in elementary classrooms were characteristically divided – and unclearly so – about whether memorizing scientific facts or exercising the scientific method was the substance of a scientific education.[51] Indeed, for most lay supporters of scientific pedagogy in the early nineteenth century, the reward of a science lesson was an appreciation of God's works. Science here meant natural theology, a philosophy wherein careful observation of nature leads to the pupil's recognition of divine design; for a school system largely controlled by the Church of England until the 1860s, such scientific lessons were appropriately religious.[52] *The Quarterly Educational Magazine and Record of the Home and Colonial School Society* for 1848 gives an example which crystallizes how detached from natural fact such lessons could be: after showing students how silver is refined, the teacher punctuates her lecture by saying, "I have given you this lesson on refining silver, to lead you to understand what Jesus Christ does for us."[53] Rejecting this kind of blatant conversion of science into theology, Spencer proposed a distinctly secular scientific education, but he was also clear that he did not intend for students to recapitulate a history of scientific thought that taught early misconceptions (like the sun's revolution round the earth) before modern scientific theory. Rather, when he placed science at the core of a recapitulative curriculum, he privileged the scientific method. In *Education*, he urges that "children should be led to make their own investigations, and to draw their own inferences. They should be *told* as little as possible, and induced to *discover* as much as possible."[54] These discoveries, in Spencer's plan, should be guided by the exercise of observation, experiment, deduction, and trial and error: the same reasoning that allowed our ancestors to evolve.

Though a quarter of a century later, Thomas H. Huxley famously debated Matthew Arnold about the merits of pursuing the natural sciences over the literary arts in the university curriculum, Spencer denounced the value of literature in the *elementary* classroom first and much more stridently. Because primitive man could not rely on books to induct him into knowledge of himself, his surroundings, or his means of survival, Spencer disparaged books that substitute reading for self-motivated discovery. In part, he was responding to the way that science lessons were conducted: without the resources or the teacher training in the sciences, early Victorian classrooms relied on texts. In his history of science education in England, David Layton says, "the dependence upon the printed word for the transmission of science led to an ironic situation in which the use of observation and experimentation to acquire knowledge was more read about than practiced."[55] In the decades following the publication of Spencer's treatise, however, school policy makers became more attuned to science not as course content alone, but as a distinct methodology for pursuing and discovering that content. The Revised Code of 1881, for instance, states that "it is intended that the instruction in the Science subjects shall be given mainly by experiment and illustration, and in the case of Physical Geography by observation of the phenomena presented in [the students'] own neighborhood."[56]

Spencer's prescriptions were eagerly adopted because they came at a time of transition for the schools. The prospect of extending formal education to working-class pupils made choosing morally edifying and socially productive school subjects even more crucial. Following the Great Exhibition of 1851, Victorian policy makers were acutely aware of the importance of scientific and technological progress to the fate of the nation. Liberal MP William Foster, the Elementary Education Act's principal defender and drafter, lamented in a Parliamentary speech that the poor state of education in England and Wales would soon leave "our work-folk . . . over-matched in the competition of the world."[57] The language of competition seems drawn from Darwinism, while the urgency of his appeal can be traced back to the shift in popular thinking around the Great Exhibition. The idea that working-class pupils, temporarily removed from the market and the factory, would be returned into the workforce as productive labor reassured middle-class parents worried about mixing their own children with those of the lower classes. Meanwhile, the promise of their children becoming skilled artisans and budding scientists helped convince working-class parents to relinquish the money that could otherwise be earned from their children's work now for the sake of greater economic prosperity later.[58] True universal education became a reality in the United Kingdom only well into the second decade of the twentieth century, and by then, the scientific, political, and pedagogical landscapes had shifted. But in the middle of the nineteenth century, the agitation for compulsory schooling and the push for scientific instruction in the elementary classroom went hand in hand, fortified by evolutionary theory and its accompanying notion of nations pitted against each other in a survival of the fittest.

Not everyone was as unequivocally optimistic as Spencer that science provided children with everything necessary to become fully formed workers, citizens, and humans. Three decades before he took on Huxley over the issue of university education, Matthew Arnold was working as a Schools Inspector and publishing near-annual reports on the state of elementary education. In this official capacity, he advocated for universal education and supported a common curriculum provided that the core was literature. He did not exclude science, proposing what he called "*Natur-Kunde*," an all-purpose course that would confine scientific instruction and limit the proliferation of specialized scientific subjects.[59] But for him, if the goal of the school was to "humanize" its students – a phrase he used often – then only literature could do the job. As early as 1852, he argued, "training [in literature] would tend to elevate and humanize a number of young men, who at present, notwithstanding the vast amount of raw information which they have amassed, are wholly uncultivated."[60] In the 1870s and 1880s, as Spencer's suggested reforms began to take effect, Mathew Arnold became more virulently critical of science, insisting that "the problem to be solved is a great deal more complicated than many of the friends of natural science suppose."[61] Talking about basic instruction in health and hygiene, for instance, he writes,

> To have the power of using, which is the thing wished, these data of natural science, a man must, in general, have first been in some measure *moralised*; and for moralising him it will be found not easy, I think, to dispense with

those old agents, letters, poetry, religion. So let not our teachers be led to imagine, whatever they may hear and see of the call for natural science, that their literary cultivation is unimportant. The fruitful use of natural science itself depends, in a very great degree, on having effected in the whole man, by means of letters, a rise in what the political economists call *the standard of life*.[62]

Without referencing evolutionary theory directly or naming Spencer, Mathew Arnold's reports nevertheless reveal his working out the claims he will later use against Huxley.[63] Evolutionary theory exacerbated the struggle between science and literature for cultural dominance – a struggle still ongoing today – first in the arena of elementary education and then in the question of children's reading. Spencer and Mathew Arnold exerted significant influence over educational policy, and though science and literature coexisted in the curriculum, their proponents continued to debate their relevance for decades.[64] During this cultural crisis about the comparative merits of literary reading and scientific experiment – sparked by the coincidence of recapitulation's reconstruction of the child and the push to mass schooling – the Golden Age of children's literature was forged.

The descent of the child

In addressing evolutionary theory and recapitulation, children's literature was toying with theories that ominously forecast its own irrelevance. Because the child was repeating the history of the species, Spencer argued, he needed to *do* and not to *read*. Recapitulation, thus, posed what might seem an insolvable problem that best be kept out of children's literature – that is, if a form of this problem had not been constitutive of children's literature from its origins. But, in fact, the conflict between doing for oneself and reading from authority is one of the genre's defining features. Drawn from the theories of Locke and Rousseau, children's literature arises from a philosophy deeply suspicious of textuality and, instead, supportive of unmediated play. In *Some Thoughts Concerning Education* (1693), Locke maintains that "Reading, and Writing, and *Learning*, I allow to be necessary, but yet not the chief Business" of the child's education.[65] According to Locke's theory of the mind as *tabula rasa*, sensory experiences of real-world physical objects are the building blocks of ideas, while reading offers the mind only derivative facts and befuddles the natural growth of rational skills. Rousseau's indictment of books is even more severe; in *Émile; or, On Education* (1762), he virulently declares that "reading is the curse of childhood," infecting the mind with information that the child has not independently acquired and hence does not really know.[66] Locke denounced all books for children except the Bible and *Aesop's Fables*, and Rousseau, slamming fabulists as little better than liars, suggested only Daniel Defoe's *Robinson Crusoe* because of its supposed fidelity to natural, untextual experience. Despite their shared derision of children's reading, however, Locke and Rousseau are rightly credited with the invention of children's literature, a genre painfully at odds with itself about what kind of experience it offers the child.

What Locke and Rousseau spawned in the eighteenth century was children's literature that tried to look as little like literature as it could, seeking to mimic raw sensation. Discussing this strange phenomenon of the antitextual children's text, Alan Richardson's *Literature, Education, and Romanticism: Reading as Social Practice, 1780-1832* (1994) cites Richard Edgeworth's preface to Maria Edgeworth's *Early Lessons* (1814). Richard Edgeworth counsels parents that in all good children's books "action should be introduced – Action! Action!"[67] Children's authors crammed texts with action rather than description and, likewise, employed dialogue to mimic real conversation; the goal of the text, it seems, was to dissolve the boundary between fiction and life. The mother narrator of Sarah Trimmer's *An Easy Introduction to the Knowledge of Nature, and Reading of the Holy Scriptures* (1780) asks her son, "is not this a charming place? You know that it is called a meadow. See how green the grass looks, and what a number of pretty flowers! Run about, and try how many different sorts of grass you can find, for it is now in blossom. One, two, three: you have got eight sorts, I declare!"[68] The familiarity of the setting (an English meadow), the narrator's imperatives ("see," "run," "try ... [to] find"), and the enumeration of potentially tangible objects ("one, two, three") elide the distinction between acting and reading and attempt to present the text as an invitation to unmediated physical experience. Other writers used the opposite tactic; instead of detextualizing their texts, they suggested that everything was text, especially their readers' own minds. Richardson shows that a number of early-nineteenth-century books encouraged "the child to take its place in a discursive universe" by "thematizing the act of reading, training the child to participate in its own textualization by writing about itself, and instilling a sense in the child of its own legibility, its status as a text open to the perusal of its parents and (ultimately) to the all-seeing eye of God."[69] Locke's idea of the child's mind as *tabula rasa* was, thus, converted – through logical contortions – into a pedagogy where reading could substitute for experience because mentation was itself textual.

Children's literature scholars who focus on the genre's enduring Romanticism rarely take up this anxiety about textuality as it continued into the nineteenth century. Since George Boas's *The Cult of Childhood* (1966) argued that the Victorian literary child "is innocent of all the arts and sciences, unspoiled by the artifices of civilization," scholars have almost universally accepted that the Golden Age children's literature is "closely bound up in the Romantic movement," according to Humphrey Carpenter, and "fundamentally affected by the Romantic concept of childhood," to quote James McGavran.[70] The most ambitious scholarship on children's literature has blamed the genre for using Romanticism to side-step questions about the child's relationship to textuality. Jacqueline Rose's seminal study *The Case of Peter Pan: or, The Impossibility of Children's Fiction* (1984) argues that children's literature is "impossible": "not in the sense that it cannot be written (that would be nonsense) but in that it hangs on an impossibility, one which it rarely ventures to speak. This is the impossible relationship between adult and child."[71] For Rose, children's literature establishes an unbridgeable abyss between adults and children (such that the latter require their own literature) but then has the adult author speaking to the child reader over the very same abyss that it has asserted. Because the adult cannot speak to the child, the author constructs a fantasy of the child (almost always of the Romantic ideal of presocial and presexual innocence) that stands in for the child he can never get. Children's literature, then, does not speak to any real children, only to the adult's desire. Rose's account is to be credited for helping to make children's literature a serious critical subject, but her insistence on the unequal relationship between the acting adult and the passive child overlooks other textual inconsistencies, such as the genre's contradictory commands that the child both do and read.

There are signs that scholarship is deviating from this model of the passive reader. Marah Gubar's thoughtful *Artful Dodgers: Reconceiving the Golden Age of Children's Literature* (2009) argues that, "rather than promoting the idea that young people are primitive naïfs, these [Golden Age] authors more often characterize the child inside and outside the book as a literate, educated subject who is fully conversant with the values, conventions, and cultural artifacts of the civilized world."[72] Gubar nicely undercuts the model inherited from Locke and Rousseau, illuminated by Rose, and assumed by so many critics, by showing off the savvy, street-smart, and articulate children populating Victorian texts. More importantly, she shows that these texts turn reading into an active, interpretive process, in which child characters manipulate, reassemble, and challenge the narratives that adults give them. Like Gubar's, my analyses will high-light a more active role for the child reader. But whereas Gubar juxtaposes the "literate, educated subject" that she examines with "the Child of Nature paradigm, which holds that contact with civilized society is neces-sarily stifling," I do not dismiss the second category as much as break it open.[73] For the second half of the nineteenth century and the beginning of the twentieth century, the "Child of Nature" was no longer the Romantic ingénue; he was not "trailing clouds of glory," as Wordsworth character-ized him, but rather dragging behind him vestiges of our savage and bestial prehistory.[74] And because, according to the scientists who defined him, this recapitulating "Child of Nature" required a developmental trajectory seemingly antithetical to textuality, his appearance inside and outside children's books became vexed.

My study is not the first critical exploration of evolutionary theory in nineteenth- and early-twentieth-century children's books, though it is the first to argue that the evolution featured in these books might actually be *for children*. The assumption that the Victorian child is an echo of the Romantic "Child of Nature" – in which both child and nature are innocent alternatives to erudite adult culture – has proven so resilient in scholarship that any scientific content of children's literature has been regarded as addressing adult, rather than child, readers. One year before Rose's book, U. C. Knoepflmacher argued that Victorian children's literature constitu-tes the genre's aesthetic zenith because it simultaneously addresses two distinct audiences: child and adult. "It is no coincidence," he writes in "The Balancing of Child and Adult: An Approach to Victorian Fantasies for Children" (1983), "that the self-divided Victorians who found them-selves 'wandering between two worlds' in their Janus-like split between progress and nostalgia should have produced what has rightly been called 'the Golden Age of children's books.'"[75] Later literary critics seem to have taken from Knoepflmacher this "Janus-like split" between the child and adult audiences and from Rose the impossibility of the child reader. The result is a children's literature criticism that dodges the question of the child reader's relationship to the text altogether. Nowhere is this more discernible than in the current work on children's literature and evolution, in part because Darwinism seems a subject beyond a child's understanding and in part because the field of literary scholarship has condoned this approach. Alan Rauch's *Useful Knowledge: The Victorians, Morality, and the March of Intellect* (2001), Tess Cosslett's *Talking Animals in British Fiction, 1786–1914* (2006), and Caroline Sumpter's *The Victorian Press and the Fairy Tale* (2008), for instance, admirably discuss the evolutionary content of Victorian children's books, but they often interpret the references and allusions to contemporary science in this literature as knowing winks to the parent reading over her child's shoulder.[76]

Despite modern critics' claims about the child's exclusion from evolutionary discourse, however, it is clear that Victorian writers and publishers were organizing the genre of children's literature around recapitulation.[77] In the second half of the century, new editions of Aesop's fables filled publishers' catalogs; some specifically attributed their relevance to the theory of evolution. The preface to Joseph Jacobs' *Fables of Aesop* (1889), for instance, admits that the ancient tales are "too simple to correspond to the facts of our complex civilisation," but for children who "pass through . . . the various stages of ancestral culture," they are just right.[78] Fairy tales, too, garnered new value because, as Sumpter recognizes, they were considered "the record of man's earliest spiritual impulses" and, thus, in line with children's development.[79] Victorian folklorist and anthropologist Andrew Lang described his twelve-book project, beginning with *The Blue Fairy Book* (1889) and concluding with *The Lilac Fairy Book* (1910), as a recuperation of prehistoric culture concurrent with the child's archaic character. In the Preface to *The Violet Fairy Book* (1901), he writes, the "tastes [of young readers] remain like the tastes of their naked ancestors, thousands of years ago."[80] And it was not only these oral traditions that received recapitulative reframing. In the United States, popular children's publisher D. Appleton reissued a number of children's texts in a Home Reading Series with a preface praising the works of Darwin, Spencer, and American evolutionary psychologist G. Stanley Hall. The introduction, written by W. T. Harris, the standing U. S. Commissioner of Education, not only affirms that "all nature is unified by the discovery of the law of evolution," but it also asserts that children's literature had best recognize that fact.[81] The Appleton series' edition of *The Story of Oliver Twist* (1897) instructs readers to analyze the initial period of Oliver's life in terms of "The Struggle for Existence" because that is the first phase of all life.[82]

Just what young readers were expected to learn about evolution (either of the species or their own) has remained largely unanalyzed in part because of the scholarly consensus that the Golden Age differentiated itself from previous iterations of the genre by eschewing education and foregrounding the readers' pleasures. This book challenges the assumption that Victorian and Edwardian literature shook off the shackles of social issues like education and science. My analysis of the genre during this period contests the connotations of purity, innocence, and proximity to the divine that the very term "Golden Age" implies. Rather, the children's texts explored here struggle with the problem of what, or even how, the prehuman, premoral, prerational, and especially preliterate child should read and, in doing so, they intensify the fissures between reading and doing at the genre's core. *Evolution and Imagination in Victorian Children's Literature* argues that many of the best-known and canonized children's works written during the period just before the publication of Darwin's *Origin of Species* until the First World War not only incorporate the figure of the bestial child into the plots and tropes of their works but also acutely understand that recapitulation's derision of literature demanded a literary response. Post-Darwinian children's writers, thus, faced a new challenge, even as they were working within a genre already immersed in the problem of textuality versus real-world experience. Unlike their predecessors, these writers were not fashioning stories to inscribe Locke's blank slate or to shelter Rousseau's untainted innocent. They, instead, sought to humanize their readers by, first, recognizing their bizarrely liminal inhumanity and, second, articulating how literature could provide the child with the principal modes of intellectual, moral, emotional, and aesthetic evolution.

This study focuses on books for young readers that entertain the theory of recapitulation but that simultaneously reject the drive to become more scientific. For that reason, I do not here examine natural histories or science readers for classroom use, nor do I explore the legions of nineteenth-century texts that introduce themselves as "encyclopedias," "conversations," "practical observations," or "easy introductions" to and about natural facts and processes.[83] My analysis, instead, turns to fanciful children's books that foreground their very literariness by inviting readers to engage with their most exaggerated unrealistic, nonsensical, and intrinsically rhetorical elements. Victorian and Edwardian children's literature is renowned for its use of impractical play, magical metamorphoses, fantastical adventures, and forays into absurdity that, for most scholars working within the field, mark the genre's abandonment of any pedagogical purpose. While these texts discard many of the familiar didactic moves and moral agendas of previous children's literature, for reasons I have hinted at above, I argue that these texts nevertheless advance an education about literature's special role in our evolution. They do not sketch out an education in *belles lettres* that, according to Matthew Arnold, teaches the child "the best which has been thought and said in the world"; such pedagogy would ignore the roots and stem of civilization and give the child only the flowers, to recall Spencer's metaphor.[84] They do, however, demonstrate how the skills acquired and enhanced by reading literature are those that humanize us, and their emphasis on their literariness suggests that this precise education is available nowhere else.

Examining scientific, pedagogical, and literary constructions of the child, *Evolution and Imagination in Victorian Children's Literature* brings together intertwined and tangled strands of an extensive interdisciplinary conversation about the child's origin, nature, abilities, development, education, and aims. My book broadens the contexts of both the current discussions of nineteenth-century evolutionary theory beyond Darwin and the literary reception beyond novel audiences. In expanding our sense of both the scientific theories and the lay readers in on the conversation about evolution, this study joins recent scholarship, such as James A. Secord's *Victorian Sensation: The Extraordinary Publication, Reception, and Secret Authorship of Vestiges of the Natural History of Creation* (2000), Geoffrey Cantor's, Gowan Dawson's, Graeme Gooday's, Richard Noakes's, Sally Shuttleworth's, and Jonathan R. Topham's collection *Science in the Nineteenth-Century Periodical: Reading the Magazine of Nature* (2004), Aileen Fyfe's and Bernard Lightman's edited volume *Science in the Marketplace: Nineteenth-Century Sites and Experiences* (2007), and Lightman's and Bennett Zon's interdisciplinary anthology *Evolution and Victorian Culture* (2014).[85] Kenneth B. Kidd's *Making American Boys: Boyology and the Feral Tale* (2004) and Dana Seitler's *Atavistic Tendencies: The Culture of Science in American Modernity* (2008) show the influence of evolutionary theory, and in Kidd's case, recapitulation, on early-twentieth-century American literature.[86] Shuttleworth's *The Mind of the Child: Child Development in Literature, Science, and Medicine, 1840–1910* (2010) superbly articulates how instrumental evolutionary theory and recapitulation, in particular, were in Victorian attempts to define childhood sexuality and insanity both medically and psychologically. My work extends her discussion of midcentury fears about the Victorian educational system in texts like *The Water-Babies* and Charles Dickens's *Dombey and Son* (1848). Unique among this excellent critical work addressing the cross-disciplinary terrain on which recapitulation redefined the child in the nineteenth and early twentieth centuries, however, *Evolution and Imagination in Victorian Children's Literature* focuses on how recapitulation altered the children of children's literature, not simply the genre's characters but also its implied readers, and the formal features invented to suit this prehuman audience.

Beyond opening up a new context in which evolutionary thought played out, my book examines the ways in which the assertion of childhood animality within evolutionary theory prompted children's authors to advocate for literature as the primary means to humanity. Here my work not only looks beyond Darwin and the novel but also challenges critical assertions about the relation between science and literature in the nineteenth century. The pioneers of Darwinist literary studies, Beer and George Levine, stressed the intersections, overlaps, and shared rhetoric of Victorian practitioners across disciplinary lines.[87] In the tradition established by Beer and Levine, Lightman's and Zon's recent *Evolution and Victorian Culture* reasserts the cross-disciplinary currents that allowed nineteenth-century scientific theories to flow smoothly within and among the diverse arenas of literature, photography, cinema, art, theater, music, architecture, and dance. Their collection's introduction states, "in a Victorian culture immersed in evolutionary thought, the culture of science and the culture of the humanities were complementary rather than oppositional."[88] However, while the sciences and the humanities may have appeared on better speaking terms then than they do today, they may not have harmonized so melodically as the "one culture" model of Beer and Levine, and now Lightman and Zon. As my book will also do, other scholars are putting pressure on this argument for interdisciplinary accord. Dawson's *Darwin, Literature and Victorian Respectability* (2007), for instance, shows how the link between science and literature was "regularly exploited and manipulated for a variety of strategic reasons" in attempts both to legitimize and to discredit Darwinism.[89] Similarly in *Moral Authority, Men of Science, and the Victorian Novel* (2013), Anne DeWitt maintains that instead of viewing science as a companion discourse, nineteenth-century "novels are attempting to delimit science, defining its concerns as distinct from fiction's – and inferior."[90] For Dawson and DeWitt, science and literature were porous to each other's influences, but simultaneously invested in defining their boundaries.

Though my study explores the ways in which children's literature adopted scientific conceptions of childhood development, which were themselves forged out of a particularly nineteenth-century collusion of evolutionary theory and narrative forms like the *Bildungsroman*, an essential part of the story that this book tells concerns a battle between science and the humanities for pedagogical dominance. The interdisciplinary encounters investigated here were not made up merely of innovative theories now open for artistic experiment or fresh tropes manipulated in novel contexts. Rather, new pressures on the mid-Victorian school system created a practical conundrum for educators and politicians, as well as a clash between disciplines for prominence in the critical questions of what children must learn and how they must learn it. For DeWitt, the novel is the most fitting literary medium to challenge the mounting cultural authority of the sciences because, she says, "moral cultivation and moral questions more broadly are claimed by the novel as its own domain of expertise."[91] Novels may very well have been the primary conduit for ethical instruction for adults, but children's literature governed the moral and intellectual education of a much more impressionable segment of the population. After the incursion of evolutionary theory into both the public awareness of and the political debates about education, children's authors necessarily confronted the threat that scientific experiment could displace the children's book as the transmitter of knowledge and the replicator of essential human experiences. From 1850 to 1915, the period this book investigates, the genre enthrallingly and ambivalently adapted science to itself and itself to science while it also competed with science as the child's first and most important teacher.

Evolution and Imagination in Victorian Children's Literature recasts the Golden Age, not as the straightforward declension of Romanticism, but as a response to scientific constructions of the animal child recapitulating the course of human evolution. This literature is not the product of a golden age, a mythological period of primordial perfection before a fall. We might say that, like Kingsley's Tom, who reverts to his animal origins so he can redirect his development along a more productive vector, Victorian and Edwardian children's literature returns to the problem at its origin – the conflict between reading and doing – in order to carve out a more formidable role for the literary in human evolution and childhood development. The classic texts of children's literature transform the multivalent meanings and inassimilable incoherencies of the bizarre analogy between individual and species into new ways to imagine the implied child reader and new plots for his ascent. Bringing together nineteenth-century constructions of evolutionary history and the complementary literary investment in the animal child, this book seeks to reveal a unique relationship between what it means to be human and what role literature plays in our humanity. Victorian children's texts made literary experience the pivotal mechanism of human evolution, capable of teaching the child how to retract his bestial "tail" and how to enter instead into a higher, distinctly human world of extraordinary, edifying, and imaginative "tales."

How the child lost its tail

The thesis that ontogeny recapitulates phylogeny – though promising a singular, all-inclusive narrative of universal development – was, in fact, a fractured and contradictory set of assumptions about the species' past and hopes for its future. Recapitulation rested on an analogy that was at best metaphorical, though it was solidified into a somewhat confused and confusing biological thesis, and then imported into pedagogical debates and youth movements. *Evolution and Imagination in Victorian Children's Literature* demonstrates how these scientific and cultural strands are interwoven through the children's literature of the period, and how this literature then offers back to popular culture and pedagogical discourse new conceptions of childhood distinct from their Enlightenment and Romantic predecessors. But more importantly, this book illustrates how the genre's incorporation of evolutionary tropes and plots was not nearly as significant as its invention of new literary styles and stratagems for both appealing to the not-quite-human reader and completing his (and later her) humanization. The textual features of these children's classics are their authors' distinctly literary mechanisms for humanizing the reader and their ingenious responses to contemporary claims that science could do it better. My chapters are not case studies illustrating either a coherent scientific theory (which recapitulation was not) or a monolithic literary rebuttal (which is similarly chimeric). They are rather linked investigations into how the child's development, the species' history, and the ways that literature could intercede in both were imagined and reimagined from the 1850s, when anxieties about human evolution and universal education merged into a newly concentrated focus on the child, until the 1910s, when concerns about the declining British empire and the impending World War renewed national and international interest in the child's fitness.

The book is divided into two parts. The authors discussed in the first three chapters –Margaret Gatty, Charles Kingsley, and Lewis Carroll – were writing just as evolutionary theory commanded popular attention and collided with the pedagogical debates about whether literature or science provides the better civilizing and more morally edifying instruction. Chapter 1, "The child's view of nature: Margaret Gatty and the challenge to natural theology," opens my discussion of post-Darwinian children's literature with a look at pre-Darwinian texts. Eighteenth- and early-nineteenth-century children's books strove to be scientific, commanding child readers to observe nature and to perform experiments. This conflation between science and literature worked (more or less) when science meant natural theology, a philosophy that saw the natural world and, by an extension taken for granted, the social world as reflections of God's benign and unchanging plan. But Gatty anticipated the disturbance that evolutionary theory's emphasis on randomness, chaos, and struggle might cause, especially if it were to become the content of universal education. In *Parables from Nature* (1855–1871), she seeks to fortify the literary tradition of natural theology against the incursion of evolutionary theory. If nature fails to display moral order, her parables suggest, then literature should not direct readers toward it, but rather point back to itself and its own visible elements of design.

Kingsley, the subject of Chapter 2, "Amphibious tendencies: Charles Kingsley, Herbert Spencer, and evolutionary education," shared Gatty's investment in divine design, but not her wish for the social and theological status quo. Eagerly accepting the political and religious potential of evolution and applauding the democratic impulse of scientific instruction, he embraced the purely scientific pedagogy initiated by Spencer and, in *The Water-Babies*, attempted to invent a children's book capable of mimicking experiential education even more forcefully than earlier children's literature had done. Whereas Gatty minimizes the "scientific" attributes of children's literature, Kingsley initially emphasizes and expands them. However, while Kingsley thought that scientific experiment could confirm Christianity's moral codes, he also thought that, to believe in God, one must first learn to believe in phenomena not available to the empirical senses. And he seems to conclude that it is literature, and not science, that grants us access to this realm beyond visible nature. Thus, while *The Water-Babies* begins as a literary manifestation of Spencer's pedagogical prescription, Kingsley ends up infusing his fairy tale with antirealist modes, like nonsense and fantasy, because these literary elements are alone capable of completing the child's evolution to full Christian humanity. Nonsense and fantasy become, for Kingsley, special kinds of didactic tools by which the child escapes scientific materialism and begins to imagine what cannot be seen or tested.

One year after *The Water-Babies*, Carroll's *Alice's Adventures in Wonderland* also employed nonsense, though not for the purpose of effecting the reader's religious conversion. Chapter 3, "Generic variability: Lewis Carroll, scientific nonsense, and literary parody," argues that Carroll was both apprehensive about evolution's destabilizing effect on man and skeptical about religion's ability to set things right. Instead, he offered his child reader language games and linguistic exercises: a focus that aligns *Wonderland* with Matthew Arnold's exaltation of literary education, in contrast to *The Water-Babies'* initial alliance with Spencer's scientific pedagogy. However, while Arnold advocated pupils' memorization of great works, Carroll celebrated his heroine's ability to parody the revered texts and conventions of children's literature, drawing the readers' attention to the way literary forms can be simultaneously altered and preserved within the new, mutated forms. In *Wonderland,* Carroll illustrates that learning to manipulate literature, especially through parody, models willed change rather than random variation and human control rather than uncontrolled chaos. *Wonderland*'s parodies turn Arnold's pedagogical prescription – of memorized recitation as opposed to Spencer's spontaneous experimentation – on its head, but they nevertheless make one of the nineteenth century's best cases for the humanizing power of literature.

The fourth chapter begins the book's second part. The effects of the 1870 Elementary Education Act were not immediate; science subjects coexisted alongside literary ones, and debates about education shifted away from curricular matters. But the issue of the child's education and its evolutionary underpinnings was revived in the last decade of the century amidst concerns about Britain's imperial prospects. Chapter 4, "The cure of the wild: Rudyard Kipling and evolutionary adolescence at home and abroad," shows that Kipling feared that British civilization, mimicking the life span of an individual, was approaching old age. *The Jungle Book* and *The Second Jungle Book* (1895) express Kipling's hope that the animal child can reinvigorate the race. His portrait of the unapologetically wild "man-cub" Mowgli garnered him admirers, among them Sir Robert Baden-Powell, who established the Boy Scouts, and Hall, through whom Kipling's recipe for British remasculinization was transported to the United States and Canada. This chapter argues that Kipling's desire to preserve the animal exuberance of childhood went much farther than his imitators allowed. *The Jungle Books* articulate a literature of deferral: prolonging, distending, reversing, and pausing the narrative of recapitulation and the traditional forward thrust of the *Bildungsroman*. Ostensibly a salve to the problems of the Empire, the poetics of the Mowgli stories disrupt the very notion of "progress" that undergirds Victorian ideas about empire, education, and evolutionary theory.

Recapitulation enabled a fantasy of cultural masculinization that had no room for little girls. Chapter 5, "Home grown: Frances Hodgson Burnett and the cultivation of female evolution," traces the corresponding evolutionary cast for the girl's development. Little girls were not encouraged to revive their natural savagery in order to fight, but they were urged to stay physically fit and to choose the right partners in order to produce healthy sons, especially in light of an impending world war. Burnett's *The Secret Garden* (1911) tackles the contradictory prescriptions for girls' education, including eugenic directives and more traditional motherhood training, and combines them in a narrative that transgenders the recapitulative plot usually reserved for boys. Transported from India to England after her parents' death, Burnett's Mary Lennox embarks on a developmental trajectory that both reverses the formula of *The Jungle Books* and expands it even further outward, shifting from the singular male hero to multiple protagonists and imagining the group as the unit of evolution. The "garden" in Burnett's title functions as a transitional stage of development, between natural wildness and gentrified cultivation, but it is the "secret" that becomes central to the girl's and the group's evolution, binding the children together and replacing physical facts with the elevating ability to tell stories about them.

My study draws together the intellectual history of evolutionary theory, the social history of educational reform, and the literary history of the burgeoning genre for children in order to enhance our understanding of all three fields. Children's literature, far from seeking to escape its historical situation and to preserve the child's innocence, instead self-consciously developed nonsense, fantasy, parody, digressive play, metamorphosis, hybrid forms, shifting perspectives, and multiple protagonists in order to counter the call that children be more versed in science for the betterment of the species. Through its investment in its pedagogical, sociological, and scientific contexts, this book is concerned primarily with the literariness of children's literature: the collective response to a new scientific conception of human history. Focusing on the adoption of evolutionary theory in child study and children's literature, on the way scientific theory influences literary form, on literature's simultaneous role in reshaping Victorian perception of scientific concepts, and on the contested value of the humanities within the rising dominance of science, *Evolution and Imagination in Victorian Children's Literature* is a project about interdisciplinarity itself and about the convergence of these discordant and multidimensional discourses around that inexorably puzzling figure: the child.

CHAPTER I

The child's view of nature
Margaret Gatty and the challenge to natural theology

William Wordsworth's Boy of Winander, "stand[ing] alone/Beneath the trees or by the glimmering lake" and blowing "mimic hootings to the silent owls,/That they might answer him," seems to represent at least a century's thinking about childhood.[1] The sensitive, solitary boy from Wordsworth's *Prelude* (1805) enjoys the sublimity of the landscape and the prospect of communication with other animals because he is a child and therefore natural and animal-like himself. But this is not the way that most nineteenth-century children were taught to experience or to appreciate nature. Their nature was populated not by enigmatic, silent owls but rather by busy bees, happy birds, and clever rabbits whose actions seemed to "speak" in moral lessons for the child to hear. Likewise, nineteenth-century literature for children rarely featured them alone; they were usually accompanied by an adult who could teach them how to read nature and to interpret its educational meaning. Nature entered children's literature not as an alternative to school, isolated from society, adulthood, and textuality, as Wordsworth presented it in his poetry. Instead, from nature, Victorian children were supposed to glean lessons like the axiom from Margaret Gatty's story "Kicking" (1864): "Animals under man – servants under masters – children under parents – wives under husbands – men under authorities – nations under rulers – all under God."[2]

Nineteenth-century nature was, indeed, a vast classroom filled with texts written by God and intended to teach children about divine design, moral behavior, and social convention. Though certain practitioners bemoaned the decline of Britain's scientific prowess in the 1830s, it was the Great Exhibition of 1851 combined with the anticipation of compulsory schooling that highlighted the need for elementary science instruction.[3] In 1852, Queen Victoria addressed Parliament, announcing, "the advancement of the fine arts and of practical science will be readily recognised by you as worthy of the attention of a great and enlightened nation."[4] The natural sciences were deemed suitable preparations for working-class students entering manufacturing professions and perfect introductions to Christianity and social order for every child. According to historian Normal Morris, the Victorian school system "exuded paternalism" and reflected "a simple desire to preserve and bring out the best in each social rank by soaking it in its appropriate ethos."[5] For this purpose, "science" meant natural theology. Natural theology is the belief that observing nature reveals the omnipotence of God and beneficence of His design. The technical knowledge gleaned from studying natural objects and processes would thus allow future laborers to assist in securing Britain's global triumphs, while the moral messages about the beneficence of the natural, political, and economic status quo also conveyed by "scientific" instruction would safeguard against any revolutionary fervor. Henry Barnard's *Object Teaching and Oral Lessons on Social Science and Common Things* (1860), exemplary of midcentury pedagogical manuals, advises, "in all these lessons the teacher should never fail to call the attention of the children to the goodness of God in accommodating each animal to the circumstances of its life."[6] Natural theology, according to science historian John Hedley Brooke, was "a visible, and enduring, symbol of an Enlightenment goal – the pursuit of science – thriving within piety."[7]

Though scientific instruction received fresh impetus in the midcentury – between the European revolutions of the 1840s and the groundwork for compulsory education in England and Wales, codified in 1870 – the 1850s concluded with a very public blow to the design argument's characterization of nature as ordered, benign, and stable. Charles Darwin's *On the Origin of Species* (1859) challenged not only the premise of natural theology but also the social conservatism that natural theology supported. Jeap-Baptiste Lamarck's "transmutation" hypothesis proposed that organisms will their own transformations, propelling themselves into higher morphological classes by what anatomist Richard Owen called individual organisms' "self-developing energies."[8] Though Darwin ultimately discarded this theory of volitionally acquired characteristics in favor of natural selection, the "struggle for existence" that he described seemed to justify – to capitalists like Andrew Carnegie, for example – cutthroat market competition similarly capable of leveling traditional economic and social hierarchies.[9] For lay readers, the distinctions between Lamarck and Darwin were subtle at best. Evolution sounded disturbingly like revolution, and if *that* was modern science, it no longer facilely conveyed the rules of social propriety, class and gender hierarchies, and unquestioning obedience to authority. Darwinism by no means wiped out natural theology; quite the opposite, natural theology maintained a prominent place in elementary education and children's literature into the twentieth century. But for some children's authors, the newly embraced sciences had changed their colors and posed a danger to the young minds now open to them.

To understand recapitulation's disruption of Victorian conceptions of the child and his education, we must first appreciate how natural theology so successfully seemed to wed science and literature and how it communicated its religious and social lessons. The centerpiece of this chapter is Gatty's *Parables from Nature* (1855–1871), a five-part series whose thirty-six stories introduced middle-class readers to the world of animals and plants through an anti-evolutionary lens. Because "Kicking" stridently upholds the social and theological stratification familiar in natural theology texts, and "Inferior Animals" (1861) famously mocks Darwin and Lamarck, Gatty gets brief scholarly mention as a staunch defender of natural theology and as a children's writer trapped in traditional ways of thinking. However, though *Parables from Nature* rejects evolution, Gatty's stories shrewdly recognize that the pedagogical methods of scientific observation and deduction – the staples of natural theology – no longer uphold the argument from design. As this chapter will show, her stories display an acute awareness that natural theology, as it was conceived and taught, could not withstand the threat that Darwinism posed. Inducting children into her social and theological vision, Gatty seems to recognize that children's literature required a refreshed pedagogical rhetoric and literary style. Thus, in antithesis to the staid natural theology lessons of the Victorian classroom that distilled science into useful knowledge with a deistic twist, Gatty's stories update the philosophy and the rhetoric of natural theology for post-Darwinian readers. In so doing *Parables from Nature* suggests that children should look to literature that explains and refashions nature, and not to nature itself, for evidence of human value, divine truth, and beneficent design.

The book of nature

In *Reconstructing Nature: The Engagement of Science and Religion* (1998), Brooke and Geoffrey Cantor discuss natural theology's use of rhetoric and catalogue its most frequently used conventions, such as analogy (between man's works and God's) and antithesis (between the perfection of the world as it is and the chaos that would occur if the world were any different).[10] In children's literature, natural theology also operated by common strategies that dissolved the boundary between text and world, directed readers to observe nature, instructed them to see proof of design, extrapolated from design in nature to design in society, and forged analogies linking the adult who designed the book, the parents who rule the home, and God who both designed and rules everything. The children's book acted as an introduction and conduit to real nature while claiming to echo, in its own formal aspects and cast of characters, the beneficent organization and social stratification that the child was meant to see there. The untutored child is not yet, as he would become in post-Darwinian accounts of recapitulation, an animal struggling to become human, but a student of nature taking careful notes in order to mimic nature's perfection in her own regulated behavior. Though evolutionary theory challenged the notion that that natural harmony could serve as a model for childhood obedience and social well-being, children's writers were slow to abandon natural theology or its rhetoric. But even the most stalwart children's literature began to reveal an awareness that natural theology's scientific instructions might not always lead to natural theology's religious convictions.

Throughout the eighteenth and early nineteenth centuries, observation was the gospel of natural theology. By observing nature, the child was meant to become acquainted with God's works. The writer who best expressed the tenets of natural theology was Isaac Watts, whose *Discourse on the Education of Children and Youth* (1760) tells parents to "shew [children] the birds, the beasts, the fishes, the insects, trees, fruit, herbs, and all the several parts and properties of the vegetable and animal world. Teach them to observe the various occurrences of Nature and Providence, the sun, the moon, the stars, the day and night ... Teach them that the GREAT GOD made all these, and that his providence governs them."[11] Watts's moral homilies about nature remained popular into the nineteenth century, and his ideas about the spiritual significance of observation were an almost ubiquitous trope of children's literature.[12] This moral was pithily summed up in the title of J. Aiken's and Anna Barbauld's "Eyes, and no Eyes; or, The Art of Seeing" (1793), the story of two brothers, one who finds nothing of interest on his afternoon ramble through the countryside and the other who discovers infinite wonders just outside his door.[13] Victorian and Edwardian children's writers continued this call to observation and affirmed its path to devotion even after *Origin of Species*. In her book of seasons, *Our Year: A Child's Book in Prose and Verse* (1860), Dinah Maria Craik encourages her readers "to keep one's eyes open to the natural things around us, and try to find out all about flowers, and trees, and living creatures – their names, and growth, and habits, and ways. For the observation of nature is an interest perpetual."[14] Half a century later,

W. Percival Westell's *Every Boy's Book of British Natural History* (1906) still declares that "the only effort, then, that is required to achieve success in Nature-study is the effort of observation" which "will lead you to Nature's God."[15]

The primacy of observation might seem to devalue the efficacy of textual instruction, and indeed the pedagogical purpose of reading at all. In his study of scientific dialogues for children, Greg Myers underscores the inherent incongruity: "the reader is taught that he or she should learn by observing things and having experiences, but he or she imbibes this wisdom by reading."[16] However, many children's writers emphasized the parallel between reading texts and observing nature (reading God's text) by making nature study the preamble to reading the Bible. The mother-narrator of Sarah Trimmer's *An Easy Introduction to the Knowledge of Nature, and Reading the Holy Scriptures* (1780) instructs her children: "all who have leisure should study the great Book of Nature ... But there is still another book in which the goodness of God to mankind is more fully displayed, I mean the BIBLE."[17] A quarter of a century later, Charlotte Smith's *Conversations, Introducing Poetry: Chiefly on the Subjects of Natural History for the Use of Children and Young Persons* (1804) renews this analogy. Her mother-narrator, Mrs. Talbot, agrees that children should be encouraged "to learn the lessons that God teaches us in his great Book of Nature, and to study these lessons as they are explained in his other great Book of Revelation. There is not a plant, or flower, or bird, but brings us some gracious message from our God."[18] For Trimmer and Smith, reading is not contrary to sensory experience; both words and objects are manufactured – either by human authors or the supreme Author, God. The metaphor of the book is used not to raise issues of interpretation or ambivalence but rather to emphasize the absolute transparency of the texts under consideration. Westell's *Every Boy's Book* succinctly sums up at least a century's worth of thinking when it refers to Nature as a "wonderful and ever-open book" that everyone can read.[19]

Though everyone can read this "open book" of nature, children must first learn how to read it. Even William Paley's philosophy-defining work *Natural Theology; or, Evidence of the Existence and Attributes of the Deity, Collected from the Appearances of Nature* (1802) admits the value of adding education to bare observation. *Natural Theology* famously opens with the author's hypothetical discovery of a watch on a heath; Paley argues that, if we know intuitively that the existence of the watch requires a watchmaker, we should also conclude that the existence of a stone necessitates a stone maker, indeed that all creation points to a Creator. But even according to

Paley, deducing a Creator demands not only "an examination of the instrument" (observation) but also "perhaps some previous knowledge of the subject" (prior education).[20] Literature was thus not only the endpoint of nature study (reading the Bible) but also the prelude, offering both previous knowledge about natural phenomena and instructions for reading nature. The preface to Priscilla Wakefield's children's book *Mental Improvement: or, The Beauties and Wonders of Nature and Art* (1794–1797), for instance, explains why, despite the perennial promptings to observe nature in the scientific dialogues that follow, her young readers first need literature. "The art of exercising the faculty of thinking and reflection upon every object that is seen, ought to constitute a material branch of a good education," Wakefield explains in her preface; "but it requires the skill of a master's hand, to lead the minds of youth to the habit of observation."[21] The "master" is both Wakefield herself, as the author of the book, and her surrogates within the text, Mr. and Mrs. Harcourt, who teach their children and their children's friends how to "read" the facts of nature. Mrs. Harcourt instructs one young houseguest to "accustom yourself to observe every thing you see with attention; consider how they are made, what the materials are, and from whence they come."[22] She does not just tell the girl to observe, but she defines what "observe" means: not simply recognizing size, dimension, or color but asking how and by whom nature was created. According to *Mental Improvement*, readers must first learn what observation entails before they can be trusted to do it on their own.

Maria Hack's *Harry Beaufoy; or, The Pupil of Nature* (1821) purports to be a child's version of Paley's *Natural Theology* that both extols the powers of observation and reminds the child reader that he needs training to exercise it properly. Hack says in the preface that she wrote the enclosed conversations between ten-year-old Harry and his parents by selecting passages from Paley's book and "arranging them so as to form a chain of argument adapted to the powers of reasoning at that age."[23] Appropriate to its purpose, *Harry Beaufoy* opens with Harry's investigation of his mother's watch, which he deems "the most ingenious contrivance that I ever saw in my life."[24] His mother instructs him to marvel not only at the skill of the watchmaker but also at "the skill of that wonderful Artist who constructed the machine we call a bird: a machine infinitely more curious and complicated than a watch."[25] But even as Mrs. Beaufoy directs Harry to "make use of those powers of reasoning and observation which a bountiful Creator has bestowed upon you," the boy's attempts to do so on his own tend to go awry. Lifting another example of God's benevolent design straight out of Paley, Mrs. Beaufoy instructs Harry to look at the underside of a cabbage leaf to see where the butterfly instinctively lays her eggs. For Paley, instinct is another attribute designed by God for the benefit of the species; he uses, as example, the butterfly's act of laying her eggs in a cabbage leaf, where her hatchlings (though not herself) will find nourishment.[26] Mrs. Beaufoy intends Harry to learn about the marvel of instinct himself, but he gets so distracted watching the fluttering butterfly that the lesson is almost lost until his mother redirects his observations along the proper channel.

The activity of observation requires even more direction when it is not only design in nature that the child is meant to see but also design in the social and familial order. One of Harry Beaufoy's lessons, when looking at the physical abilities of the different animals, is to admire "the exercise of voluntary power within just bounds," and that lesson is quickly extrapolated to include people.[27] The Talbot children in Smith's *Conversations, Introducing Poetry* likewise learn that "every day is lucky in which we possess strength of mind and body to do our duty, in whatever line of life we are placed."[28] In *Mental Improvement*, piety to God for His organization of nature is predicated by the Harcourt children's gratitude to their parents for creating such wonderful lessons about nature: "how happy we are," exclaims sixteen-year-old Sophia, "to be blessed with such parents, who devote so much time to our instruction and amusement!"[29] The care that the children's parents take in their lessons is analogous to "the wisdom and goodness of that divine Being, who careth for all the works of his creation, and has provided for the respective wants of each."[30] Nature study persuades the children to respect their parents and God for so arranging their world and their pedagogical induction into it, and it additionally teaches them to model themselves after such perfected arrangements. After learning that God has so designed the animal kingdom that those species useful to humans reside in and around Great Britain, while the noxious beasts inhabit foreign lands, twelve-year-old Cecilia says, "Now I am convinced of what you have often told me, that nothing can be well done without order and method. I will endeavour to be more attentive to this point, and do every thing with greater regularity in the future."[31] Growing into a proper young lady, here, means seeking to mimic the tidiness of nature, to recognize that everything has its natural place relative to other elements, including children and parents, girls and boys, and the lower and upper classes.

This pedagogical pattern – (1) learn to observe nature, (2) appreciate design, (3) infer God, (4) regulate oneself – appears almost ubiquitously in "scientific" lessons for children in the first half of the nineteenth century, and plenty in the second half. Darwinism was perhaps so pernicious because it began from the same starting point but arrived at very different conclusions. In *Origin of Species*, Darwin uses cognates of "observe," "see," "look," and "find" multiple times and on almost every page.[32] Like Wakefield, Barbauld, Hack, Craik, and Smith's readers, Darwin's audience is urged to observe, but what it can expect to see has radically altered. In the decades after *Origin of Species*, even texts that preserved natural theology began to admit that man's supremacy cannot be based solely on observable fact. Worthington Hooker's *The Child's Book of Nature* (1874), for instance, admits that "man can climb, but he can not do it as well as a cat or a monkey. He can swim, but not as well as a fish. The frog and the grasshopper are better jumpers. The horse and the dog can run faster than he can."[33] The child discussant in Mrs. C. C. Campbell's *Natural History for Young Folks* (1884) likewise points out that "a man cannot run so fast as a dog or horse, mamma; and he is not so strong as a lion or an elephant."[34] Though admitting man's physical limitations, neither text leaves us in the inferior position for long; Campbell soon asks the children to recall Genesis, wherein "man was made in the image of God" and "was made a living soul." Reverend J. G. Wood's *The Boy's Own Natural History* (1861) celebrates the human hand and man's erect posture but locates our real superiority in "the human spirit indwelling in Man."[35] While claiming the importance of observation, these post-Darwinian texts reach for the unobservable, suggesting that when humans are the objects, observation alone cannot justify our specialness.

If looking at man does not unreservedly convince the observer of his superiority in the animal kingdom, the child presented an even tougher case. Hooker's *Child's Book* dwells on the child as a figure oddly straddling the divide between man and animals. The author tells his readers: "hands were made for useful work and innocent play; but they are often used to strike with. Teeth are given to us to eat with; but children, and even men sometimes, bite with them like an angry beast. Nails are given us for various useful purposes, but I have known children to use them in fighting, as beasts do their claws and spurs."[36] While praising man's development and use of tools, then, Hooker compares children's use of their hands, teeth, and nails to the behaviors of precivilized beasts. Searching for a defense of human specialness not based on observable anatomy, children's writers often remind children that they alone can read and appreciate stories. Hooker explains, "you never would think of telling a story to a dog or a cat as you would to a child, for you know that it would not be understood."[37] James Johonnot's *Friends in Feather and Fur, and Other Neighbors, for Young Folks* (1884) similarly insists, "nothing but a human being has been able to get thought from a written or printed page and convey it to others."[38] Children's bodies may not seem that different from animal bodies, but their ability to read at least reassures late-century authors that even hitting, biting, and scratching children are human.

Midcentury children's literature in the tradition of natural theology posited that reading books would lead the child to observe nature, which would then bring the child back to reading *the* Book, the Bible. The child's first texts trained the young eye to see everywhere in nature what was already true in society: that everything is designed and that maturation means mirroring in one's own personal comportment, domestic relations, social encounters, and religious devotion the perfect arrangement one finds in nature. These children's works, even and especially after Darwin, attempt to sidestep the interpretive ambiguity of Nature's book, the chaos and waste that appears alongside beneficence, and the visible weakness of man, but many also recognize that undirected observation may not provide unquestionable evidence of natural and social design. It was to be expected that much of nineteenth-century children's literature superficially looked the same before and after Darwin. Children's literature would follow the culture at large in holding onto a philosophy in which science merely seconded what religion already knew. But children's literature was hardly the escapist genre that critics have assumed, and indeed it could not be. Science was entering the school system and gaining fresh eyes, and there was a dawning sense that the scientific program of encouraging the child to observe nature must be tempered with other kinds of instruction. None of the works so far discussed, however, sufficiently theorize this problem or seek to solve it until Gatty's *Parables from Nature*.

To see or not to see

Upon first reading, Gatty's *Parables from Nature* seems to retread the familiar territory of pre-Darwinian natural theology. "A Lesson of Hope" (1855) introduces an owl who preaches to the other forest birds that nature is designed to bring happiness to all its inhabitants: "Life, order, harmony, and peace," he says, "means duly fitting ends; the object, universal joy. This is the law. Believe in it, and live!" (1: 38). In "The Law of Authority and Obedience" (1855), Gatty uses that old staple, the hardworking and seemingly class-conscious hive bee, to exemplify the importance of doing one's duty in a stratified society. The caterpillar in "A Lesson of Faith"

(1855) and the frog in "Not Lost, But Gone Before" (1857) illustrate nature's metamorphoses analogous to human transformation after death. In "Gifts" (1864), the rain drops murmur to the plants that they water that "each [is] good after its kind, each bearing a part in the full perfection of the kingdom which is boundless, the plan which is harmony – peace, peace, peace upon all!" (II: 53). This applause for God's perfect design has served to characterize Gatty's fiction. In *Darwin's Plots: Evolutionary Narrative in Darwin, George Eliot and Nineteenth-Century Fiction* (1983), Gillian Beer uses Gatty's tales as an example of the stubborn persistence of "older world orders" even as Darwinism was pushing them aside.[39] Subsequent scholarship about Gatty tends to echo Beer. Bernard Lightman's reassessment of Victorian women writers affirms "Gatty's perpetuation of the natural theology tradition," and Alan Rauch's article on *Parables from Nature* likewise contends that her stories are "always firmly rooted in the tradition of natural theology" and "always grounded in the observable and the empirical."[40] Though this insistence on Gatty's uncritical adoption of natural theology has set the tone for recent discussions of *Parables from Nature*, the collection does not keep the faith as staunchly or naively as critics have claimed.

Undoubtedly Gatty's biography seems to support these critical interpretations of her works. As the daughter and the wife of Anglican clergymen, the mother of ten children, a teacher in the parish school erected by her husband, an amateur naturalist with a passion for seaweeds, and an avid anti-evolutionist, Gatty neatly fits the mold of the Victorian middle-class Christian.[41] It was while recovering from the birth of her seventh child in 1848 that a trip to the English coast introduced her to the pleasures of collecting and classifying seaweeds, which in turn led to her acquaintance with professional scientists. Though her interest in natural history took her outside the conventionally feminine domestic sphere, and even gained her notoriety as an expert with her publication of *British Seaweeds* (1862), Gatty always placed the pursuit of science in the service of Christianity. In her profile of the author in *Revealing New Worlds: Three Victorian Women Naturalists* (2001), Suzanne Le-May Sheffield says that Gatty's professional and personal writings "suggest that she had completely internalized societal norms about her proper place as a woman in middle-class Victorian society and within the scientific hierarchy," but that Gatty also considered the time she spent collecting seaweeds on the beach to be "a refuge from the gendered conventions of societal expectations."[42] My reading of Gatty's work does not make her a pioneer for feminism; as Sheffield admits, she was invested in reinforcing social hierarchies and anxious about science's potential for toppling them. Gatty's innovation, rather, emerges from her awareness of evolution's precise threat and her reinvention of a natural theology fortified against the amoral and revolutionary consequences of modern science.

Though proclamations of visible design are scattered liberally throughout *Parables from Nature*, Gatty's stories repeatedly register a deep suspicion of natural theology's reliance on observation. In *Parables from Nature*'s most critically discussed tale, "Inferior Animals," a parliament of rooks debates whether or not man is the superior life form or, indeed, a devolved species of bird. To make their case that "man . . . is neither more nor less than a degenerated brother of our own race!" (II: 30), the rooks rely on observable fact. The head of the rook caucus declares, "I venture confidently to look back thousands on thousands of generations, and I see that *men* were once *rooks!*" (II: 30), drawing attention to the acts of looking and seeing. The team of "experts" who bear witness likewise bases its theories on direct observation: "now all common observation is against the superiority of man. While we fly swiftly through the sky, behold him creeping slowly along the ground. While we soar to the very clouds, a brief jump and come down again is all his utmost efforts can accomplish" (II: 28). Others of Gatty's rook assembly add similar arguments gathered from observable evidence: man's blackening himself (with dark suits and coal pollution) and his attempt to regain an arboreal life (by erecting multistory buildings) attest to men's desire to become rooks again. All of this, according to the head rook, is "common observation," which may be different from intelligent or informed observation, but the critique of observation is clear. Looking will not demonstrate incontestable proof of human superiority, and is likely to yield the opposite. Gatty's satire does not seek to unseat man from his place at the head of the animal kingdom; the rooks' reasoning is foolish, as we are meant to understand. But it may not be their erroneous conclusions that are the butt of the satire but rather their faulty methods. In "Inferior Animals," Gatty pokes fun at both evolutionists and natural theologians by asking the essential question of the collection: can we trust our own eyes?

For those critics who wish to make Gatty's *Parables from Nature* a clear example of natural theology for children, "Inferior Animals" is given a special place: a story for adults craftily snuck into a child's collection. Rauch maintains that "Gatty's tale of the rooks . . . presupposes an understanding, if not an appreciation of, evolutionary development" that "would resonate with adult readers only."[43] In *Talking Animals in British Children's Fiction, 1786–1914* (2006), Tess Cosslett agrees, claiming that "Inferior

Animals" invokes "a very adult debate" about biological progress and degeneration; because "one of the purposes of the *Parables from Nature* is to counter scientific naturalism and its attendant disbelief, and evolutionary thought in particular," she writes, "this purpose leads Gatty to address adults as well as children."[44] For both critics, the satire of "Inferior Animals" – like the rooks themselves – flies straight over younger readers' heads to alight only in the more sophisticated minds of older readers. It illustrates the "dual address" of Victorian children's literature notably described by U. C. Knoepflmacher's essay "The Balancing of Child and Adult: An Approach to Victorian Fantasies for Children" (1983).[45] Knoepflmacher, Rauch, Cosslett, and Lightman, among other scholars, have skillfully shown how Victorian women writers used children's literature to speak to women readers about scientific and political theories they could not so openly discuss. The recognition that children's literature simultaneously addresses child and adult readers is essential to understanding the genre, but determining what content is addressed to which audience must take into account contemporary readers' expectations and not just our own. Nineteenth-century schoolchildren, we should remember, were steeped in literature that valorized observation. They likely could have understood the parody perfectly well.

That Gatty had an adult reader at least partially in mind for "Inferior Animals" is clear. Gatty's narrator appeals to the reader: she asks, "shall you and I become children in heart once more?" in order to hear the birds speak (II: 25). Cosslett reads this moment as an illustration that neither the narrator nor the implied reader is rendered as a child. Biographical evidence also shows that Gatty understood "Inferior Animals" as a rebuttal of Darwinism for educated readers. She admitted in a letter to Dr. William Harvey, "of course Darwin's theories are the moving cause of my attempting the subject," though the rooks' account of man's degeneration from the disuse of their wings shows that Gatty did not distinguish Darwinism from Lamarckism.[46] The rooks' reasoning also echoes (though surely coincidentally) a parody made thirty years earlier by German embryologist Karl Ernst von Baer. In *Entwicklungsgeschichte der Thiere* (1828), von Baer imagines a group of scientifically savvy birds observing humans and thinking that men "bear many resemblances to [bird] embryos, for their cranial bones are separated, and they have no beak, just as we do in the first five or six days of incubation," and "there is not a single true feather on their body, rather only thin feather-shafts, so that we, as fledglings in the nest, are more advanced than they shall ever be."[47] In other words, the birds reverse the recapitulation paradigm that deems humans as the only fully developed organisms and places all the others as versions of arrested men. The birds believe instead that they have passed through an anterior human stage and are thus the more evolved being. Just as Gatty uses the rooks to argue against evolution, von Baer poses this parody as an argument against recapitulation. The satire is a complex one and, related this way, almost assuredly flew over the heads of the Victorian child reader.

But a child reader need not have read Darwin or von Baer to recognize that Gatty is poking fun at the reliance on observation: an undisputed value pervasive in their school lessons and leisure reading. The warning against observation runs throughout *Parables from Nature*. The series opens with "A Lesson of Faith," a story that could easily be renamed "A Lesson against Observation." Here, a caterpillar cannot understand why a dying butterfly has put her in charge of soon-to-be-hatched butterfly eggs. When a lark tells the caterpillar that she will one day become a butterfly herself, she does not believe it: "I know what's possible, and what's not possible . . . Look at my long green body and these endless legs, and then talk to me about having wings and a painted feathery coat!" (I: 4). When the caterpillar takes a "look" at her anatomy, she reaches the obvious but erroneous conclusion that a "long green body" and "endless legs" are antithetical to prismatic, gauzy wings. Her vision is limited, "for, poor thing! she never could see very far at any time, and had a difficulty in looking upwards at all, even when she reared herself up most carefully" (I: 2). This emphasis on limited vision anticipates the rest of Gatty's parables. In "The Deliverer" (1861), the narrator says, "we strive after signs and wonders, we look for visible manifestations, we long for sensible experiences, and when unanswered we fall back without a hope" (II: 23). And vision, according to *Parables from Nature*, is not our only deficient sense. In "The Cause and the Causer" (1871), a story that interrogates the possibility of instinct working without divine direction, Dr. Earwig tells the insect academics assembled before him that "human ears, whatever human beings may think of them, take in but a few octaves of the great gamut of the universe. To all below and above these they are insensible, and hence often speak of silence when the silence exists only for themselves" (II: 94).

Not only are our senses flawed, for Gatty, but so is the evidence we gather even when they are working. For a collection ostensibly promoting natural theology, *Parables from Nature* is surprisingly filled with chaos, destruction, and the absence of design. Messages like those in "A Lesson of Hope" and "Gifts" about "order, harmony and peace" or "peace, peace, peace upon all," though prevalent, are in the minority. More common are stories like "Whereunto?" (1861), in which two men walk across the beach at low tide, marveling at all the sea life stranded on the sands and suffocating in the air. One of the men says, "Here again, you see; the same old story as before. Wasted life and wasted death, and all within a few inches of each other! Useless, lumbering plants, not seen half-a-dozen times in the year; and helpless, miserable sea-creatures, dying in health and strength, one doesn't know why" (1: 97). The vegetal matter and animal life still think the world is made for them, but the story mocks their narcissism, and the argument about design is ambivalent at best.[48] In an earlier story, "Training and Restraining" (1855), nature without human intercession is chaotic: the wind wreaks havoc on a villa garden, leaving, "the shattered Carnations ... rotted with lying in the wet and dirt on the ground," "the white Lily ... languishing, discoloured on its broken stalk," and "the Convolvulus' flowers ... coated over with mud-stains" (1: 26). Even in "A Lesson of Hope," the owl feels the need to insist that "life, order, harmony, and peace ... is the law" because all visible evidence is to the contrary; after a storm has razed the birds' nests, all is "disorder, death, destruction" (1: 38). Such stories do not deny God's omnipotence or beneficence, but they suggest that observation alone does not inevitably lead the viewer to that Christianizing conclusion.

Instead, *Parables from Nature* admonishes readers who think that nature is an open book that readily and clearly answers our questions. Toward this end, the series challenges not only the efficacy of observation but also the utility of another narrative strategy familiar to children's literature: the scientific dialogue. "Inferior Animals" opens with a frame in which the narrator reflects on the childhood desire to hear animals speak and the childhood conviction that such communication is possible. And though we do eventually hear the transcription of the birds' debate, the narrator lingers for a moment on the impossibility of actual dialogue between humans and animals:

> What do they say? – what do they say? – what do they say? –
>
> What can they *have* to say, those noisy, cawing rooks, as they sail along the sky over our heads, gathering more and more friends as they go, to the appointed place of meeting?
>
> What have *they* to say? – What have *we* to say? they may equally ask. (II: 24)

In "The Child's Place in Nature" (2002), her first version of the argument she takes up in *Talking Animals*, Cosslett intriguingly speculates about this frame: "it is as if evolutionary thought raises too uncomfortably the idea of animal/human kinship, and causes [Gatty] to examine what she is doing using the talking animal convention."[49] However, Cosslett misses that this moment also allows Gatty to examine the convention of the scientific dialogue. Myers has demonstrated that the scientific dialogue is a chief ingredient of natural theology texts because it delivers the perfect "symmetry of questions and answers."[50] In most of these dialogues, the child asks a question about the nature of the world around him, and the parent demonstrates her ability to answer it fully and without fail; according to Myers, this symmetry imparts a "sense that the world was made for man's education." Nothing falls outside the child's curiosity, as nothing falls outside the parent's knowledge. But in "Inferior Animals," the narrator repeats her inquiry three times in vain: "what do they say? – what do they say? – what do they say?". The story of "What the rooks say" is a parody of evolution, but the frame's broken dialogue pokes fun at the rhetoric of natural theology that expects nature to speak to us, to answer all our questions about its origins and its processes. The rooks' "noisy cawing" is "discordant and confused" (II: 24), and rather than hearing any truth in this cacophony, we receive only the echo of our own desires and preconceptions. "What have *they* say" becomes "what have *we* to say," as advocates of evolution and design alike extract from nature precisely those ideas they impart to it.

If *Parables from Nature*'s distrust of observation and its ridicule of the scientific dialogue mark its break with the philosophical and rhetorical tradition of natural theology, as I have been claiming, this legacy is not a simple one. Beginning in 1865, editions of Gatty's stories, appearing as *Parables from Nature, with Notes on the Natural History*, preserve natural theology's practice of using fiction to lead the child to nature. Appended notes to each tale, written by Gatty herself, draw from scientific authority, often quoting correspondence between Gatty and men of science like Richard Owen and Phillip Henry Gosse. Elaborating the tale "Purring When You're Pleased" (1861), Gatty says she has written to Owen and asked him to explain why cats purr, to which he responded that purring is caused by "the delicate membranes attached to the 'vocal chords' of the *larynx*, or voice-organ . . . set in vibratory motion under a placid sensation of comfort."[51] To "Cobwebs" (1864), Gatty adds a quotation from Gosse, saying that "the spinning apparatus [of the spider] consists of four little teats or warts at the hinder extremity of the body."[52] These notes reinforce the idea that the stories' real meanings lie in opening up the readers' eyes to the intricacy of design, while other notes direct the reader to perform his own experiments and make his own observations. After "Red Snow" (1861), one of the collection's most explicit Christian allegories, the note instructs readers how to grow and to examine the algae the story describes: "Place such fragments in a common sandstone vase, such as are frequently to be found in gardens, and pour a little soft water over them. In time – it may be days or weeks, or months even – the plant is sure to make itself observed."[53] In this edition, at least, reading about nature leads the child into nature with an eye to nature's wonders: the principles of natural theology seem preserved.

However, even in the Bell and Daldy edition, where *Parables from Nature* seems most interested in engaging the child reader in nature study, Gatty's longest note – appropriately to "Inferior Animals" – quotes John Henry Newman's "The Invisible World" (1838) in order to muse at much greater leisure on the limits of observation:[54]

> We are in a world of spirits as well as in a world of sense, and we hold communion with it, and take part in it, though we are not conscious of doing so. If this seems strange to any one, let him reflect that we are undeniably taking part in a third world, which we do indeed see, but about which we do not know more than about the angelic hosts, – the world of brute animals. Can anything be more marvellous or startling, unless we were used to it, than that we should have a race of beings about us whom we do but see, and as little know of their state, or can describe their interests or their destiny, as we can tell of the inhabitants of the sun and moon? It is indeed a very overpowering thought, when we get to fix our minds on it, that we familiarly use, I may say hold intercourse with, creatures who are as much strangers to us, as mysterious as if they were the fabulous, unearthly beings, more powerful than man, yet his slaves, which Eastern superstitions have invented. We have more real knowledge about the angels than about the brutes.[55]

Newman's thoughts complicate the ease of natural theology and the pedagogical program that it asserts, moving us smoothly from observing natural fact to appreciating design and then onto inferring a Designer. Instead of the world of sense leading us to the world of spirits, sense and sprits are two opposite ways of knowing the world that are not sequentially accessible. Observation, experiment, and science constitute a way of living in the world that is juxtaposed with religion and spirituality. Furthermore, there is a "third world" that appeals neither to sense nor to spirits but to an unsolvable mystery: the world of animals. Taking Newman's position as a gloss on *Parables from Nature* as a whole only further complicates what purpose Gatty's talking animals are serving. They are neither fact (sense) nor symbol (spirit) but may point to a third way of knowing that Gatty's stories aim to manifest.

Like Newman's sermon, *Parables from Nature* contrasts observation with faith through a third term: the figure of the animal. In "Knowledge Not the Limit of Belief" (1855), a seaweed and a zoophyte discussing their own categorical instability – caught between taxonomies of plant and animal – are interrupted by a bookworm who tells them they must accept what they do not know and trust their superiors because "*Observation and Revelation are the sole means of acquiring knowledge*" (1: 21). But in Newman's sermon and in *Parables from Nature*, this is not the whole story. Newman suggests that animals are a third way of knowing, or rather a way of knowing that is not knowing. In Gatty's "Knowledge Not the Limit of Belief," the intercession of the bookworm adds a third member to the previous binary of seaweed and zoophyte, and as a third figure he suggests that there might be a possibility in addition to observation and revelation. There is no such animal as a "bookworm"; the word is merely a metaphor for a bibliophile. Thus the bookworm is the epitome of the fictionalized animal, the literary animal, which exists (in more ways than one) only in books. "Knowledge Not the Limit of Belief" suggests a way of knowing and not knowing, of foregrounding the mysterious that we cannot know by either observation or revelation. Having debunked observation, Gatty slyly inserts living in books – like the bookworm himself – as the way out of the trap of scientific materialism and social disorder.

Leaving nature behind

Gatty's critics are not wrong that she maintains the design argument of natural theology. However, while she upholds natural theology's conclusions, she dispenses with its methods. In "Inferior Animals," the rooks' deductions about man's inferiority are dangerous: they upset the precept "animals under man" and thus threaten to capsize all the analogous hierarchies: "servants under masters – children under parents – wives under husbands – men under authorities – nations under rulers – all under God." Beyond the evolutionary allegory, the caucus of rooks also suggests the Chartist Working Man's Association agitating for economic equality as well as a group of children (who, Gatty's narrator says, believe they have access to the birds' speech) taking too seriously their own role-play. The rooks' dangerous conclusions are derived from the unsophisticated observation of nature that children's books of the time were encouraging their readers to perform, even as some were notably anxious about observation without guidance. Children's literature, especially when working within the framework of natural theology, contained the contradictory appeals to readers to *do* while making them *read*. Gatty solves this paradox, not by insisting on the transparency between text and world, but rather by making the path from one to the other more opaque. She encourages her young readers, mostly middle- and upper-class children, to look to the text – rather than to nature – as not only evidence of man's design but also an indication of God's even greater design. *Parables from Nature* suggests that it is fiction, not science, that presents a faithful analogy of God's plan and that should therefore drive the child's moral, intellectual, and (paradoxically given Gatty's position) evolutionary education.

Not only does "Inferior Animals" emphasize the mistakes that result from unguided observation, but the frame story also departs from natural theology by disparaging instinct. Paley's *Natural Theology* and Hack's *Harry Beaufoy* present instinct as akin to the morphological adaptations designed by God for the organism's well-being and happiness. They use the butterfly's instinct to lay her eggs on a cabbage leaf as proof that God has equipped the insect with a means to provide for her young that well exceeds her knowledge. In "A Lesson of Faith," Gatty uses the same example of the butterfly, but her focus is not the butterfly that acts by instinct but rather the caterpillar that, by the story's end, "had learnt the Lark's lesson of faith" (1: 5). If faith must be learned, then it is not instinct. Indeed, apart from the dutiful bees in "The Law of Authority and Obedience," instinct in *Parables from Nature* is more often a misleading impulse in need of correction. In "Inferior Animals," the narrator refers to the child's desire to talk with animals as an "instinct" that she must "unlearn":

> Alas, for the barriers which lie so mysteriously between us and the other creatures among whom we are born, and pass our short existence upon earth! – Alas! – for a desire for intercommunication is one of the strong instincts of our nature, and yet it is one which, as regards all the rest of creation but our human fellow-beings, we have to unlearn from baby-hood. (II: 24)

The child's instincts are erroneous and, if not corrected, threaten to topple the animal hierarchy that places man at the top. Gatty does not adhere to any theory of evolution or recapitulation, but her fiction nevertheless seeks to guide the child away from the instincts that link her to the animal world and replace them with something else – faith perhaps – that makes the child fully human. Keeping Darwinism at bay and yet at the same time painfully aware of its consequences, *Parables from Nature* aims to teach the child that becoming human means being unnatural.

"Training and Restraining" makes this lesson explicit in its address to the middle-class girl who must doubly submit, as both female and child, to her superiors in accordance with the Victorian social structure. In the story's Miltonic allegory, the wind (an agent of nature) is a "Wicked Wind"; with a satanic cadence, it seductively blows through the prettily ordered rows of Eve-like flowers, tempting them to throw off the shackles artificially erected by the gardener and to return to their natural postures and proclivities. The wind slyly tells the convolvulus that "you surely cannot suppose that in a natural state you would be forced to climb regularly up one tall bare stick such as I see you upon now," and to the Lily, he says that "Nature who had done so much for her that the fame of her beauty extended throughout the world," would not have "left her so weak and feeble that she could not support herself in the position most calculated to give her ease and pleasure?" (1: 23–24). The flowers make a mistake when they decide to recover their "nature"; unmoored from the artificial constraints of the garden, they are knocked into the mud. Whereas Cecilia from Wakefield's *Mental Improvement* declares that she will strive to mimic the "order and method" and "greater regularity" that she sees in nature's design, the girl in Gatty's "Training and Restraining" learns the opposite lesson. Arriving home to see her garden spoiled by the wind, she learns that nature is disorder:

> [N]ow, at last, I understand what you say about the necessity of training, and restraint, and culture, for us as well as for flowers . . . The wind has torn away these poor things from their fastenings, and they are growing wild whichever way they please; and I might perhaps once have argued, that if it were their *natural* way of growing it must therefore be the best. But I cannot say so, now I see the result. They are doing whatever they like, unrestrained; and the end is, – my beautiful GARDEN is turned into a WILDERNESS. (1: 26)

Gatty's protagonist offers a correction to Wakefield's Cecilia and, indeed, to the tradition of natural theology that precedes her. Instinct is dangerous; female nature is chaotic. By attending to the restraints erected by the male gardener, the girl rearranges herself to fit God's *unnatural* but beneficial and improving design.

This realization in "Training and Restraining" epitomizes the pedagogy behind *Parables from Nature*. Nature shows us discord and destruction, and thus cannot provide a model for religious devotion or socially constructive behavior. But man (the Gardener, acting as God's surrogate) converts nature into artifice and, in doing so, reveals design. Growing up, and becoming moral citizens and socialized adults, means becoming unnatural. Ironically, Thomas H. Huxley repeated precisely this idea, and even the same metaphor, at the end of the century in *Evolution and Ethics* (1893–1894). Huxley describes human culture as a rejection of the "cosmic process" of competition and self-preservation in favor of a "horticultural process" of ethics and attention to the social good: "not only is the state of nature hostile to the state of art of the garden; but the principle of the horticultural process, by which the latter is created and maintained, is antithetic to that of the cosmic process."[56] Such a statement could be a coda to Gatty's story. Nature is violence, struggle, and destruction, but the man-made garden is the realm of ethics and, more important for Gatty than for Huxley, social propriety. Though Gatty would surely find this serendipitous consensus with "Darwin's bulldog" a distortion of her intent, by equating the child with impulsive, instinctual, selfish nature and pre-scribing an education that can elevate her out of this original primitiveness, *Parables from Nature* asks the child reader – as sure as Huxley imagines society at large has done – to evolve out of nature and into art.

Though Gatty could not have predicted Huxley's use of the garden, *Parables from Nature* anticipates the symbols that Darwinism and Christianity share. In "The Law of the Wood" (1857), a spruce-fir luxuriously spreads its branches, carelessly crowding its arboreal neigh-bors and using its compliance with its own "nature" as an excuse for selfishness. When the other trees complain, the fir responds, "we grow in the way which Nature dictates; and our right to do so must therefore be unquestionable" (1: 50). The branching tree, which in *Origin of Species* represents the genetic relations among species and the history of struggle, adaptation, survival, and extinction, in Gatty's story also embodies a similar competition among neighboring organisms for nat-ural resources. One of the fir's neighbors, an old silver-barked birch foretells the impending danger of the sapling's capricious and unchecked expansion: "if [the trees] all go on, shooting out their branches in that manner, how hot and stuffy they will get! Not a breath of air will be able to blow through them soon, and that will be very bad for their health; besides which, they are absolute pests to society, with their unaccommodating ways" (1: 48). This image of branches crowding out other branches, sucking up the sunlight, rainwater, and fresh air that could otherwise be available to adjacent branches, remarkably recalls Darwin's arboreal illustration of the struggle for existence.

The conclusion of "The Law of the Wood," however, replaces this Darwinian image of internecine competition with a Christian moral of mutual cooperation. Into the wood intrudes "the occasional sound of an axe-stroke . . . for the owner was attended by his woodman" (1: 53). God, the supreme proprietor of designed nature, and his human attendant cull the forest, felling those whose selfishness thwarts the prosperity of their more vulnerable neighbors. Once hewn, the tree ceases its struggle for resources and becomes a Christmas tree: the symbol of Christ's birth and ultimate sacrifice. The metaphor of the tree is momentarily redeemed for its Christian use, but then Gatty adds another twist, and the fir becomes a mouthpiece for post-Darwinian ideas once again. In its last moments, decorated and on display in a public hall, the fir comes to understand "the moral of its fate" by watching ill-behaved children push and jostle each other, reenacting its own egoistic extensions in the forest:

> But then, when the crowds of children were collected in the brightly-lighted hall, where he stood covered with treasures and beauty, and when they all rushed forward, tumbling over one another, in their struggles to reach his branches; each one going his own way, regardless of his neighbour's wishes or comfort; and when the parents held back the quarrelsome rogues, bidding them one give place to another, – "in honour preferring one another," – considering public comfort rather than individual gratification – then, indeed, a light seemed to be thrown on the puzzling subject of the object and rules of social life; and he repeated to himself the words of the silver-barked Birch, exclaiming –
> "Mutual accommodation is certainly the law of the wood, or its inhabitants would all be wretched together."
> It was his last idea. (1: 54)

This "law" of mutual accommodation may seem to counter the laws of struggle and competition that Darwin made an indelible part of nature. But Gatty only anticipates theories by evolutionists like Peter Kropotkin, who claimed that "Mutual Aid and Mutual Support" constitute the "feature of the greatest importance for the maintenance of life, the preservation of each species, and its further evolution."[57] By the century's close, Gatty's resistance to the theory of evolution by natural selection would become its bedfellow.

Stranger still is the picture of the children in "The Law of the Wood." Not quite the middle-class girl from "Training and Restraining" who instantly recognizes the benefits of submission to adult, male authority, the unruly mass of "quarrelsome rogues" pushing and shoving in the public hall in "The Law of the Wood" evokes a revolutionary intensity. Gatty's uneasiness about the results of teaching lower-class pupils to observe nature and to adopt a morality based on natural precepts is here obvious. Rushing, tumbling, and struggling, the children are presented as animals without the dignity that Gatty elsewhere grants even animal characters. Furthermore, it is the tree who divines its moral lesson from watching the children rather than, in the conventional formulation of natural theology, the other way around. And yet, there is no irony in the tree's conclusions, as there is for the rooks' observing man in "Inferior Animals." On the one hand, then, "The Law of the Wood" suggests that disobedient children and working-class mobs are at the bottom of the moral hierarchy, below plant matter, and do not deserve a subjectivity even within her story. But on the other hand, this rhetorical device of presenting the children's bad behavior only through the mediating consciousness of the talking tree – which has itself already been converted from its natural state into a holiday houseplant weighted with religious meaning – presents a complex reformulation of the function and power of fiction. The tree mediates between the rambunctious children in the story and the reading children outside the story; to learn the moral of the story is to accept the judgment of the de-natured tree. And this is a voice only available in fiction.

A kindred scenario of rowdy children judged by a tree appears in the final story of Gatty's *Parables from Nature*. "See-Saw" (1871) introduces a tree stump, used as the base for a see-saw, complaining about the children who ride the plank and "do nothing but play pranks and enjoy themselves" (II: 120). Wakened by this grumbling residuum of a felled tree, a snail named Sir Helix Hortensis comforts the stump by telling him that he performs a noble duty "holding them both [the plank and the children] up, which is more than they can do for themselves" (II: 121). In "The Balancing of Child and Adult," Knoepflmacher chooses this story to illustrate the genre's appeal to a dual audience: the children are, straightforwardly, careless children, the stump acts the crabby adult, and the snail mediates between them with something for everyone. "The child reader," Knoepflmacher writes, "is clearly expected to relish [Gatty's] anthropomorphism," while "older readers, who might even be expected to know the Latin name for 'garden snail,' can cherish the mock-heroic touch in the author's dubbing of her mini-knight: 'Sir Helix Hortensis – so let us call him,'" as well as similarities between the snail and Satan of John Milton's *Paradise Lost*.[58] But, again, this easy division too neatly classifies the story's elements as either adult- or child-centered appeals, existing simultaneously in the text but never overlapping. In *Parables from Nature*, it is not so clear that the child reader is meant to enjoy anthropomorphism, which like the talking animal is rendered suspect in "Inferior Animals," nor that the child reader is supposed to be unaware of Milton, so essential to "Training and Restraining."

The problem in "See-Saw," as in "The Law of the Wood," is not what content is meant for whom but rather to which order – either the natural or the social – the children belong. Knoepflmacher says, "in their careless indifference, the children become outsiders, uneducatable and unattractive."[59] If the children do indeed remain "uneducable and unattractive," then, this penultimate story from Gatty's five-part series written and published over a sixteen-year period can be read as an admission that the entire edifying project of *Parables from Nature* has been a failure. The children are aloof, deaf to the snail's conversation with the stump, and thoughtless as ever in their actions. "See-Saw" seems to recognize that Gatty has not solved the problem of the child. While trees and flowers and caterpillars have learned their lessons and curbed their lower natures, the children of the final story have not. Sir Helix tells the stump, "they're all light-minded together, and don't think ... Up in the sky one minute, down in the dust the next" (II: 121). With more at stake than mere selfishness and inconsideration, the children see-saw up and down between spiritual and material possibilities of existence. The snail's words pose a question about whether the children will end up as angels in heaven above or only "dust" underground. The most draconian of Gatty's stories, "See-Saw" forces the child readers to take one more look at themselves through the eyes of another inhuman creature: the snail.

In making his case for Gatty's appeal to dual audiences, Knoepflmacher looks at Sir Helix's eyes. Gatty's narrator describes the snail as he approaches the stump and the children playing on the see-saw:

> [H]is horns turning hither and thither as those wonderful eyes at the end strove to take in the full state of the case. And his are not the eyes, you know, which waste their energies in scatter-brained staring. He keeps them cool in their cases till there is something to be looked at, and then turns them inside out to do their destined work.
> And thus he looked, and he looked, and he looked ... (II: 120–121)

According to Knoepflmacher, "it is the eyes of the snail itself, 'those wonderful eyes at the end' of his probing horns, that the reader, now at last overtly addressed as 'you,' is invited to behold," and these eyes perform the "Janus-like split" of a children's literature that looks both back to childhood and forward to adulthood.[60] The snail's eyes are indeed the focal point of the story, but within this collection obsessed with observation and its limitations, how the snail sees is as important as the directions in which he looks. Since Knoepflmacher's reading of Gatty's story extracts it from the rest of *Parables from Nature*, he does not mention that Gatty's readers have met Sir Helix before in "The Cause and the Causer," one of the stories that insist on the inadequacy of the knowledge gained from the human senses alone. In this earlier story, Sir Helix proclaims, "the more you think, the less you see; that is, the more you think, the more you find out how little you are able to see" (ii: 102). The snail is the one creature in *Parables from Nature* whose vision includes this recognition of the poverty of observation.

Sir Helix's eyes are important, not because they embody the gaze of both child and adult, but because they see in a way that is distinctly inhuman. *Parables from Nature* shows Gatty's interest in alternate, nonhuman ways of seeing. In her comments for "Whereunto?" in *Parables from Nature, with Notes on the Natural History*, for instance, Gatty tries to account for the spots clustered on the arms of starfish: "some naturalists have concluded these to be eyes, or organs of vision of some sort."[61] She quotes Rymer Jones, saying that the starfish "perceive[s] what is going on in the world around them" and apprehends its surroundings not through vision as we experience it but "by some sense analogous either to smell or vision." Gatty continues, citing "the late Dr. Johnston" from a lecture on the subject: "it was wrong to conceive that because we had only five senses, starfishes or other animals could have no more, or none which was not analogous to ours ... [W]e knew that many of them wanted senses which we have, but we could not tell but they might possess senses which we had not." The fictional concoction of the talking animal, for Gatty, highlights the central error of both natural theology and Darwinism: the assumption that nature speaks to us in any simple and direct way that we can easily hear and interpret. But imagining the seeing animal – not just the animal that we see according to the tenets of natural theology but the animal that sees in ways that we cannot – opens up the mysteries of nature and the potential for realizing a grander design than our faulty organs can perceive.

Parables from Nature forces readers out of the conventional habit of looking at nature in order to see design. Throughout the collection, Gatty repeatedly admits that the raw visual data gathered from nature will more likely present chaos rather than arrangement, misunderstanding rather than revelation, and destruction rather than design. This paucity of vision does not mean that there is no Designer, but that God's design eludes our limited powers of observation. The multiple animal perspectives in *Parables from Nature* – some of them more trustworthy than others – correct for our partial vision, insist on a divine plan beyond what we see, deliver morals about self-sacrifice, and judge the child readers for their own short-sighted behaviors. Gatty, thus, leads readers back to a now fortified natural theology, but her methods appear post-Darwinian. Literary critic Cannon Schmitt has recently argued that evolutionary theory raised doubts that human language was up to the task of representing prehuman and extra-human processes. In "Evolution and Victorian Fiction" (2014), he suggests that "to think evolutionarily requires putting aside an anthropocentric point of view, admitting (more: taking to heart) the likelihood that humans, the product of evolution, may not be equipped to comprehend or fully describe its workings."[62] Surprisingly for a work of natural theology, *Parables from Nature* repeatedly criticizes anthropomorphism, not only reminding readers of the plenitude of other organisms but also taking to heart their distinctly nonhuman powers of perception. But despite Schmitt's sense that evolutionary theory made fiction writers skeptical about their medium, Gatty's stories reassert the unique ability of man-made artifice – the tended garden, the culled forest, and the children's story – to reveal the deep design that only appears missing from nature because of our imperfect sight. Gatty's stories have a special place within children's literature, which was henceforth influenced by and responsive to the post-Darwinian landscape. Updating natural theology, Gatty's *Parables from Nature* encourages readers to see through other animals' eyes not to accept their status as just another of nature's animals but rather to start appreciating the panoply of visual perspectives available only through art. Chaos and destruction are the effects of nature on our compromised perceptions, but art can reveal the all-encompassing totality and perfection of God's design.

Gatty's importance in both the formation of the children's canon and the intersection between scientific theory and literary technique should not be forgotten. As the founder and editor of *Aunt Judy's Magazine* (which she ran from 1866 until her death in 1873), Gatty helped to shape children's literature and to build the reputations of other notable authors like Lewis Carroll and Hans Christian Andersen. In his autobiography, Rudyard Kipling fondly recalls reading Gatty's animal stories and imitating them when writing his own.[63] *Parables from Nature* was immensely popular, reaching its eighteenth edition by 1882 and continuing to be reissued until 1950.[64] In 1876, *The Young Lady's Book* recommended *Parables from Nature*, alongside the works of Charles Kingsley and Lewis Carroll, for awakening both "the spirit of inquiry and wonder" and the "love for what is beautiful," a combination of scientific and aesthetic values.[65] As the next stage of Victorian children's literature ostensibly left behind the didacticism, religiosity, and social conservatism of Gatty's fiction, it remained indebted to the subtle readjustments she makes between the natural world and the human subject, between environment and education, and between natural experience and cultivated faith.

Perhaps Gatty's most important contribution to natural theology and children's literature is her meditation on the significance of literariness itself. *Parables from Nature* exploits the apprehension that natural theologians had long felt about the need to train the human observer to see nature correctly and to repackage nature as easily digested, ethically efficacious, affirmably Christian consumables. In the midst of the publication of *Origin of Species* and the "Darwinian Revolution" in biology and geology, Gatty faced alternate interpretations of natural facts that further challenged natural theology's confidence in our ability to read nature without external guidance or religious mediation. Her "parables" are thus not *of* nature or *about* nature, but very much "from nature" – marking, even in the series' title, a movement away from the direct, unmediated access that natural theology espoused. The literary process, here the conversion of natural fact into the fictional form of the parable, mirrors the efforts of the gardener and the woodman to improve upon an imperfect nature and, in so doing, to act as God's attendant on earth. In other words, what child readers learn through Gatty's stories is not to follow nature but rather to reshape their own natures to fit a higher purpose, and like the tales they read, to achieve their place within God's infinite plan by extracting themselves *from nature*. With Gatty's work, children's literature became both the mechanism and the model for this transformation to a higher humanity.

CHAPTER 2

Amphibious tendencies
Charles Kingsley, Herbert Spencer, and evolutionary education

In *The Water-Babies: a Fairy Tale for a Land-Baby* (1863), Charles Kingsley offers a parody of Victorian education. His hero, a chimney sweep named Tom who morphs into a newt and embarks on an underwater journey, comes to the Isle of the Tomtoddies. Here the young pupils are so crammed with useless information that they have been literally turned into vegetables with "all heads and no bodies," sticking out of the ground and quaking in fear of the regular visits from "their great idol Examination."[1] Unable to process their lessons or to answer any of the Examiner's questions, one of the overfilled botanicals bursts open: "Tom thought he was crying: but it was only his poor brains running away, from being worked so hard; and as Tom talked, the unhappy turnip streamed down all over with juice, and split and shrank till nothing was left of him but rind and water" (301–302). This image is a reaction to the Revised Code of 1862 that linked school funding to student performance on state-set examinations.[2] Many critics of the Code, including Charles Dickens and Matthew Arnold, projected that this system of "Payment by Results" would have disastrous pedagogical consequences, though none painted the prospect so luridly as Kingsley.[3] The Victorian school, according to *The Water-Babies*, was ignoring the student body and, more pointedly, the students' literal bodies to the detriment of the nation.

By what the Tomtoddies' school omits, this episode articulates Kingsley's vision of a more sound education. Tom learns that the pupils' "foolish fathers and mothers, instead of letting them pick flowers, and make dirt-pies, and get birds' nests, and dance round the gooseberry bush, as little children should, kept them always at lessons, working, working, working. . ." (303). This prescription for active, outdoor education was familiar to Kingsley's audience; children's literature had been encouraging readers to make their own explorations in nature for at least a century. But Kingsley promoted natural history and scientific instruction at all levels. In lectures delivered to military officers and working men's clubs, he hailed science as the vital discipline for the modern age, not only because it brings man into an intimacy with God's works according to the tenets of natural theology, but also because learning scientific principles (especially about health and sanitation) would toughen soldiers and enable the working classes to improve their lot.[4] Unlike the children's authors discussed in the last chapter, Kingsley was a Chartist and an evolutionist; he launched himself into political and scientific movements and embraced the fluidity of social and biological systems. When he exclaimed, in an anonymous poster addressed to workers, "a nobler day is dawning for England, a day of freedom, science, industry," he voiced the interconnection of these promises.[5] But his poster also warns that the right kind of education is necessary to fulfilling these joint futures: "Workers of England, be wise, and then you must be free, for you will be *fit* to be free."[6]

The Water-Babies' Tom is an untutored, orphaned chimney sweep who works for a cruel taskmaster, aptly named Mr. Grimes. The opening pages of the book let us know, quite clearly, that he is not fit for much of anything. Politically, *The Water-Babies* helped effect the 1864 Chimney Sweepers Regulation Act, which reinforced penalties for master sweeps who ignored (as most of them did) an 1840 law prohibiting climbing boys.[7] Kingsley's polemic against this abuse of child labor was not without its complementary focus on child education, a hotly debated issue in the decade leading up to the 1870 Elementary Education Act making school available and compulsory school for pupils aged five to twelve years in England and Wales. As the Isle of the Tomtoddies shows, Kingsley was skeptical about the Victorian school, and the practice of examinations seems beyond redemption. Instead, Kingsley develops throughout *The Water-Babies* a pedagogical program for his protagonist capable of reforming society's least fit (as chimney sweeps unarguably were) into able minds and bodies. The answer for Kingsley lay in the theory of evolutionary recapitulation: the idea that the development of the individual repeats the evolution of the species. By transforming Tom into an amphibious eft (a baby newt), *The Water-Babies* rewinds the process of human civilization that has rendered him a foolish and feeble chimney sweep and begins his evolutionary progress anew in order to ensure a more successful maturation. Only by recapitulating, receiving a "natural" education as he travels downriver, can Tom finally become a man. *The Water-Babies* does not so much suggest that children naturally *do* recapitulate the evolution of the species than that they systematically *should* in order to ensure a healthier, fitter, and nobler human future.

Kingsley's enthusiasm for science's reformatory power was unparalleled among authors of his era. Like Margaret Gatty, he wanted to hold onto the central precepts of natural theology, including the argument from design. Unlike her, however, he adopted evolution (and its theological and social consequences) as an extension of natural theology rather than its nullification. *The Water-Babies* is, I argue, an experiment in how far a literary text could offer a scientific education. In this, Kingsley is indebted to Herbert Spencer, who argued that because children recapitulate the ascent of the species, they must learn as early humans did. *The Water-Babies* begins by fervently assenting to Spencer's pedagogy, thrusting its hero out of society and into nature. For the child reader, Kingsley's fairy tale seeks to provide experiences that, though textual, can mimic Tom's naturalistic education in accordance with Spencer's prescriptions. But as the novel goes on, Kingsley seems increasingly doubtful about the efficacy of the natural sciences to complete the child's recapitulation. Missing for Kingsley is knowledge of God and human distinctness that only the expansion of the imagination yields. Imagination, however, requires a literary education: fairy tale, fantasy, and nonsense provide the essential lessons for Tom's final leap into humanity. Thus adopting Spencer's theory of recapitulative education only to transform it entirely, *The Water-Babies* makes evolution an essential part of children's literature and complementarily makes literature the crucial step in human evolution.

Education goes evolutionary

In the middle of the nineteenth century, not merely the progress of the natural sciences but also the status of elementary education was at a crossroads. For the previous century, schools were largely run by church associations, rather than by the state, and focused on instruction in the three "Rs" – reading, writing, and arithmetic – with little interest in the natural sciences.[8] But three important trends were developing that would change the pupils, the subjects, and the methods of Victorian education. First, the early nineteenth century experienced a boom in the number of schools established, many enrolling economically disadvantaged children previously excluded from formalized education. Though these schools were created by religious societies, usually arms of the Church of England, there was by midcentury a growing opinion that these schools required state intervention to fulfill their missions. Second, this new population of students engendered a reconsideration of school subjects. Educators sought lessons based on everyday objects and practical skills, and the natural sciences suggested a profitable supplement to the traditional curriculum.[9] The Great Exhibition of 1851 also emphasized the technological strengths of other nations and convinced many Britons that they had to catch up. Movements for better scientific apparatus in classrooms and more coherent teacher preparation began throughout Great Britain. And third, child-centered pedagogies developed in Europe were making their way across the Channel, and new ideas about the child's nature were supplanting John Locke's blank slate model of the young mind. Literary critics define the Golden Age of children's literature as the genre's move away from its eighteenth- and early nineteenth-century didacticism, but this shift occurred within a larger social and pedagogical context.

As a discourse about intellectual development, pedagogy in the midcentury anticipated its own intersection with evolutionary theory. Typical of such discussions is Johann Gaspar Spurzheim's *Education: Its Elementary Principles, Founded on the Nature of Man* (1847), which claims that a coherent educational system depends on answering three questions: (1) whether human nature is in a state of degradation or perfection; (2) whether humans constitute one or several species; and (3) whether children are born as blank slates or come into existence with innate tendencies and dispositions. Education, according to Spurzheim, must take into account what is universal about human nature. This system requires, as later pedagogues would even more forcefully insist, a methodical approach drawn from the emerging sciences of biology, psychology, and anthropology. In *Education*, Spurzheim – a Viennese academic associated with the Royal College of Physicians – determines that humans are perfecting that they constitute a single species, and that "education must fail, as long as we continue to think that children are born alike."[10] The blank slate thesis, therefore, errs by misunderstanding human nature and human history. Indeed, "the first thing to be done," Spurzheim argues, "is to trace back the faculties of children to their origin."[11] He does not mean that we should trace human faculties back to their animal origins, as Charles Darwin would do in *The Descent of Man, and Selection in Relation to Sex* (1871) and *The Expression of the Emotions in Man and Animals* (1872). For Spurzheim, educability depends on a more proximate heritability, but the openness of these questions to evolutionary answers is undeniable.

Like much of the European and European-influenced pedagogical theories in the early Victorian period, Spurzheim is indebted to the work of Johann Heinrich Pestalozzi, a Swiss pedagogue who extended Jean-Jacques Rousseau's reappraisal of childhood into school reforms. Pestalozzi built his pedagogical theories by carefully observing and analyzing his son during his first few years, an activity that Darwin would also pursue in "A Biographical

Sketch of an Infant" (1877).[12] Though he admired Rousseau's vision of an education driven by the child's inherently good nature, he found himself continually frustrated at his unsuccessful attempts to follow the advice Rousseau lays out in *Émile; or, On Education* (1762). In a series of letters published as "How Gertrude Teaches Her Little Ones" (1801), Pestalozzi argues that establishing a meaningful pedagogy calls for a reexamination of our educational development, "the beginning of which must be adapted to the very first unfolding of the child's powers"; only then will we be capable of "determining with the greatest accuracy, what is calculated for every age and every stage of development."[13] Because the child is not a blank slate open to any inscription, education must be based on a child-study that can nail down, with an unprecedented exactitude, what powers the newborn infant has during his first days and in what order he acquires subsequent skills. Pestalozzi's theories were influential throughout Europe and in England, though his concept of the "child nature" upon which all educational principles should be based remained more a vague notion than a scientific definition. According to Edward Biber's 1831 introduction of Pestalozzi for English-speaking educators, what Pestalozzi means by "nature" is "more the expression of a mysterious something than of an idea, or of a being, clearly apprehended."[14]

For Spencer, evolution and the theory of recapitulation gave the mystery of "child nature" a concrete expression and a precise pedagogical sequence. He converted the metaphors already inherent in pedagogical discourse into causal explanations. Like many continental and British Romantics, Pestalozzi considered untaught man an animal. At man's birth, he wrote, "the animal is entirely formed, and something above the animal is awakened."[15] This idea reappears repeatedly in midcentury pedagogical treatises. Henry Edwards's *Elementary Education: The Importance of Its Extension in Our Own Country* (1844), for instance, attests that "we are born but *animals*; it is knowledge and education, which make us *men*."[16] Neither Pestalozzi nor Edwards are making evolutionary arguments. In fact, Edwards explicitly denies that there is any genetic relation between man and the lower animals. Pestalozzi's philosophy notably flavored Friedrich Froebel's establishment of the kindergarten: an innovation in education that shared with Spencer's plan the equation between children and nature and the attention to identifying discrete stages of child development.[17] Unlike Edwards, Pestalozzi, and Froebel, however, Spencer seized on the language of childhood animality and literalized it. His signature treatise, *Education: Intellectual, Moral, and Physical* (1860), asserts that "people are beginning to see that the first requisite to success in life, is to be a good animal."[18] Though Spencer picks up on the Romantic notion of man's animality, he is clear to distinguish his argument from previous pedagogical theories. Man does not, at birth, begin to shed the animal; quite to the contrary, man spends the beginning of his life perfecting the animal that is his genetic inheritance. Our first lessons, then, should be those that "directly minister to self-preservation"; second, training to meet the necessities of life outside of sheer survival; third, instruction for rearing healthy offspring; fourth, practice in social bonding; and last, leisure activities like art and literature.[19] Education must work through the animal to raise the man.

The fact of human evolution, then, gives Spencer the starting point of his educational system, but it is the theory of recapitulation that contours the curriculum. "The development of children in mind and body rigorously obeys certain laws," he writes in *Education*, and "only when they are completely conformed to, can a perfect maturity be reached."[20] These laws, according to Spencer, have been determined for the individual by the evolution of the species. In much of his writings but especially in "Progress: Its Laws and Its Cause" (1857), Spencer maintains that all progress – of individuals, societies, species, ecosystems, planets, and indeed the universe as a whole – operates according to the same law of differentiation from simpler to more complex forms and functions.[21] Three years later, he applied this theory of general progress to the specific needs of elementary school children. *Education* insists: "if there be an order in which the human race has mastered its various kinds of knowledge, there will arise in every child an aptitude to acquire these kinds of knowledge in the same order ... and hence the fundamental reason why education should be a repetition of civilization in little."[22]

Spencer's pedagogy seeks to follow an established series of developmental stages and considers not merely the content but also the methods of instruction. Taking seriously the idea that the child must attain knowledge not only in the *order* that early man attained it but in the same *manner*, he urges that "children should be led to make their own investigations, and to draw their own inferences. They should be *told* as little as possible, and induced to *discover* as much as possible."[23] Theories of self-motivated education had been floating around for nearly a century, but Spencer's influence brought these ideas into the Victorian classroom. The Code Reform Association of 1881 adopted Spencer's dictum, officially stating that "if these subjects are taught to children by definition and verbal description, instead of making them exercise their own powers of observation, they will be worthless as a means of education."[24] The Reform

Commission took Spencer's other suggestions and rationalizations to heart as well, specifically about the importance of hygiene to self-preservation and thus to elementary education. It likewise included provisions for school meals, physical education, self-taught observation and experiment, and education for girls – all of which Spencer deemed both necessary for the survival of the species and essential for the continuation of national progress.

There is an irony in the fact that Spencer became such an influential voice in government-mandated school reforms. As a firm believer that progress is only attained by the processes of natural selection, Spencer famously denounced government intervention, social programs, and a centralized school system.[25] But his arguments for what children most needed to learn answered a prescient question just at the moment that the government was taking the control of the schools away from the Church and as the call for mandatory elementary education was gaining ground. If the British school system was going to be responsible for teaching all children, many asked what subjects were universally applicable. Spencer's answer was science. Science, he argued in *Education*, not only helps keep the pupil alive but also offers the building blocks for all further knowledge: "the constant habit of drawing conclusions from data, and then of verifying those conclusions by observation and experiment, can alone give the power of judging correctly."[26] Every pupil does not necessarily need to know the *facts* of science, but he must be versed in the *scientific method* because, according to Spencer, scientific method mimics the trial-and-error experimentation by which early man learned about his world and his powers in it. Spencer was not alone in this evaluation of science. Mathematician Augustus De Morgan wrote in *Remarks on Elementary Education in Science* (1830), "all human knowledge ... is based upon experiment."[27] Likewise Thomas H. Huxley told the audience of his lecture "On the Educational Value of the Natural History Sciences" (1854) that "science is, I believe, nothing but *trained and organized common sense*, differing from the latter only as a veteran may differ from a raw recruit."[28] "Science" was not a part of a liberal education; it was the whole of the pupil's educability.

Spencer's recapitulative pedagogy subjugated literature and textual instruction to the status of "ornament," added on only in the last stages of human evolution and thus inessential, even distracting, in modern education.[29] In the absence of books to transmit codified knowledge, early man, according to Spencer, faced every experience wholly on his own. Spencer's imagined human progenitor learned purely through immediate sensory and cognitive contact with his natural environment and, thus, so must the child educate himself in and through nature alone. When Spencer insists that children should discover on their own rather than being told, he means to privilege scientific method over textual instruction. Based on "immediate cognition" rather than the "mediate cognition" gained from reading books, scientific education was identical with an experiential one; guided by pleasure and self-motivated discovery, the child authentically reproduces both the method and the occasion of early man's first contact with his natural environment.[30] Literature and art, if they were to enter into the curriculum at all, must come into the child's education only in the final "leisure" stages, after self-preservation, health, success, reproduction, and cognition have all been accounted for by direct means. Since art was the result of civilization, rather than its cause, literature and art were the endpoints, rather than the building blocks, of education.

Literature is not, for Spencer, even necessary for the development of our moral sense; in this he makes scientific education both primary and sufficient. In *Education*, he devises a method of disciplinary education that requires no more than the child's unmediated observation of nature: not the pleasant pictures of moral nature drawn by natural theology but rather the most violent and unruly scenes of wild existence. Taking from Locke's *Some Thoughts Concerning Education* (1693) a scenario in which the child impulsively sticks his hand in an open flame, inevitably gets burned, and therefore learns prudence, Spencer uses this imagined event to explain the child's first lesson in ethics.[31] The impetuous act and the resultant pain teach the child, according to Spencer, "that there are rewards and punishments in the ordained constitution of things, and that the evil results of disobedience are inevitable."[32] This recognition, he argues, was for the species, as it must be for the child, an introduction to the foremost principle on which all ethical systems are based: justice. Parents should allow their children to burn their hands because "the child, suffering nothing more than the painful effects brought upon it by its own wrong actions, must recognise more or less clearly the justice of the penalties."[33] Pain and pleasure take center stage because the physical body is the primary medium through which nature has taught its lessons. Introducing terms like "evil," "disobedience," "punishment," and "justice," however, Spencer executes the most ambitious part of his argument. To survive, all extant species must have learned to avoid the behaviors that nature punishes and thus incorporated into their habits the basic idea of justice. Maintaining natural selection's fundamental Darwinian indifference, Spencer assigned it a crucial disciplinary role in instructing the species.

By the time Kingsley wrote *The Water-Babies*, he was embroiled in many of the same social concerns and pedagogical quandaries that Spencer's *Education* sought to solve. He had established his reputation as a literary writer – with works like *Alton Locke, Tailor and Poet* (1850), *Westward Ho!* (1855), and *The Heroes; or, Greek Fairy Tales for My Children* (1855) – as well as a prolific author of sermons, essays, and lectures, written in his capacities first as rector of the Eversley parish in Hampshire and later as Professor of History at Cambridge.[34] In the last of these roles, Kingsley was growing increasingly worried about the physical well-being of his fellow country-men, especially the working class, and convinced that modern civilization was in decline. Ideas brewing through the 1850s and the 1860s are best summed up in his 1874 essay, "The Science of Health," in which Kingsley recalls Spurzheim, asking "whether the British race is improving or degenerating?"[35] The answer Kingsley gives, however, is decidedly the latter. The Napoleonic Wars, he says, took "our stoutest, ablest, healthiest young men," leaving "the weaklier man to continue the race."[36] Pointedly borrowing the language of "fitness" from evolutionary discourse, Kingsley prophesies a national crisis. But worse than the war that killed the would-be fathers of a strong future race, he says, so-called social "improvements" preserve feeble bodies that would have been weeded out in more savage days: "every sanatory reform, prevention of pestilence, medical discovery, amelioration of climate, drainage of soil, improvement in dwelling-houses, workhouses, gaols: every reformatory school, every hospital, every cure of drunkenness" unnaturally insures that the weakest among the nation survive and allows them to breed the next, even weaker, generation.[37] "If war kills the most fit to live," Kingsley writes, "then we save alive those who – looking at them from a merely physical point of view – are most fit to die."[38] What is left of the "British race" is in desperate need of rejuvenation.

Kingsley was no advocate of the austere antiwelfare and eugenic pro-grams that would come to be called Social Darwinism; he supported government intervention to ensure clean water and pure air for the British public. But to offset the ill effects of welfare that protects the socially "unfit," he argues in "The Science of Health," there must be a universally available educational system that strengthens the weak and reinvigorates the nation in every new generation:

> We must teach men to mend their own matters, of their own reason, and their own free-will. We must teach them that they are the arbiters of their own destinies; and, to a fearfully great degree, of their children's destinies

after them. We must teach them not merely that they ought to be free, but that they are free, whether they know it or not, for good and for evil. And we must do that in this case, by teaching them sound practical science; the science of physiology, as applied to health.[39]

The call for the exercise of passion and free will is broad enough, but when Kingsley gets into practical pedagogy, he shares Spencer's pedagogical principles: that a sound mind must first possess the knowledge to preserve a sound body. In a lecture entitled "How to Study Natural History" (1846), Kingsley recommends that any system of education begin "at the beginning" – with science.[40] In a lecture simply called "Science" (1866) Kingsley echoes De Morgan and Huxley but adds his loftier goals; scientific method, he says, "is simply common sense, combined with uncommon courage, which includes uncommon honesty and uncommon patience."[41] He connects nature study to his desire for a pedagogical program that could remasculinate Britain: one that would come to be known as "muscular Christianity."[42] His Glaucus; or, The Wonders of the Shore (1855), for example, seamlessly combines nature study, natural theology, and muscular Christianity, presenting the naturalist as a "perfect knight-errant," "strong in body" and willing "to fight for his life."[43] In Town Geology (1872), Kingsley articulates his most optimistic hopes that scientific education could create democracy: "in becoming scientific men, in studying science and acquiring the scientific habit of mind, you will find yourselves enjoying a freedom, an equality, a brotherhood, such as you will not find anywhere else just now."[44]

In writings like these, Kingsley agrees with his scientific contemporaries that science will provide the cure to many of England's social and moral ills. As a refinement of common sense, the scientific method was the means to acquiring knowledge that anyone could exercise. As an instruction in health and hygiene, scientific education informed the populace how to stave off the degenerative trend in Victorian culture. As a self-motivated discipline invested in experiment and observation rather than textual description and rote memorization of facts, it propelled the pupil to make his own discoveries, to learn to judge properly for himself, and to mold himself into an active citizen and formidable man. Finally, as the way our ancestors supposedly advanced from animalistic primates to human builders of civilizations, science prescribed a tried and true course of development that now determines both the means and the order in which individual minds mature. Therefore, in The Water-Babies, when Kingsley imagines his protagonist, a poor chimney sweep, thrust into nature and recapitulating an evolutionary path from eft to man, he establishes this vision for a purely experiential education that can reinvigorate the species.

Becoming a beast through nature

The Water-Babies' adoption of evolutionary theory has been well noted by literary critics but, surprisingly, little analyzed. Gillian Beer's seminal study *Darwin's Plots: Evolutionary Narrative in Darwin, George Eliot and Nineteenth-Century Fiction* (1983) uses Kingsley's book to demonstrate the arrested development of science in nineteenth-century children's fiction. For Beer, *The Water-Babies* attempts "to naturalise the new theories back into creationist language," naively clinging to the individualism and teleology that Darwinism relinquished.[45] Both Beer and Alan Rauch group *The Water-Babies* with Gatty's *Parables from Nature* (1855–1871) because, according to Rauch, both writers interpret "the metamorphoses of animals to be evidence of a consistent providential pattern."[46] But the plot of *The Water-Babies* also contains a recapitulative trajectory that suggests that Kingsley took seriously the potential for the new forms of scientific education. Though much scientific theorizing is mocked in *The Water-Babies*, the recapitulation that contours the plot is the only hope that Tom has of attaining productive adulthood. Tom reenters nature and evolves via the very methods that Spencer prescribes: observation, experiment, and trial and error. And in an even more deft narrative turn, *The Water-Babies* invites its reader to recapitulate along with Tom. Despite the reader's very different social, economic, and circumstantial position, Kingsley manufactures textual scenarios through which the reader can exercise the same skills that Tom is accruing in his naturalistic education. Kingsley's fairy tale ingeniously fashions a recapitulative education that seamlessly merges modern science and a new kind of children's literature – at least for a while.

At the beginning of *The Water-Babies*, Victorian culture has failed to educate Tom. We learn that "he could not read nor write, and did not care to do either; and he never washed himself . . . He had never been taught to say his prayers. He had never heard of God, or of Christ" (1–2). When he accompanies his employer, Mr. Grimes, to clean the flues of a country manor, he looks in a mirror for the first time and thinks the reflection of his soot-covered face is that of "a little black ape" (26). In his own self-image, the boy is a degenerate representative of the urban poor whose ignorance and infirmity suggested, for Kingsley, symptoms of national decline.[47] Once in the country, Tom runs away and, though he finds temporary refuge in a small schoolhouse presided over by a charitable dame,

Kingsley's tale suggests that a different education is warranted for Tom's safety, health, and ultimate salvation. Escaping out of the school's window, Tom runs "with four hands instead of two" to the edge of a river, falls in, drowns, and is transformed into an eft (50). Wrenching the child out of the putrid and unhealthy streets of London and flinging him into a "natural" world and thus back to a prehuman stage of morphological and moral development, *The Water-Babies* answers social degeneration with evolutionary recapitulation.

Readers have wondered whether Tom's transition to this aquatic state is a magical transformation or a physical death.[48] Beer writes, "of course, he is drowned, though it was not until I read the book as an adult that I recognised that."[49] This belated recognition leaves open the idea that, for the child reader, Tom is only transformed. But his ambiguous status as both alive and dead is also written into his new form: an amphibian who, as Kingsley's jocular narrator says, was "supposed by our ignorant ancestors to be compounded of a fish and a beast; which therefore, like the hippopotamus, can't live on the land, and dies in the water" (83). Either doubly living or doubly dead, Tom begins a new course of instruction from the animals he sees underwater. Some lessons suggest that Tom is better off dead, and that his physical transformation symbolizes a spiritual metamorphosis in a straightforward tradition of natural theology. A dragonfly, who is "a very ugly dirty creature" with "six legs, and a big stomach, and a most ridiculous head with two great eyes and a face just like a donkey's," emerges from its chrysalis as "the most slender, elegant, soft creature" and thus engenders Tom's desire for heavenly transcendence (94–95). As the dragonfly rises out of its cocoon, "the most lovely colours began to show on its body, blue and yellow and black, spots and bars and rings; out of its back rose four great wings of bright brown gauze; and its eyes grew so large that they filled all its head, and shone like ten thousand diamonds." Reminiscent of the miraculously morphing caterpillar of Gatty's *Parables from Nature*, the dragonfly is meant to make Tom want to be a good boy in a traditionally Christian sense so that he too can earn his angel's wings.

Though some of Kingsley's underwater animals serve as exempla of natural theology, others offer lessons in Darwinian self-preservation and, thereby, indicate that Tom's metamorphosis is not death. In these moments, *The Water-Babies* does not, like Gatty's *Parables from Nature*, seek to fortify a design argument against visible evidence of evolution, extinction, and struggle. Rather, Kingsley's departure from natural theology signals his eager adoption of evolutionary recapitulation. Originally without the survival skills necessary for his new environment, Tom observes how the caddis flies gather food and how a crablike creature builds his home: "one wonderful little fellow . . . had two big wheels, and one little one, all over teeth, spinning round and round like wheels in a thrashing-machine," and Tom watches the "clever fellow" spin mud into bricks (90). A terrifying encounter with an otter, showing "such a set of sharp teeth in a grinning mouth," likewise hastens Tom's learning to take cover and to run away (104). There are no moral lessons here, no analogies between the animal's physical body and man's immortal soul. The crab shows Tom how to transform one's environment into a home, and the otter illustrates Spencer's survivalist pedagogy in which being a good animal (and future human) means knowing how to provide for and to protect oneself. Tom's transformation into an eft also communicates more explicit lessons about evolution. Explaining the basic principles of evolutionary theory to his young audience, Kingsley's narrator connects Tom's transformation to similar bodily changes in the amphibian and attacks head-on the hubris that says that humans alone were specially created: if your tutor "says (as he most certainly will) that these transformations only take place in the lower animals, and not in the higher, say that that seems to little boys, and to some grown people, a very strange fancy" (74–75).[50]

Transformed into an animal fighting for his survival, Tom begins the "natural" education that Spencer prescribed. In *Education*, Spencer insists that the child "should be *told* as little as possible, and induced to *discover* as much as possible," and *The Water-Babies'* narrator likewise assures readers that Tom must learn everything "for himself by sound and sharp experience" (92). This natural education is watched over by Mrs. Bedonebyasyoudid, a fairy who lives in the river, but she is initially invisible to Tom, refusing to interfere with his natural education. In explicit accordance with Spencer's directions for schoolmasters, Kingsley's fairy says that she "wishes people to keep their fingers out of the fire, by having them burned" (214). Critic Naomi Wood identifies Mrs. Bedonebyasyoudid as the embodiment of "the orderly workings of natural law."[51] More specifically, I argue, she is Spencer's disciplinary nature, a personification of cause and effect who bears few of the qualities we would expect from a benevolent tutor; she is not, after all, Mrs. Bedonebyasyou *would*. Explaining her sovereignty over all other organisms only much later in the narrative, she voices Darwinian selection's utter disavowal of conscious agency: "I cannot help punishing people when they do wrong . . . For I work by machinery, just like an engine; and am full of wheels and springs inside; and am wound up very carefully, so that I cannot help going" (196–197). Though invoking comparison with William Paley's famous watch analogy, which demands that we accept not only the existence of a watch maker but also a divine and beneficent Creator of all natural phenomena, Mrs. Bedonebyasyoudid is not a merciful God.[52] Entertaining neither excuse nor appeal, the clockwork fairy represents the absolute justice that Spencer ascribes to an indifferent nature, where "there are rewards and punishments in the ordained constitution of things" and consequences are "inevitable." Lest Kingsley's young reader "think that she is going to let off you, or me, or any human being when we do wrong, because she is too tender-hearted to punish us," the narrator warns, "you will find yourself very much mistaken" (214).

Nature's automatic responses turn evolutionary selection into a disciplinary system, and here Kingsley extrapolates Spencer's pedagogy into social parables. Early in his journey, Tom meets the king of the salmon who explains the differences between his own noble species and the degenerate trout: "a great many years ago [the trout] were just like us," but "instead of going down to the sea every year to see the world and grow strong and fat, they chose to stay and poke about in the little streams" (125). As a result of their laziness, "they have grown ugly and brown and spotted and small; and are actually so degraded in their tastes, that they will eat our children." Later Mrs. Bedonebyasyoudid tells Tom a similar story about the Doasyoulikes, a race of idle and ignorant humans who "are grown so stupid now ... They have almost forgotten, too, how to talk. For each stupid child forgot some of the words it heard from its stupid parents ... [T]hey will all be apes very soon, and all by doing only what they liked" (235). Their devolution pointedly recalls Tom's earlier identification of his reflection as that of a "little black ape" and the problem of working-class degeneration that recapitulation aims to solve. Kingsley's merging of natural theology and evolutionary theory is impressive. Nature is not designed to be perfect and unchanging, as the natural theologians would have it, but is instead constantly designing itself. Evolution (here moral progress) depends on the individual's enthusiasm for keeping up with nature's continual change and the physical challenges through which nature offers opportunities for self-improvement.

Nature alone – even and especially evolving nature – teaches morality. Spencer claims that nature provides an education in justice: organisms acting in accordance with nature's laws are rewarded, while those in ignorance or defiance of those laws are punished. For Kingsley's fish and Doasyoulikes, positive actions result in morphological advance and disobedience with degradation, and both are inherited by the next generation.[53] While drawing from, and jumbling together, various evolutionary theories, Kingsley's examples already start to deviate from

Spencer's "natural justice." *The Water-Babies* quietly displaces, indeed inverts, the relationship between natural law and morality that was the purpose of such education to enshrine. For Spencer, nature is premised on the attitude of the Doasyoulikes: organisms endeavor first to survive, seeking pleasure and avoiding pain are as good guides as any to self-preservation, and self-preservation instills the basic principles of a moral education. But Kingsley's nature penalizes offenses such as sloth, cowardice, and selfishness not because they interfere with survival – selfishness and cowardice can work to an organism's advantage – but because they are violations of Protestant virtues.[54] Rather than indifferently constituting justice, Kingsley's natural selection is already constituted by it. Re-creating Spencer's school of cruelty within an antithetically benign moral universe, Kingsley makes ethics the cause rather than the result of evolution.

Kingsley's insistence on the organism's choice to evolve is justified in part by his seeming ignorance of any distinction between the theories of Darwin and those of Jean-Baptiste Lamarck. In an 1871 lecture, tellingly titled "The Natural Theology of the Future," Kingsley displays his blend of natural theology and evolutionary theory: "we knew of old that God was so wise that He could make all things; but behold, He is so much wiser than even that, that He can make all things make themselves."[55] God has instilled in every organism the willed volition that Lamarck granted to the giraffe purposely stretching its neck to reach the higher leaves or the crane lengthening its legs to walk in deeper waters.[56] Illustrating the same principle of divinely-delegated design, *The Water-Babies* presents a fairy named Mother Carey who sits at the center of creation, not "snipping, piecing, fitting, stitching," etc. (271), as Tom expects but rather "mak[ing] things make themselves" (273). Likewise, merging Spencer's pedagogy, Lamarck's willed adaptations, and conventional Christian morality, Tom's "natural" education involves opportunities for him to stretch his moral muscles, and Kingsley's fairy tale makes it clear that he must make the choices that will drive his evolution forward. Upon entering the river, for example, Tom initially delights in harassing other smaller creatures, giving the narrator an occasion to reprove:

> But I am sorry to say, he was too like some other little boys, very fond of hunting and tormenting creatures for mere sport. Some people say that boys cannot help it; that it is nature, and only a proof that we are all originally descended from beasts of prey. But whether it is nature or not, little boys can help it, and must help it. For if they have naughty, low, mischievous tricks in their nature, as monkeys have, that is no reason why they should give way to those tricks like monkeys, who know no better. (91)

What begins as proof of zoological continuity – that "we are all originally descended from beasts of prey" – is invoked merely to be denied by an insistence on moral difference – "little boys can help it, and must help it." Passages like this one suggest that the recapitulative content of *The Water-Babies* is merely a gimmick: a sugar-coating that makes Kingsley's sermonizing pill easier to swallow. Governing terms like "animal" and "man" masquerade for what are really only religious, rather than biological, categories in a conventional Christian homily.

Such moments may persuade us to agree with Beer and Rauch that *The Water-Babies* provides a shiny scientific gloss to an all-too-familiar religious didacticism. However, Tom is not the only child whom Kingsley seeks to educate with his fairy tale. It is in Kingsley's unique addresses to the reader that *The Water-Babies* seems to imbibe Spencer's pedagogy most deeply. Tom and the reader seem to have little in common. One is untutored and illiterate, while the other ostensibly recognizes the names of Darwin and Huxley. Tom learns his lessons "by sound and sharp experience," while the reader gains the same by reading, or having a parent read to him. Ensconced in his cozy nursery filled with books, the reader is surely not recapitulating human evolution from its animal origins. But through his storytelling, Kingsley's narrator merges these two experiences. Tom's great moral act, which enables him to graduate from eft to water-baby, occurs when he figures out how to release a captive lobster caught in a fisherman's trap, and immediately the river is filled with other water-babies who had previously been invisible to him. Surprisingly self-restrained, the narrator refrains from delivering the moral we might expect and asks instead,

> Now, was not that very odd? So odd, indeed, that you will, no doubt, want to know how it happened, and why Tom could never find a water-baby till after he had got the lobster out of the pot. And, if you will read this story nine times over, and then think for yourself, you will find out why. It is not good for little boys to be told everything, and never to be forced to use their own wits. (185)

The narrator leaves it to the reader to deduce the relation between cause and effect; without being told, the reader must discover for himself the laws – if not natural laws, then narrative ones – that determine the events of the story. The anticruelty moral of the episode seems drawn from Samuel Taylor Coleridge's "The Rime of the Ancient Mariner" (1798), the conclusion to which forms the epigraph to Kingsley's third chapter: "He prayeth best who loveth best/ All things both great and small" (82).

The moral may be Coleridge's, but the method for learning it comes from Spencer. The reader is asked to engage with the text in a manner that is analogous to Tom's application of the scientific method underwater. If Tom has to learn everything for himself, then so then does the reader.

The Water-Babies announces that literature, for Spencer pejoratively associated with didacticism and moral exegesis, can provide commensurate occasions for the same self-directed cognitive progress that recapitulative pedagogy celebrated. The literary text usurps the place of scientific experiment in the child's miniaturized evolution. This conversion of Spencer's scientific program into an exercise of reading does not annul the fairy tale's recapitulative plot; it provides its crucial extension. Reading a literary text can reproduce the opportunities for self-motivated discovery just as well as, if not better than, the natural environment. But Kingsley's avocation of reading, and the importance of literature, in the development of both ontogenic and phylogenic humanity, goes even further than this. The key term in the above passage, and for Kingsley's entire enterprise, is "wits." The narrator refrains from explaining why the water-babies suddenly appear in order to force the reader to use his "own wits" to decipher the causal connection between Tom's good deed and his reward. It is telling that the narrator repeats the same word that he had previously employed to describe Tom's disabling the trap: "having more wit than the lobster, he saw plainly enough what was the matter," says the narrator, and he then adds that "experience is of very little good unless a man, or a lobster, has wit enough to make use of it" (177). Put in such proximity, Tom's mechanical manipulation of the trap and the reader's intellectual handling of the plot are linked as equivalent, interchangeable uses of "wit."

At the high point of Kingsley's invention of a literary form capable of replicating self-directed discovery and conveying Spencer's recapitulative pedagogy, however, *The Water-Babies* announces its most obvious departure from it: the existence of fairies. The paradoxical personification of impersonal nature in Mrs. Bedonebyasyoudid shows that the tale incoherently combines Spencer's model of a hands-off, self-propelled, natural education with a didactic model of the parent or teacher who intrusively directs the child's behavior. Here *The Water-Babies* fully departs from the pedagogical program, which it really never adhered to in the first place. After rewarding Tom for rescuing the lobster, Mrs. Bedonebyasyoudid inducts him into an underwater Sunday school that propagates traditional moral lessons and cedes her role as Tom's teacher to her sister, Mrs. Doasyouwouldbedoneby. This second fairy, her name rearranging her predecessor's hard causality into the formula of the Golden Rule, dispatches Tom on a journey to aid in the redemption of Mr. Grimes. From this point forward, the plot ceases to follow evolutionary recapitulation and adopts the form of a religious pilgrimage. Even adding an ethical and intentional element to nature did not satisfy Kingsley; in the second half of the fairy tale, he creates a purely religious realm of existence separate from that already moralized nature. Mrs. Bedonebyasyoudid tells Tom that her sister "begins where I end, and I begin where she ends, and those who will not listen to her must listen to me" (206). Becoming a man means following nature only so far.

On one level, *The Water-Babies* provides an exaggerated example of the incoherency within nineteenth-century children's literature that encouraged readers to discover for themselves while at the same time communicating their lessons through schoolmarmish fairies and egregiously didactic narrators. But on another level, in adopting Spencer's educational paradigm and supplementing it with Christian moralizing and literary conventions, Kingsley is rewriting not only the narrative of child development but also the story of human evolution. The fairies represent a divine presence that, for Kingsley, has always been working behind the scenes. Rejecting the doctrine of special creation in favor of an evolutionary theory, he holds on to a Christian sense of divine omnipotence that his text overdetermines in at least three fairies and one narrator. In "The Natural Theology of the Future," Kingsley admits that nature study alone cannot be the whole of our worldview; here he distinguishes "natural theology," which he defines as "what can be learned concerning God himself" by looking at the physical evidence of nature, from "natural religion," which is "what can be learned from the physical universe of man's duty to God and to his neighbor."[57] About the latter, he says, "I do not even affirm that a natural religion is possible." Some other education is necessary, but *The Water-Babies* does more than simply layer religion onto science. In his evolutionary fairy tale, Kingsley seeks to locate the fundamental and uniquely human transformation during which science gives way to religion in the developing mind of the child and, accordingly, in the history of man. His answer is literature: in particular, fantasy, fairy tale, and nonsense.

Nonsensical nature of man

In *The Water-Babies*, the scientific method, applied to natural phenomena, teaches the recapitulating child lessons about health, survival, design, and even morality and justice. Children do not need to look beyond nature to reform their behavior into socially acceptable and morally beneficial forms.

Tom's altruistic act of saving the lobster shows that ethics can develop "naturally." However, becoming moral is just the first step to becoming Christian, which for Kingsley is the end point of humanity. Becoming Christian requires knowledge of the Divine beyond what can be seen or inferred from natural phenomena. This next step necessitates an education that lies outside of the observation and self-motivated experiment that Spencer prescribed as the whole of children's learning. For Kingsley, God is the unobservable, the omnipresence that makes experiment possible, but who does not reveal Himself through rational deduction. Believing in God means believing in entities that cannot be scientifically proven and that are thus understood only through the exercise of the imagination. Literature and art, not science, prepare the human mind for religious devotion to this unseen Divinity. The fairies in Kingsley's fairy tale – indeed the fairy tale itself – both introduce the child reader to a realm of fantasy that supplements his scientific education and replicate that era of our history in which the ability to imagine beyond what could be seen and tested marked our evolution into a distinct humanity.

Critical assessment of *The Water-Babies* frequently bisects Kingsley's fairy tale into nonsensical fantasy for children and evolutionary allegories for adults. In *The Victorian Press and the Fairy Tale* (2008), Caroline Sumpter suggests that its references to scientific theories are really not for the child readers – who could not understand them – but for the adults who encountered *The Water-Babies* in its first appearance serialized in *Macmillan's Magazine*. She reminds us that Kingsley's adult readers would have become familiar with his scientific references "simply through browsing the pages of *Macmillan's*."[58] The Doasyoulikes, for instance, would be understood in the contexts of *Macmillan's* "wider explications of philological and ethnological, Christian and scientific constructions of mankind." Jonathan Padley amplifies Sumpter's point and argues that, because *Macmillan's* was "an adult-focused journal," it is "transparently clear that this story is anything but an example of typical Victorian writing for children."[59] Sumpter's and Padley's considerations of *The Water-Babies'* publication history invaluably complicate the category "children's literature," but their division of *The Water-Babies* into two discrete halves (one for children and the other for adults) merely turns into an asset which former critics have seen as a failing. Humphrey Carpenter's *Secret Gardens* (1985) faults the book for too many ideas: "it managed to discover and explore almost all the directions that children's books would take over the next hundred years. And in exploring them it usually fell flat on its face."[60] Similarly, in *The Natural History of Make-Believe* (1996), John Goldthwaite says, "*The Water-Babies* is a story divided against itself," and wonders "why Kingsley willfully burdened his parable with so much that impeded its progress."[61] Whether Kingsley's book is an incoherent mess, as Carpenter and Goldthwaite assert, or an avant-garde experiment on "the margin between (potentially incompatible) audience expectations," as Padley claims, critics agree that its two registers have nothing to do with each other.[62] In contrast, I am arguing that, through the opposition between Spencer's empirical pedagogy conveyed by the evolutionary plot and the fantastical elements of the fairy tale, Kingsley lays out his unique vision of human development.

Despite modern scholars who feel the need to clarify Kingsley's intended audiences, *The Water-Babies* already explicitly tackles questions about its own readership. The narrator continually asks who is reading, how much knowledge that reader needs, and how he is receiving the tale. This focus on the implied reader allows Kingsley to foreground the act of reading as a pedagogical event that can, at once, mimic empirical experience and make up for its deficiencies. According to *The Water-Babies'* initial chapters, the implied child reader is weirdly savant. While working-class Tom "could not read or write," the reader clearly has an education, and a good one. The narrator anticipates that his reader will protest – "there are no such things as water-babies" (67) and "a water-baby is contrary to nature" (69) – to which he responds:

> You must not say that this cannot be, or that that is contrary to nature. You do not know what Nature is, or what she can do; and nobody knows; not even Sir Robert Murchison, or Professor Owen, or Professor Sedgwick, or Professor Huxley, or Mr. Darwin, or Professor Faraday, or Mr. Grove, or any other of the great men whom good boys are taught to respect. (69–70)

If Kingsley meant for the evolutionary content of his story to bypass child readers – who made up at least one of the book's intended audiences – then the decision to craft these references within direct addresses to a child is oddly provocative. Rather, Kingsley suggests that literary texts can do something that the scientific method cannot. The narrator here effectively reclaims nature from the naturalists, recruiting the scientific method's own principle of observation on behalf of an argument for possibilities that escape its reach. When his reader objects that "surely if there were water-babies somebody would have caught one at least," the narrator counters, "no one has a right to say that no water-babies exist, till they have seen no water-babies existing; which is quite a different thing, mind, from not seeing water-babies" (68). *The Water-Babies* thus offers its own rationale for its two competing pedagogical modes: empiricism allows the individual to evolve only so far, and literary fancy is required to take him the rest of the way.

Throughout *The Water-Babies*, Kingsley's narrator repeatedly insists that scientific explanations are inadequate unless supplemented by aesthetic ideas. The description of Tom's transformation into an eft, for instance, is cheekily couched in scientific terms: Tom is suddenly "about four inches, or – that I may be accurate – 3.87902 inches long, and having round the parotid region of his fauces a set of external gills" (67). To illustrate Tom's consciousness of being remade, however, the narrator quotes William Wordsworth's "Intimations" Ode:

> *Our birth is but a sleep and a forgetting;*
> *The soul that rises with us, our life's star,*
> *Hath elsewhere had its setting,*
> *And cometh from afar:*
> *Not in entire forgetfulness,*
> *And not in utter nakedness,*
> *But trailing clouds of glory, do we come*
> *From God, who is our home.* (85)

Spencer's animalistic child and Wordsworth's angelic child make a sharp contrast. The latter is not merely nonevolutionary but antieducational; the maintenance of his perfection depends on eschewing any and all change, especially what Wordsworth's next line calls the "shades of the prison-house" of formal schooling.[63] But there is a theoretical logic to Kingsley's juxtaposition of these two ideas. *The Water-Babies* presents the Romantic child not as a truism but rather as a fiction necessary to resist the scientific materialism that was reducing men to mere animals. "There," the narrator says, concluding his recitation with "you can know no more than that. But if I was you, I would believe that. For then the great fairy Science, who is likely to be queen of all the fairies for many a year to come, can only do you good, and never do you harm."[64] Linley Sambourne, Kingsley's illustrator for the fourth textual edition, punctuates this threat with a picture of Huxley and his rival, anatomist Richard Owen, examining Tom, now a specimen trapped in a glass jar [Figure 4]. Science, it seems, will turn the little boy into an animal every time, unless he believes in the alternate version of humanity provided, and performed, by art.

To emphasize the necessity of aesthetic education, Kingsley introduces another child: a little girl, upper-class, educated, Christian, and opposite in every way to Tom. The fairy tale first introduces Ellie when Tom, on the job with Master Grimes, inadvertently enters her bedroom and watches her

Figure 4 From Charles Kingsley, *The Water-Babies: A Fairy Tale for a Land-Baby*, 1863, 4th ed., illustrated by Linley Sambourne (London: Macmillan and Company, 1890), 69.

sleep before he flees to the river's edge, and she renters the story just as Tom is getting used to his underwater existence. From the river below, Tom overhears Professor Ptthmllnsprts (Kingsley's parody of Huxley) walking with Ellie, his pupil, on the cliffs above. She is bored with the professor's nature lessons that concern only the dry facts of animal life and inquires whether there are any animals that talk. Like the overscientific reader, Ptthmllnsprts insists that science admits no such possibility. While he speaks for science, Ellie presents the opposing voice of an art that envisions mermaids, mermen, and water-babies. She says that she has seen them "in a picture at home, of a beautiful lady sailing in a car drawn by dolphins, and babies flying round her, and one sitting in her lap" (152). Though the picture itself cannot prove the veracity of its vision, she claims, "it is so beautiful, that it must be true." Her assertion is the central contention of Kingsley's fairy tale, and the first editions of the text underscored her claim. Taking Ellie's side, the narrator expresses his partiality for art: "Ah, you dear little Ellie, fresh out of heaven! when will people understand that one of the deepest and wisest speeches which can come out of a human mouth is that – 'It is so beautiful that it must be true?'"[65] Truth is not restricted to observable and testable fact. "Fresh out of heaven" like the subject of Wordsworth's ode, she advances an aesthetic standard for truth transcendent of scientific reason. As Tom is the practical child predicted by natural law, Ellie is the prophetic child created by poetic inspiration.

The tale brings them together rather inelegantly: Ellie leans over the rocks to see if there are any water-babies despite her tutor's resolve, slips, and drowns like Tom, but she does not transform into a lower animal. Her state of grace seems preternaturally unchangeable; just before she dies, the narrator says, "here she comes, looking like a clean white good little darling, as she always was, and always will be" (145). Ellie drowns simply so that she can teach Tom the next lessons in his moral development: self-restraint, honesty, and forgiveness. Disappearing on Sundays, presumably to visit some more heavenly realm that her soul, but not Tom's, can access, Ellie gives Tom a new goal, and his relationship with her prepares him to embark on a pilgrimage to rescue Grimes, his former abuser, from a Dante-esque inferno, where he has been encased in a chimney. That Ellie is fully evolved and faithfully represented by her pure white garb and skin reveals Kingsley's views on femininity. In the lecture "The Tree of Knowledge" (1879), Kingsley sought to vindicate Eve by arguing that her decision to take the forbidden fruit illustrated the best of humanity: the striving for knowledge. In eating the apple, "she proved herself thereby – though at an awful cost – a woman, and not an animal."[66] Refusing to limit her knowledge to her tutor's restrictions, Ellie may replicate the qualities of Kingsley's Eve, who is not the little beast that Tom is. The girl's place in the late Victorian recapitulation narrative was deeply problematic, and Kingsley sidesteps the question of female bestiality by making Ellie the result, rather than the origin, of our ancestors' ascent to humanity.[67]

In *The Water-Babies*, Ellie expresses the state of mind that is key to evolution: she exercises her imagination, which is also her wit. In the ambidextrous sense that Kingsley gives the term "wit" when Tom opens the lobster trap and the reader figures out why this act makes the water-babies appear, wit is also another word for imagination. "Without imagination," Kingsley argues in "How to Study Natural History," "no man can possibly invent even the pettiest object . . . [I]t is one of the faculties which essentially raises man above the brutes, by enabling him to create for himself."[68] A scientific education in the facts of nature – without the imaginative creation of counterfacts – is not enough to make the species, or the child, fully human. Kingsley's connection of wit and imagination seems drawn from Locke, whose *Essay Concerning Human Understanding* (1689) contends that wit synthesizes ideas, giving way to "pleasant Pictures, and agreeable Visions in the Fancy."[69] But if we are supposed to recognize Locke here, we are not meant to accept his hierarchy of intellectual faculties that ranks wit lower than judgment.[70] When Ellie speaks of the truth communicated by aesthetic beauty, in *The Water-Babies*' first edition, Kingsley's narrator explicitly claims that we will only see this truth when we "give up believing that Mr. John Locke . . . was the wisest man that ever lived on earth."[71] Revising Spencer's natural education, Kingsley also rejects Locke's dependence on reason – and the tradition of children's literature rooted in his empiricism – in favor of the Romantic enshrinement of the imagination as the supplement to Darwinian science.

And if imagination is necessary for the child's development, then literature (Kingsley's own fairy tale) steps in to supply that very faculty. Awareness of the fairies within the text elevates Tom, and likewise, appreciation of the fairy tale constitutes the most important stage of the reader's evolution. Casting Huxley as Professor Ptthmllnsprts, the "very great naturalist, and chief professor of *Necrobioneopalaeonthydrochthonanthropopithekology*" (148–149), Kingsley engages Huxley's notorious disagreement with Owen. In an 1857 paper delivered to the Linnaean Society, Owen had argued that the unique possession of three cerebral features – the *hippocampus minor*, the posterior cornu, and the third lobe – distinguished human beings from apes sufficiently enough to justify our inclusion in a separate subclass.[72] But after studies revealed the same structures in simian brains, Huxley repeatedly challenged Owen in print and speech, insisting in 1863 that the discovery proved beyond any doubt "the impossibility of erecting any cerebral barrier between man and apes."[73] Mocking the significance that scientists were giving to this minuscule cranny, Kingsley's narrator addresses the reader:

> You may think that there are other more important differences between you and an ape, such as being able to speak, and make machines, and know right from wrong, and say your prayers ... but that is a child's fancy, my dear. Nothing is to be depended on but the great hippopotamus test. If you have a hippopotamus major in your brain, you are no ape, though you had four hands, no feet, and were more apish than the apes of all aperies ... No, my dear little man; always remember that the one true, certain, final, and all-important difference between you and an ape is, that you have a hippopotamus major in your brain, and it has none. (153)

Though the savvy reader will see through the faux protests of Kingsley's narrator and conclude that humanity does, in fact, lie in the unique abilities to speak, to make machines, to know right from wrong, and to say one's prayers, the real power of humanity for *The Water-Babies* is expressed through our ability to create and to enjoy this kind of nonsense. Whereas Owen's and Huxley's scientific arguments threaten to turn humanity into anatomy, Kingsley's fairy tale – substituting "hippocampus" for its more familiar sound-alike "hippopotamus" – retaliates by turning anatomy into nonsense. This moment of silliness is, indeed, a recipe for completing the reader's recapitulation: the scientific self yields to the literary, fantastical, nonsensical self. In contrast, the fully scientifically minded Professor Ptthmllnsprts does not acknowledge the possibility of "*nymphs, satyrs, fauns, inui, dwarfs, trolls, elves, gnomes, fairies, brownies ... angels, archangels, imps, bogies*" (154). The inclusion of angels and archangels suggests that the professor's dependence on empirical science rules out the possibility of Christianity. As punishment, Huxley's alter ego is made to believe in "*unicorns, fire-drakes, manticoras, basilisks, amphisbænas, griffins, phœnixes, rocs, orcs, dog-headed men, three-headed dogs*, [and] *three-bodied geryons*" (155). This punishment is a blessing according to the logic of the book, for it is the ability to believe in impossible things that finally makes us human.

"Am I in earnest?", the narrator asks the child reader of *The Water-Babies*; "Oh dear no! Don't you know that this is a fairy tale, and all fun and pretence; and that you are not to believe one word of it, even if it is true?" (76).[74] Children's literature, as Kingsley was renegotiating it for the post-Darwinian era, must invite the child to use his wits, spark his imagination, and provide opportunities for "fun and pretence." Not entirely abandoning Spencer's recapitulative pedagogy, *The Water-Babies* reserves a privileged place for nature study and self-exploration. But far from being primary, natural education is secondary to the more essential education in fantasy and nonsense. According to Kingsley's lecture "How to Study Natural History," nature study introduces to us "a class of objects which may excite wonder, reverence," but in *The Water-Babies*, Kingsley's more extensive exploration of how nature study might work in the instruction of chimney sweep and reader alike, becoming human entails using this wonder to imagine far more than nature can offer.[75] In fact, that which develops after our "natural" growth and which is most "artificial" about us – which, like the water-babies themselves, is "contrary to nature" – is the core of our humanity. There is thus no overlap between Mrs. Bedonebyasyoudid (illustrating the principle of Spencer's mechanical nature) and Mrs. Doasyouwouldbedoneby (the conventionally didactic Golden Rule), nor need there be. The divide between the two sisters – nature and morality – is already bridged by the fairy tale in which they are both contained. Imaginative literature performs the defining moment of the child's recapitulative transition, from picturing nature in fairy form to believing in a fairy who transcends nature and dictates conduct beyond purely natural need.

Fairy tales, and other fantastic fictions, not only held a primary place in Kingsley's ideas about individual development but also served as an essential stage in his idiosyncratic version of human history. In the same year that *The Water-Babies* began to appear in *Macmillan's Magazine*, Kingsley wrote a letter to Darwin reporting that, at a hunting party where theories of human descent came under attack, he defended the evolutionist. But, then, Kingsley quickly moves on to his hypothesis that myths and legends retain evidence of the "missing link," and thereby makes a singular claim for the place of literature in human evolution:

> I want now to bore you on another matter. This great gulf between the quadrumana & man; & the absence of any record of species intermediate between man & the ape. It has come home to me with much force, that while *we* deny the existence of any such, the legends of most nations are full of them. Fauns, Satyrs, Inui, Elves, Dwarfs – we call them one minute mythological personages, the next conquered inferior races – & ignore the broad fact, that they are always represented as more bestial than man, & of violent sexual passion . . .
>
>   I hope that you will not think me dreaming – To me, it seems strange that we are to deny that any Creatures intermediate between man & the ape ever existed, while our forefathers of every race, assure us that they did.[76]

Congratulating European culture for suppressing "inferior races," Kingsley's letter can, and perhaps should, be dismissed as late Victorian racism and despicable imperialist ravings. The fallacy of transforming myth into history, furthermore, exemplifies an illogical and unscientific leap by which, as Cannon Schmitt has recently accused Kingsley, "supposition provide[s] proof."[77] Nonetheless, Kingsley's idea that imagination – the "collective unconscious" if we want to be generous to him – carries clues to our evolutionary past intriguingly recasts recapitulation from a process of physiological development to an unfolding of our mental, and in particular aesthetic, faculties. Schmitt says that Kingsley "fetishize[s] the past, worshipping it precisely because it cannot be brought back."[78] But for Kingsley, the past is brought back in a safe and usable form through the literature that preserves it and delivers it to the child. If this curious version of a proto-human prehistory rife with mythological and magical half-humans were converted into a corresponding narrative of sequential recapitulation, we would get something like *The Water-Babies*. The recapitulating child first goes through successive animal stages during which he learns directly from nature, as Spencer prescribes, but then he must pass through a fairy tale stage in which he is either himself a mythological creature (like a water-baby) or believes in fantastic beings (like fairies). The fairy tale is the essential transition from bestiality to humanity for both the individual and the species.

Even with the calls for more scientific instruction in elementary school, in 1905 the centralized Board of Education hoped that English lessons, and especially composition, would "be the common bond which unifies the whole curriculum," and soon, *The Water-Babies* appeared on its short-list of recommended reading.[79] Which version of Kingsley's novel the Board of Education meant, however, is unclear. While *The Water-Babies* was common school reading in both England and the United States, students' abridged versions often omitted all overt references to evolution and thus presented Tom's miraculous metamorphosis and underwater journey as pure fairy tale. In one *Water-Babies, Adapted for Use in Schools* (London, 1908), the Professor "gave [Ellie] a succinct compendium of his famous paper at the British Association, in a form suited for the youthful mind" but its elision of the paper – as well as Kingsley's joke about the "hippopotamus major" – suggests that scientific satire was not so suitable.[80] The even more abridged *Kingsley's Water-Babies, Arranged for Youngest Readers* (Boston, MA, 1898) includes the Professor's disbelief in water-babies but gives no explanation for his resistance, introduces Tom to the noble salmon but erases their degenerating trout kin, and describes Mother

Carey but grants her no creative power to make animals make themselves.[81] Culling Kingsley's 300-page rambling tale had obvious merits for the writers of Boston's Public School Publishing Company, who claimed in 1916 that "the teacher whose superintendent or whose board chooses *The Water Babies* for her [to teach] is lucky," even though "the amount of scientific knowledge that children gain from reading [it] is of about as much importance as the bubbles of the sea."[82]

Not all students' engagements with Kingsley's arguments about evolution were so clipped, nor were the scientific uses of his fairy tale so evanescent. A 1913 Infant Teacher's Edition of *The Water-Babies* put out by the Pitman Readers series advertised Kingsley's text "adapted and re-told with copious natural history notes and a scheme of correlated lessons and handwork."[83] With an extensive appendix including facts about the flora and fauna that appear in the novel, this edition instructs teachers: "each story should be followed by easy conversational lessons dealing with the plants and animals mentioned."[84] When pupils read Kingsley's allegory of the salmon, for instance, the episode was to be supplemented with information about piscine morphology and activities in which students constructed clay models of fish. Even though Pitman's version still excludes Professor Ptthmllnsprts's complicated discovery of the "hippopotamus major," the students' experience of reading *The Water-Babies* in the context of nature study and art lessons still allows them to move between scientific and aesthetic registers and, thus, preserves some of the tale's explorations into contrasting disciplines. And these abridged versions were not the only encounters children had with Kingsley's novel. Literary biographers have noted that *The Water-Babies* introduced writers as diverse as nineteenth-century American naturalist Theodore Dreiser and twentieth-century science fiction author Robert Heinlein to evolutionary theory.[85] It is impossible to gage the extent of Kingsley's influence, but *The Water-Babies'* mingling of natural science and fairy tale constituted many generations' first encounter with evolution.

Scholars who divide *The Water-Babies* into a nonsensical fantasy for child readers and an evolutionary allegory for adults miss the central place that Kingsley assigns to fiction within evolution. His attempt to blend evolutionary theory with natural theology, nature's impartial justice with Christianity's concern with mercy, proves unwieldy, even dizzying, and without satisfactory harmonization. But *The Water-Babies* more successfully integrates diverse philosophies in the place it gives to the literary imagination – and the activity of reading – within the child's recapitulation. Against Spencer's purely experiential pedagogy, Kingsley illustrates that literature allows for the mental play that mimics the trial-and-error stage of the species' intellectual evolution, introduces the child to possibilities outside those verified by scientific fact, opens a space for the divine, and inducts the child into a stage of mythological existence that constitutes the essential link between animals and humans. When his narrator says that "no one has a right to say that no water-babies exist, till they have seen no water-babies existing" (68), Kingsley turns the criteria of empiricism against itself. Scientific investigation can confirm but can never disprove existence. Meanwhile, literary fancy, in positing entities outside visible reality, provides a portal to acts of faith. *The Water-Babies'* lessons about evolution and scientific instruction are is separable from its fantastical and nonsensical elements.

For Kingsley, the very mythic quality of literature enabled – and continues to enable – the essential fulcrum in the species' ascent to humanity and in each individual's miniaturized repetition of the same process. In his understanding of natural history, Kingsley was deeply influenced by noted naturalist and anti-evolutionist Phillip Henry Gosse, with whom he corresponded as he wrote *The Water-Babies*. Though Kingsley disagreed with Gosse about evolutionary theory and its consequences for Christianity, we may hear Gosse's words running through Kingsley's recapitulative fairy tale. In *Romance of Natural History* (1860–1861), Gosse writes,

> There are more ways than one of studying natural history. There is Dr. Dryasdust's way, – which consists of mere accuracy of definitions and differentiation; statistics as harsh and dry as the skins and bones in the museum where it is studied. There is the field observer's way: the careful and conscientious accumulation and record of facts bearing on the life-history of the creatures . . . And there is the poet's way, who looks at nature through a glass peculiarly his own; the aesthetic aspect, which deals, not with statistics, but with the emotions of the human mind, – surprise, wonder, terror, revulsion, admiration, love, desire, and so forth, – which are made energetic by the contemplation of the creatures around him.[86]

This poet's way of sympathy and the moral relations to other animals and things are part of what Kingsley seeks to convey in *The Water-Babies*. But in addition to the poet's way, Kingsley explores the fabulist's way, the way of fantasy, unreality, and nonsense; these modes of thinking raise us above the brutes. Thus ushering in a new age of children's literature, *The Water-Babies* ultimately offers a subtle but persuasive argument that children's fiction must become more fantastic, more satirical, and more nonsensical to remain pedagogically effective for the animal child struggling to become human.

CHAPTER 3

Generic variability
Lewis Carroll, scientific nonsense, and literary parody

Lewis Carroll's parody of Victorian education begins early in *Alice's Adventures in Wonderland* (1865). Falling down the rabbit hole, Alice tries to recall the distance to the earth's center and the precise location of the antipodes: "for, you see," the narrator's parenthetical interjection says, "Alice had learnt several things of this sort in her lessons in the schoolroom."[1] From Alice's desperate attempt to recite her school lessons in *Wonderland* to the Red and White Queens' preposterous examination at the end of *Through the Looking-Glass, and What Alice Found There* (1872), the *Alice* books repeatedly mock common pedagogical practices. It might then seem that, in forcing his protagonist out of the Victorian schoolroom, sending her on an underground journey, and introducing her to a cast of talking animals, Carroll initiates a project like Charles Kingsley's *The Water-Babies: A Fairy Tale for a Land-Baby* (1863), discussed in the last chapter. A handful of literary scholars have gestured toward this reading. Eighty years ago, William Empson's *Some Versions of Pastoral* (1935) provocatively asserted that *Wonderland*'s opening posits an allegory of recapitulation: the Pool of Tears is "the sea from which life arose . . . it is also the amniotic fluid," suggesting the analogy that "ontogeny then repeats phylogeny."[2] If we take Empson's position that *Wonderland* opens with Alice's recapitulation, birthing her anew alongside the birds and rodents with whom she crawls out of this amniotic sea of life and subjecting her to a natural education, *Wonderland* might seem another experiment in Herbert Spencer's pedagogy.

Scholars other than Empson have highlighted the Darwinian hints lurking in *Wonderland* and *Looking-Glass*. Nancy Lacey Schwartz, for instance, maintains that the Dodo's role as the orchestrator of the Caucus-race "makes fun of the Darwinian themes of extinction."[3] Donald Rackin calls both the Caucus-race and the Mad Tea-Party "graphic metaphors for the Darwinian model of nature's instinctual, unthinking, amoral, and endless round of self-preservation."[4] U. C. Knoepflmacher extends this

86

network of evolutionary references, seeing the Dodo, Caterpillar, and Pigeon as "imports from a Darwinian world of aggression, voracity, and sexual selection."[5] *Wonderland* has been particularly amenable to Darwinian readings, but *Looking-Glass* is not immune. According to Robert Polhemus, Tweedledum's and Tweedledee's poem "The Walrus and the Carpenter" offers "a comic microcosm of 'nature red in tooth and claw' . . . as if Herbert Spencer had been spliced with Machiavelli and then articulated and rhymed by Edward Lear."[6] Furthermore, for Rose Lovell-Smith, John Tenniel's illustrations in both texts draw directly from "the life sciences, natural history, and Darwinian ideas about evolution," giving the *Alice* books a further evolutionary gloss.[7] That Carroll toys with Darwinian figures and themes is undeniable, but their effect is ultimately more ambiguous than elucidating.

Though both the Darwinism of the *Alice* books and the similarities between *Wonderland* and *The Water-Babies* have been noted, an experiment in natural education hardly seems an apt interpretation of the hearty plays with language, logic, and social convention that abound in Carroll's texts.[8] Nature is hardly a meaningful category in either *Wonderland* or *Looking-Glass*. Rather, Carroll's allusions to Darwinism or the natural world draw attention to the attenuated relationship between textual allusion and extra-textual referent. To rephrase the array of critics previously quoted, the *Alice* books are full of "graphic metaphors" and "imports"; they offer a "comic microcosm," "mak[ing] fun" of the figures they include and contort. This literary contortion is especially evident in Alice's muddled version of Isaac Watts's "Against Idleness and Mischief" (1715), a nugget of natural theology memorized and recited by Victorian schoolchildren. Instead of reproducing Watts's poetic praise of the industriousness of the bee, Alice delivers *Wonderland*'s first parody, "How doth the little crocodile." Watts's "busy bee" who "labours hard" and "skillfully . . . builds" her hive is transformed into a predatory crocodile who "seems to grin" in order to trick fishes into his "smiling jaws" (19).[9] This moment might herald a transitional moment for science education in England: in the 1860s, the lessons in natural theology's benignly designed universe were under threat of being usurped by Darwinian images of self-preservation and the survival of the fittest. But more important than the transformation of the poem's subject (from bee to crocodile), I argue, is the method of that transformation. It is the promise of parody, not the destructiveness of Darwinism, that *Wonderland* teaches.

Wonderland responds to the Darwinist turn in the biological sciences, not by fortifying natural theology like Margaret Gatty's *Parables of Nature*

(1855–1871) or by adding a humanist education onto a scientific base like Kingsley's *The Water-Babies*. Carroll more radically dismisses the value of nature study altogether, finding in nature no viable model for human agency and creativity, and opts instead for an education in linguistic nonsense and literary forms. Whereas Kingsley began his fairy tale in deference to Spencer's prescriptions for a purely empirical recapitulative pedagogy, Carroll takes the side of Matthew Arnold, who opposed science's growing dominance at every level of education and championed, in particular, literature, grammar, and memorization. In focusing on language games rather than nature study, Carroll experiments with the kind of education that Arnold, in his capacity as Schools Inspector, recommended in his biannual reports, but in emphasizing parody over rote recitation, nonsense over grammar, and playful mockery over humble respect for the canon, Carroll devises a literary pedagogy that revels in fluidity and adaptation. For Carroll, a noted skeptic of evolution, evolutionary theory destabilized the natural order, even our sense of self, but it offered no methods by which to manage the disturbance that it created. Parody, and to a lesser extent nonsense, in contrast, negotiate questions of change and continuity, language and meaning, and self and volition. *Wonderland* demonstrates that adeptness with language and literature recovers the human agency that new biological theories were threatening to take away.

Nonsense of naming

A half century ago, literary critic A. Dwight Culler's "The Darwinian Revolution and Literary Form" (1968) argued that *Wonderland* is Darwinian not "because it contains evolutionary materials (as in abundance it does) nor despite the fact that its author is known to have detested Darwin (as he certainly did)" but "because, like Darwin, [Carroll] subjects the rigidities of an ethical, social, and religious world to the fresh natural vision of a child and to the destructive analysis of formal chance."[10] This new "analysis," according to Culler, is none other than the literary mode that Carroll perfected: nonsense. For Culler and for later critics, figures like Carroll and Darwin share the notable distinction of defying the sacred orders of Victorian thinking, and this is sufficient to posit a relation between them. Nonsense, even from the pen of an anti-evolutionist, still seems Darwinian because it does not let the old world order stand. Though nonsense challenges conventional ways of making sense, and both Carroll and Darwin were contemporaneously engaged in challenging Victorian thought, the easy conflation of these two mavericks overlooks how non-sense was commonly marshaled in anti-Darwinian, pro-natural theology children's texts throughout the century. The tension between, but inter-dependence of, nonsense (logical or semantic disorder) and design (natural order) wed this supposed revolutionary literary mode to a far more tradi-tionalist scientific conception than Culler wants to admit, but of which, as we will see, Carroll himself seems well aware.

By the time Carroll composed *Wonderland*, nonsense had long been one of the most useful and well-worn rhetorical tools of natural theology. William Paley introduces his argument from design in *Natural Theology; or, Evidence of the Existence of Attributes of the Deity, Collected from the Appearances of Nature* (1802) with his famous analogy of the watch. If upon examining a watch, we deduce automatically that there must be a Watchmaker, he argues, then we must make the same conclusions about a stone, the earth, and the flora and fauna on it. To look at the fine construction of the watch and think that anything other than a conscious Maker could account for it is nonsense, according to Paley. "Can this be maintained without absurdity," he asks, and thus characterizes atheism as the belief in the patently ridiculous notion that the design could exist without a Designer.[11] Elsewhere in his argument as well as in the children's books that applied natural theology, readers are encouraged to appreciate design in nature by recognizing that any other configuration of nature's elements would be nonsensical. Even before Paley, the mother-narrator of Sarah Trimmer's *An Easy Introduction to the Knowledge of Nature, and Reading the Holy Scriptures* (1780) teaches her child-auditors to appreciate the benevolent design of the earth's oceans by looking at a globe and "suppos[ing] the places which stand for water were really dug hollow"; if this were the case, she says, "we should never be able to reach parts beyond [the] sea."[12] Earlier, she explains the benevolence of God's four-legged animal design by imagining the absurdity of a bipedal cow, "whose food is on the ground . . . [and thus] would always be stooping, which would tire them sadly."[13] Grounded ships and crouching cows are the silly, nonsensi-cal results of altering God's creation. Such images lead the child to the only logical conclusion: the world is designed by an omniscient and compassio-nate Designer.

Even texts that are calculated homages to the *Alice* books, self-conscious imitators of Carrollian plays on language and logic, often use *Wonderland*-like nonsense to convey explicit morals about the sensibility of design. In Tom Hood's fantasy *From Nowhere to the North Pole: A Noah's Ark-Æological Narrative* (1875), for example, a boy named Frank encounters a subterranean menagerie of talking animals and composite beasts, like the Buffalant, Tigeroceros, Elegoapard, and Armaskullamus. The mutants tell Frank that they are his creation; in his waking life, he tore apart the figures in his Noah's Ark set and mingled their parts because "he began to fancy that he could improve upon them, or design others of a superior kind."[14] His Frankensteinian experiments demonstrate the nonsense of deviating from God's design. Unlike God, Frank "had not proceeded to construct [his animal creations] with any regard to the mutual fitness of the various proportions he had designed to join together."[15] For instance, the Armaskullamus – part armadillo and part hippopotamus – has internal organs but no skin, and as a result, its "brains inside have shrivelled up into a little dry lump, and roll about into odd corners" of its skull.[16] This illustration of non-design is straightforward natural theology: any other arrangement than God's looks "as if you had shaken up the Zoological Gardens and the Natural History collections at the British Museum in a bag, and had then glued the pieces together haphazard in the dark."[17]

At one point in Hood's underground adventure, Frank encounters a group of elves who try to determine what kind of a creature he is; this episode is reminiscent of kindred scenes from *Wonderland* and *The Water-Babies*. In *The Water-Babies*, an otter wondering whether the recently transformed Tom is an edible treat for her pups decides that he is only "a nasty eft," and he is unable to convince her that he is a boy.[18] Similarly in *Wonderland*, the Pigeon, this time afraid that Alice will eat her eggs, exposes Alice's failure to explain what makes her a little girl as opposed to a serpent, or indeed any other kind of animal. In Hood's text, the elves debate Frank's digestibility and finally insist that he is an earthquake with unaccountable appendages. Frank's response, however, turns the encounter into a lesson about innate human specialness:

> "I've no hind legs, and I'm not an earthquake or anything of that kind," [Frank] said, in an offended tone.
> "Then what are you?" asked one little man who had climbed on to the roof of his toadstool.
> "What am I? Why, a boy, of course."
> "A booooy!" shrieked all the little people in chorus. "It says it's a boooy! What *is* as boy?"
> "I shall be a man some of these days," added Frank, proudly.[19]

Unlike Kingsley's Tom who says he's a boy but then asks "what are men?" or Alice who stutters, "'I – I'm a little girl,' … rather doubtfully" (48), Frank tells the elves that he is a boy "of course" and "proudly" gives a definition of a boy as someone who "shall be a man" – as if the latter term cannot be questioned.[20] Thus, rather than display any uncertainty about what constitutes humanity, Hood's Frank quickly recovers the category. Potential nonsense is quickly dispelled in favor of good sense, where manhood is an unquestioned essence, even if boyhood is a bit tentative. In showing that it is the very questioning of the integrity of humanity – and certainly not the category itself – that is nonsense, Hood's text demonstrates the fundamental sense of species in general and human specialness in particular.

Hood's translation of *Wonderland*-like scenarios into defenses of natural theology is not unique. Albert and George Gresswell's even more overtly derivative *The Wonderland of Evolution* (1884) attempts to ventriloquize Carroll's sardonic voice in order to unmask the nonsensicality of evolution. Again seemingly incorporating attributes of both Carroll and Kingsley's texts, the Gresswells' book opens with an adult narrator recapitulating from a polyp to an ant, a fish, a frog, and so on while interviewing his fellow creatures about how they achieved their current forms. The goal of these inquiries is to show that any description of gradual adaptation, if interrogated, will prove to be preposterous, and that special creation is therefore the only sensible explanation for the diversity and perfect functionality of animal morphology. A cuttlefish explaining the existence of his ink sac, for instance, says that generations ago one of his forefathers was just about to be eaten by a larger predator when "suddenly . . . recollecting that he had recently come into the possession of several small pigmentary particles, he began to bethink himself how he might use them in self-defense."[21] The cuttlefish's story is intended to mock Darwin's theory of random variation and natural selection, questioning how pigments could have magically appeared before the organism had any use for them and then how such a simple creature as a cuttlefish could have self-consciously "began to bethink himself" to take advantage of them. This supposed absurdity illustrates what the Gresswells deem the ridiculousness of unguided, non-teleological evolution.

Put in this context, Kingsley's employment of nonsense in *The Water-Babies* is indeed revolutionary. Instead of asserting that only theological arguments from design make sense and that evolution (or any theory besides special creation) is illogical, Kingsley suggests that theories based on scientific empiricism, like evolution, are perfectly rational and that it is the belief in an unseen Creator that is akin to nonsense. As discussed in the last chapter of this book, Kingsley contrasts the sensible science of nature that discovers and classifies natural phenomena with the unfounded – but not invalid – leaps of faith that bring us into contact with the unscientific, spiritual dimensions of existence. When Kingsley's narrator anticipates his skeptical reader's dismissal of the possibility that there are water-babies, he offers this rebuttal: "You must not say that this cannot be, or that that is contrary to nature."[22] At stake here is not just whether we believe in water-babies but whether we believe in God, who is also "contrary to nature," a Being about which "nobody knows," and who according to purely scientific logic is nonsensical. Nonsense in *The Water-Babies* is not the opposite of design, as it is for Paley, Trimmer, Hood, and the Gresswells, but rather its companion. Science proves the factual, but nonsense attests to the counterfactual, which for Kingsley is just as genuine.

In *Wonderland* and *Looking-Glass*, Carroll uses nonsense neither to buttress the natural theology argument about design nor to encourage his readers' deistic hypothesizing. Though Carroll comes closest to Kingsley when, in *Looking-Glass*, the Unicorn offers to Alice, "if you'll believe in me, I'll believe in you. Is that a bargain?" (201) or when the White Queen insists that "sometimes I've believed as many as six impossible things before breakfast" and encourages Alice to do the same (174), Carroll's brand of nonsense more often turns its focus on the quotidian details of our social and linguistic realities than to alternate realms of speculative belief. But his interrogation of language also remarks on the categories to which such language refers, and the idea of species is one target of Carroll's linguistic mockery. In *Looking-Glass*, the Gnat's insect taxonomy includes the "Rocking-horse-fly," who is "made entirely of wood, and gets around by swinging itself from branch to branch" (149), the "Snap-dragon-fly," whose "body is made of plum-pudding" (150), and the "Bread-and-butter-fly," whose "body is a crust, and its head is a lump of sugar" (151). As Humpty Dumpty explains when Alice asks him to translate the poem "Jabberwocky," these names are "like a portmanteau," in which "there are two meanings packed up into one word" (187); joining "rocking-horse" and "horse-fly" or "bread and butter" and "butterfly" achieves this compound effect. Carroll's nonsense resembles Lear's *Nonsense Botany* (1888), which, showcasing specimens like "Armchairia Comfortabilis" and "Manypeoplia Upsidedownia," attaches faux-Latinate suffixes to common words to poke fun at scientific taxonomy.[23]

Surely, Carroll's and Lear's creations are ridiculous and, like Trimmer's stooping cattle or Hood's Armaskullus, could be used to bear witness to the absurdity of any order other than the nature that God designed. But Carroll and Lear resist this familiar move. While *Nonsense Botany* presents one taxonomic absurdity after another without comment, the Gnat's nonsense entomology ends when he asks Alice, "I suppose you don't want to lose your name?" (151). The reader is brought back to a recurrent problem throughout the *Alice* books: Alice's trouble maintaining a coherent sense of self despite changes, gains, or losses such as the alterations to her size wrought by the cake and potion in *Wonderland*, her situation in unfamiliar settings in both books, or her temporarily forgetting names and classifications in *Looking-Glass*. The *Looking-Glass* insects cleave the possibilities of language from the realities of nature. Tenniel's illustration of Carroll's "Rocking-horse-fly" draws attention to the physical incompatibility of each of the linguistic parts: the insect is pictured with rockers that, though they might heave up and down, would make forward movement impossible, while the wings, though sized appropriately for the equine torso, are wholly inadequate to lift the bulky rockers. We can say "Rocking-horse-fly" and have that name conjure up an image in our minds, but, while this image appears in our imagination, it cannot exist in nature. More like Kingsley than the straightforward natural theologians, Carroll uses nonsense to point to an alternate realm that is "contrary to nature," but unlike Kingsley's contrariness, Carroll gestures not toward the existence of divine agency but rather toward the possibilities of human language.

In these moments of nonsense naming, the *Alice* books foreground the gap between language and nature in order to question whether we understand ourselves primarily as linguistic constructions or as physical realities. When the elves of Hood's *From Nowhere to the North Pole* prompt Frank to declare that he is a "boy" rather than an earthquake, his easy act of naming himself convinces his interlocutors and makes his utterance so. Alice's encounter with the Pigeon lacks such a definitive resolution. Rather, if names and classifications mean only by their real-world applications, Alice loses the argument. Having eaten too much of one side of the Caterpillar's mushroom, she grows precipitously, and her elongated neck invades the expectant Pigeon's nest. The Pigeon, familiar with long necks, accuses her of being a serpent in search of eggs, and Alice unsuccessfully struggles to sway the mother bird:

> "I – I'm a little girl," said Alice, rather doubtfully, as she remembered the number of changes she'd gone through, that day.
>
> "A likely story indeed!" said the Pigeon, in a tone of the deepest contempt. "I've seen a good many little girls in my time, but never *one* with such a neck as that! No, no! You're a serpent; and there's no use denying it. I suppose you'll be telling me next that you have never tasted an egg!"

"I *have* tasted eggs, certainly," said Alice, who was a very truthful child; "but little girls eat eggs quite as much as serpents do, you know."

"I don't believe it," said the Pigeon; "but if they do, why, then they're a kind of serpent: that's all I can say." (48)

The Pigeon has a perfectly serviceable definition of serpent: an animal with a long neck that eats eggs. If this is the extent of her definition – and for her purposes, it is all that is necessary – then Alice is a serpent. As long as Alice agrees to argue on the Pigeon's terms, in which the word "serpent" signals real-world referents like appearance (long neck) and behavior (eats eggs), then she cannot defend any distinction between "little girl" and "serpent," just as she earlier fails to differentiate herself from her classmates Ada (who has curly hair) and Mabel (who lives in a pokey house) based on physical criteria alone. The Pigeon is right when she says, "You're looking for eggs, I know *that* well enough; and what does it matter to me whether you're a little girl or a serpent." But Alice is also right, though she does not know it yet, when she responds, "It matters a good deal to *me*." The answer to the problem of species lies in Alice's insistence on a "*me*": a linguistic marker with no consistent real-world referent.

Alice's position relative to the other animals is a problem that *Wonderland* and *Looking-Glass* must solve, and Tenniel's illustrations underscore the heroine's species confusion, which children in natural theology texts like Hood's *From Nowhere to the North Pole* do not have. Hood's frontispiece [Figure 5] resembles Tenniel's illustration for *Wonderland*'s third chapter [Figure 6], though with significant differences. In both pictures, the child sits in a corner of the frame, with his or her legs spread, surrounded by fantastic creatures. In Tenniel's illustration, Alice seems just one of the birds, rodents, and crustaceans (to say nothing of the mysterious monkey) who have all crawled together out of the Pool of Tears and are now gathered to hear the Mouse's tale. [24] Alice's face is turned away from the viewer, and her wet, disheveled hair makes her difficult to pick out from among the other bedraggled feathers and fur. Since Alice creates the Pool of Tears by crying about her perceived loss of identity, her indistinctness from the bestial company is appropriate. Hood's Frank, despite being positioned like Alice among animals, shares none of her problems. While Alice is turned from us, Frank is presented by a full frontal headshot, with the full-cheeks and luxurious mop of hair typical of Victorian child portraits. He is separated from the animal company not only by his human countenance and unspoiled appearance, but also by the map that he holds before him. Frank is not attending to the animals but

FRONTISPIECE.

Figure 5 From Tom Hood, *From Nowhere to the North Pole: A Noah's Ark-Æological Narrative*, illustrated by W. Brunton and E. C. Barnes (London: Chatto and Windus, 1875), Frontispiece.

Figure 6 From Lewis Carroll, *Alice's Adventures in Wonderland*, illustrated by John
Tenniel, 1865 (London: Macmillan and Company, 1866), 29.

commanding the whole scene that surrounds and faces him; remember
that the miscreant creatures pictured here – the fly with a bulldog's face or
the pelican with a dragon's torso – are explicitly products of Frank's
imagination. From the first image of Hood's book, then, even as it refers
to Carroll's, human children are special creatures who can read, create, and
direct, while Alice begins her adventures unsure of her prerogative as
a human or as a "little girl." She cannot take her identity for granted as
God's design, but must acquire it through language.

Though nonsense is by no means the unambiguous indicator of revolutionary rhetoric that Culler wants to believe it is, Carroll's particular brand
of nonsense distinguishes his children's fiction from the natural theology
that precedes and follows it. In her study *nonsense* (1979), Susan Stewart
defines nonsense as a decontextualized metaphor or signifier without
referent.[25] Expanding on Stewart a decade later, Wim Tiggs calls nonsense
a negative construction that "balances a multiplicity of meaning with
a simultaneous absence of meaning."[26] The natural theologians used the
nonreferentiality of nonsense to signal the perfection of the referential and

empirical world. Kingsley used the same nonreferentiality to point to a possibility beyond the empirical world. Carroll, in contrast, turns our focus away from the absence of meaning or referent in the real world to the "multiplicity of meaning," that Tiggs discusses, entirely within language. Alice's repeated identity crises, from her inability to distinguish herself from other little girls to her failure to posit little girl as a category discrete from other animals, reveal our vulnerability to scientific classifications. Nonsense in the *Alice* books, particularly of naming and classification, disrupts the coherency of categories like the "self" and the "human." It exposes what, in his Preface to *Curiosa Mathematica* (1888), Carroll admitted he feared would be the result of the "state of constant flux" inherent in Victorian science, especially biology.[27] But the fun that Carroll has with scientific taxonomy in the wake of Darwinism shows that words might be even more flexible and are certainly more productive than biological forms. Nonsense reveals the instability of meaning, but the means of negotiating and controlling human specialness and coherent personal identity within change will come from another literary modality: parody.

Potential of parody

Once down the rabbit hole, Alice attempts to recite a familiar poem, Watts's "Against Idleness and Mischief," and instead presents the book's first parody, Carroll's "How doth the little crocodile." This experiment comes just after she has failed to establish her identity on physical facts (her hair and her house). So instead, she tries her memory, particularly of school lessons: "'I'll try if I know all the things I used to know' . . . and she crossed her hands on her lap, as if she were saying lessons, and began to repeat' Watts's poem (18). While Empson's claim that *Wonderland* opens as an allegory of recapitulation seems an interpretive stretch, Alice's predicament does suggest a destabilization caused by midcentury science. Its title is reminiscent of Gideon Mantell's *The Wonders of Geology* (1838) and Peter Parley's (Samuel Griswold Goodrich's) identically labeled *The Wonders of Geology* (1846). *Wonderland* drops its heroine into the earth, thereby making her confusion seem to be the result of a geological shift.[28] Alice's concern that morphological changes (growing and shrinking) have altered her identity, anticipating her later uncertainty about her species, further implicates her in post-Lyellian, post-Darwinian doubt. To alleviate her disorientation, Alice tries to recite poetry that she has learned in school, which according to at least one of Carroll's contemporaries makes perfect sense. Starting in the 1850s, Arnold, who like Carroll was both skeptical about evolution and critical of Victorian schooling, argued that literary lessons (especially grammar and recitation) would provide the mental, moral, and aesthetic cultivation lacking in modern science. Alice's attempt to use poetry to reassert her identity appeals to an Arnoldian sense of value, while Carroll's ensuing parody offers a wholly new model for how linguistic and literary education can reassert the human specialness that science threatens.

Arnold's foray into the late Victorian culture wars, which pitted science against the arts and humanities, produced his famous exchange with Thomas H. Huxley. Huxley argued in an 1880 lecture, titled "Science and Culture," that Britain's future depends on embracing scientific education, and Arnold famously responded with an impassioned defense of the humanizing effect of literature.[29] Arnold's essay "Literature and Science" (1882) maintains that literature alone answers our inherent "need of relating what we have learnt and known to the sense which we have in us for conduct, to the sense which we have in us for beauty."[30] Though this essay usually serves as Arnold's essential statement on the humanities, his thoughts on the comparative merits of scientific and literary education began to foment thirty years earlier. In his capacity as Schools Inspector, Arnold proposed limiting science in the elementary curriculum; science, he argued, filled the pupil with facts, but true cultivation is achieved by reading literature, learning the rules of grammar, and memorizing and reciting great works. "The true aim of a boy's mental education," he says in his 1861 report, is "to give him the power of doing a thing right."[31] Grammar yields this lesson better than mathematics because grammar "is not only exact . . . but it also compels him, even more than arithmetic, to give the measure of his common sense by his mode of selecting and applying, in particular instances, the rule when he knows it."[32] Recitation enhances this pedagogical discipline; in repeating by rote a work of literature, "you have, first of all, the excellent discipline of a lesson which must be learnt right, or it has no value; a lesson of which the subject matter is not *talked about*, as in too many of the lessons of our elementary schools, but *learnt*."[33] Memorizing great poems introduces the student to the beauty of human thought; reciting them without any inaccuracies fosters his sense of physical and moral conduct.

When Alice demurely folds her hands in her lap and adopts a compliant posture for the dutiful recitation of Watts's moral homily, "Against Idleness and Mischief," she seems to be fulfilling Arnold's pedagogical directive. Buffeted by changes in her external circumstances, Carroll's protagonist thinks her question – "who am I?" – might be answered by poetry. Watts's poem, the one she means to perform, thematizes discipline and design: it promises, if only Alice could get the words right, to bolster her sense of her own strength and continuity of character through the unchanging exemplar of the common bee. A staple of natural theology, "Against Idleness and Mischief" aims to teach the child to emulate nature and absorb its lessons, through the act of recitation, into her own bodily conduct:

> How doth the little busy bee
>   Improve each shining hour,
> And gather honey all the day
>   From every opening flower!
>
> How skillfully she builds her cell!
>   How neat she spreads her wax!
> And labours hard to store it well
>   With the sweet food she makes.
>
> In works of labour or of skill,
>   I would be busy too:
> For Satan finds some mischief still
>   For idle hands to do.
>
> In books, or work, or healthful play
>   Let my first years be past,
> That I may give for every day
>   Some good account at last.

In Watts's verse, and in natural theology generally, nature is generative, purposeful, and permanent. The flowers continually produce pollen, and the bee is ceaselessly busy transforming that pollen into "sweet food." All action works to "improve" the natural materials; the labor is "skillfully" wrought, and the end result is a "neat" and orderly home. Just as the pollen is converted into useful domestic products, the entire exemplum of the bee is similarly translated into a homily that children can easily digest and regurgitate in preparation of their own neatly ordered homes. The first two stanzas of illustration thus easily give way to the second two stanzas of moral application, and this application of the poem is just another product of the bee's industry; nature is for human use, both nutritionally and pedagogically. If Alice were able to recite this poem as she wishes to do, she would prove her memory intact and her self-discipline undamaged. She would also show that natural theology's tenet of stable nature extends to herself as well, that she is still the same Alice, and that reciting poems about nature brings the child's body in line with God's moral precepts.

But Alice does not recite this poem. Instead, she delivers a parody that maintains part of the structure and some of the wording of Watts's description of his bee, but turns the bee's noble industry – and all its implication for stable identity and ethical meaning – inside out. Instead of Watts's original, we get Carroll's poem about the crocodile:

> "How doth the little crocodile
> Improve his shining tail,
> And pour the waters of the Nile
> On every golden scale!
>
> "How cheerfully he seems to grin,
> How neatly spread his claws,
> And welcomes little fishes in,
> With gently smiling jaws!" (19)

An inverse of the bee, the crocodile is greedy, indolent, selfish, duplicitous, and vain. "Cheerfully" rather than "skillfully," he improves his own "shining tail" rather than "each shining hour," spreads deadly claws rather than nutritional wax, and tricks the fish into his treacherous "smiling jaws" rather than sincerely provide for others. This reptilian mutation of Watts's noble insect suggests that the beneficent design of natural theology has been replaced by the self-interested predation of Darwinism. As a rejection of nature's endemic morality, the new poem notably supplies no lesson to the child reader. Carroll parodies Watts's first two stanzas of description, but entirely omits the last two stanzas of application. Thus, the predatory crocodile does not provide any succor to Alice. The double loss of the natural theology espoused by Watts's poem and the moral edification that Arnold finds in accurate recitation leaves Alice convinced that she has changed. She cries, "I'm sure those are not the right words," unable to see any connection between Watts's original and her mutated verse, and she immediately decides that "I must be Mabel after all" (19). If the bee can become a crocodile – if such radical evolution were possible – then Alice could just as easily become Mabel, or anyone else.

Alice's reaction to her distortion of Watts's poem, however, is a misunderstanding of how parody works. Parody and nonsense are related and, according to literary scholars, rely on similar strategic moves. Stewart, for instance, includes reversal and inversion as types of nonsense, and Linda Hutcheon characterizes parody as an "ironic inversion" of the original object.[34] Both modes work by turning something – a previous work of art, a conventional way of thinking – on its head. We might say that parody uses nonsense as a tool to remake (or reverse) another text, and that nonsense is a parody not of a specific work or genre but of the very conventions of sense or language. But the two forms have an important distinction: parody must maintain conspicuous signs and echoes of the parodied object within its own form if the reader is to understand the work as parody. Parody maintains a connection with the "original" that it parodies, repeating certain elements and changing others in order to allow the reader to see both old and new at the same time. As a palimpsest between a past and a present object, between moments in time, between related but nonidentical forms, parody illustrates evolution. Samuel Johnson defined parody as "a kind of writing, in which the words of an author or his thoughts are taken, and by a slight change adapted to some new purpose."[35] Johnson's use of "adapted" (though a century before Darwin's *Origin of Species*) is significant: slight variations transform an older literary form to fit a new receptive environment. Though critics do not agree on how much parody preserves and how much it contorts, they concur that parody maintains an essential relationship between two literary forms and literary periods.[36] Two centuries after Johnson, Hutcheon writes that "a new form develops out of the old, without really destroying it; only the function is altered"; parody, she says, is "a way to preserve continuity in discontinuity."[37]

Carroll's parodies, then, are not the same as what Arnold would characterize as mistakes in recitation, not simply because the errors are purposeful (if not for Alice, then for Carroll), but because change has value. In *Wonderland* and, to a lesser extent, in *Looking-Glass*, parody both articulates Alice's identity crisis and stands in for its solution: a solution that neither natural theology nor evolutionary theory seems able to offer. When she falls down the rabbit hole into Wonderland, Alice thinks that she must remain completely unaltered in order to be the same person; for her, any change threatens to turn her into another girl altogether. She thinks the same of the poem that she tries to recite; either she replicates its wording perfectly, or she and it become entirely different entities. But Carroll's "How doth the little crocodile" is not an entirely different entity from Watts's "Against Idleness and Mischief"; if it were, we would not be able to recognize it as parody. "How doth the little crocodile" may not achieve the disciplinary effect that Arnold celebrated in recitation, nor do the grammar lessons in the *Alice* books illustrate exactitude. Far more often, Carroll's grammatical nonsense points out the arbitrariness of linguistic conventions. But for Alice's negotiation of identity and species, and her particularly post-Darwinian expression of these problems, parody's deviation from the original shows that change and continuity can coexist, that being the old Alice and the new Alice are both part of being Alice, and that species is a sliding category capable of both maintaining and accruing meaning. Most importantly – here Carroll's linguistic education differs sharply from Arnold's – parody illustrates human agency to conduct purposeful change.

Alice does not understand this yet. Only later in *Wonderland* does she revise her conception of parody, and this is an important (but critically overlooked) part of her education underground. After she botches Watts's poem and fears for the continuity of her identity as a result, the Caterpillar invites her into one of *Wonderland's* many seemingly unproductive and circular exchanges. "Who are *you?*" he asks, and she replies, "I – I hardly know, Sir, just at present – at least I know who I *was* when I got up this morning, but I think I must have changed several times since then" (41). The caterpillar, a member of a species accustomed to transformation, frequently functioned as an example of morphological change in both natural theology and evolutionary theory. In *Parables from Nature*, Gatty uses the caterpillar's metamorphosis into a butterfly to symbolize man's transformation after death.[38] In contrast, Darwin's Notebooks use the caterpillar as an analogy for man's progress from child to adult.[39] In the context of both these discourses, Carroll's Caterpillar would be the right creature to ease Alice's anxiety about her own physical changes, but *Wonderland* is not an allegory of either natural theology or evolutionary theory. Perhaps expecting the Caterpillar to take his familiar role, Alice tries to find common ground with the soon-to-be-butterfly and says, "when you have to turn into a chrysalis – you will some day, you know – and then after that into a butterfly, I should think that you'll find it a little queer" (41). Despite her invitation to empathize, however, the Caterpillar emphatically responds, "Not a bit." Refusing to provide an analogy for human experience, however, the Caterpillar furthers Alice's education in parody.

When Alice tells the Caterpillar about her failure to recite Watts's poem, he invites her to try another poem: this time Robert Southey's "The Old Man's Comforts, and How He Gained Them" (1799), or as the Caterpillar refers to it, using Southey's first line, *"You are old, Father William."* Southey's poem delivers a moral about industriousness, parsimony, piety, and faith similar to Watts's homily, and likewise, Carroll gives us another parody that turns Southey's original on its head, literally, by endowing the main character with the tendency to stand on his head. Southey's Father William, when asked why he is so cheerful on the threshold of death, explains that "in the days of my youth I remembered my God."[40] Carroll's Father William is, instead, asked why he chooses inversion and responds,

Figure 7 From Lewis Carroll, *Alice's Adventures in Wonderland*, illustrated by John
Tenniel, 1865 (London: Macmillan and Company, 1866), 63.

"in my youth . . . / I feared it might injure the brain;/ But, now that I'm
perfectly sure I have none,/ Why, I do it again and again" (43). "You are
old, Father William" goes on to play with the relationship between youth
and old age by showing how the latter becomes an absurd parody of the
former: when young, William feared to injure his brain, but now he stands
on his head; when young, he kept physically fit, but now he constantly does
somersaults; when young, he argued law cases with his wife, but now his
jaw is so robust he eats the flesh, bones, and beak of his supper goose.
Tenniel's illustrations, even more than Carroll's verse, present the relationship between old age and youth as inversion, visually demonstrating for the
child reader how parody works. Two of the four panels feature a thin and
suitably vertical youth next to an obese and overturned Father William
[Figure 7]. The contrast between an upright young questioner and an
upturned older respondent mimics the relation between the original text
and the topsy-turvy inversion produced by parody. Adulthood is a parody
of youth. In the mutation of natural theology's bee into Darwinism's

Figure 8 From Lewis Carroll, *Through the Looking-Glass, and What Alice Found There*, illustrated by John Tenniel (London: Macmillan and Company, 1872), 172.

crocodile and the maturation of the youth into the adult, development in *Wonderland* takes the form of parody.

Carroll and Tenniel return to this image of the standing youth next to the upside-down adult in *Looking-Glass*, which is itself a kind of distorted return to and revision of the characters and themes of *Wonderland*. In the later text, Alice is the upright youth next to the aged White Knight who has toppled off his horse almost immediately after saving Alice from being taken by the rival Red Knight [Figure 8]. When the White Knight falls off his horse headfirst into a ditch, Alice drags him out and sets him right, though he seems fundamentally incapable of staying right-side up. As in "You are Old, Father William," the physical inversion in *Looking-Glass* highlights the many ways in which the White Knight's behavior is a variation on Alice's; she falls into Wonderland, and he likewise topples into *Looking-Glass*, and we watch both actively considering how best to be prepared for their respective journeys, though Alice's wish to control her size once down the rabbit hole is more practical than the Knight's plan to arm his horse's legs with barbs to keep sharks away. The White Knight has been considered a figure for Carroll, and therefore the right counterpart to represent age against the youth of the "real" Alice, Alice Liddell. But as an inversion of youth, adulthood is importantly not its negation; to use a metaphor more apropos to *Looking-Glass*, adulthood is youth's distorted mirror image. The White Knight, after all, produces one of *Looking-Glass*'s best parodies – of William Wordsworth's "Resolution and Independence" – and the book's most sentimental wish for the preservation of memory – when the narrator, seemingly ventriloquizing the Knight, says that "years afterwards [Alice] could bring the whole scene back again" (214). The Knight, then, ostensibly the figure for Carroll, unites preservation and parody as parts of the same impulse.

In *Looking-Glass*, this encounter with the upside-down Knight ushers Alice into the final square, where she meets the Red and White Queens.[41] In *Wonderland*, her recitation of "You are old, Father William" prompts a significant, though subtle, reevaluation of how parody works. After she performs "How doth the little crocodile" at the beginning of the book, Alice thinks to herself, "I'm sure those are not the right words." At this early moment in the book, then, she thinks that there is no relation between the poem she intended and the one she actually delivers, in the same way that she then immediately thinks that she must have become Mabel, no longer Alice, after all. But later, at the end of her twisted rendition of "You are old, Father William," it is the Caterpillar who makes this kind of evaluation of her poem; he scolds her with the criticism "that is not said right ... it is wrong from beginning to end" (45), suggesting, as Alice did previously, that the two poems have no relation to each other. But though Alice's poem may be "wrong," or revised, in parts, it does not so totally depart from the original as the Caterpillar claims. And in contrast to her own response to her previous recital, Alice now seems to sense the inadequacy of the Caterpillar's assessment. She offers a more nuanced understanding of the rapport between the two poems: "'Not *quite* right, I'm afraid,' said Alice, timidly: 'some of the words have got altered.'" Here, she implies that other words have remained the same and that the poem she recites still retains a relation to the original. This might be a small adjustment to the book's pronouncements about how parody works, but it is an important one. Alice has started to think that change does not radically divide, and as a result, she walks away from the Caterpillar with a slightly stronger sense that she is still Alice – a fact she does not doubt again – even if in the next moment she fails to convince the Pigeon that she is a little girl.

Alice's self-knowledge is partial and gradual throughout both books. In *Wonderland*, she tells the Pigeon that, even though the difference between little girls and serpents does not matter to the bird, "it matters a good deal to *me*." Though she does not know how to define "little girl" objectively outside the Pigeon's classification, she seems to know more that she did when she thought she might be Ada or Mabel; she knows that there is a "*me*" and that this identity is, at least in part, constituted by what "matters" to her. But Alice starts to learn that "me" stays constant even as physical dimensions, external circumstances, and even what matters change through Carroll's use of parody. Arnold argued that only literary instruction could accomplish education's civilizing mission; his 1872 report on elementary schools states that the coursework "at most gives to a child the mechanical possession of the instruments of knowledge, but does nothing to *form* him ... [W]hat practically will be found to contribute most towards *forming* a pupil is familiarity with masterpieces."[42] Carroll's parodies, appropriately, reverse this formula: they allow the pupil to form a coherent and agential self by reforming the masterpieces. Literature and language are malleable, and this malleability gives the child an opportunity to control change. The "me" that results – a pronoun that works nothing like a taxonomic classification – is fluid but, nevertheless, made meaningful by the speaker. The speaker gives form to language and to the self by appropriating and reappropriating the lessons of a literary education.

Language's ability to show gradual change, and to highlight questions of rupture and continuity, was a continuing motif in Carroll's work. In a logical game called "Doublets," which he published in *Vanity Fair* in 1879, players are asked to transform certain words into other words in a prescribed number of links; the instructions say that, to play the game, contestants must do so by "interposing other words, each of which shall differ from the next word *in one letter only*."[43] One paired beginning and end point directs players to "Evolve MAN from APE" with five "links," while another round challenges players to metamorphose "FISH to BIRD" in four, again choosing only letters that ensure a valid intermediary word at every stage of the game.[44] Without exaggerating the importance of these imbedded evolutionary jokes, we can safely say that, as a logician and a children's writer, Carroll was interested in both linguistic and biological variation, especially when they could be so cleverly intersected and manipulated. "Doublets" shows how one linguistic form can be converted into another, without losing sense. But unlike the two words on either side of the Doublet, parody does not completely obscure the earlier words in its transformations. This more sophisticated version of preservation and change, and its application to both poems and persons, constitutes the educational trajectory – loose and veering as it may be – of the *Alice* books.

Turning the tables on deep time

Alice does not recapitulate animal forms to arrive at a higher humanity like Kingsley's Tom, in part because the animals may be less "animals" in Carroll's text than ways of thinking about language and how literary forms negotiate change. *Wonderland* and *Looking-Glass* do not progress in any straightforward way; Alice, for instance, may be no more able to articulate who she is at the end of her adventures than at the beginning. Indeed, toward the end of *Wonderland*, when the Mock Turtle requests of Alice, "come, let's hear some of *your* adventures," she responds, "I could tell you my adventures – beginning from this morning . . . but it's no use going back to yesterday, because I was a different person then" (91). But while Carroll's heroine may never gain a full sense of how one can change and yet retain continuity of self, Carroll's texts demonstrate how this might be conceived and enacted within literature. In Alice's misremembered verses, in the parodies that her memory lapses create, in her attempts to defend her humanity against the Pigeon, and in her failure to find an animal analogy in the Caterpillar, *Wonderland* toys with more and less successful ways to think about human development. In episodes like "A Mad Tea-Party," Carroll expands his investigation of individual change to broader questions about temporality and human agency, and again parody steps in as a means for both representing contemporary scientific questions and diffusing science's attempts to answer them. In the face of biological and geological schemes that decenter man, *Wonderland* enacts parody as a way of reinstating human agency.

One may object to my argument, stating that only a fairly sophisticated reader could recognize in the *Alice* books this potential for parody. But even a quick reading suggests that Carroll expected his younger readers to see how *Wonderland* and *Looking-Glass* manipulate the conventions of children's literature. The humor of "How doth the little crocodile" works best when the reader is familiar with "Against Idleness and Mischief," as many of Carroll's midcentury child readers were sure to be. Alice herself recalls "several nice little stories about children who had got burnt, and eaten up by wild beasts, and other unpleasant things, all because they would not remember the rules their friends had taught them" (13). In both these moments, the text encourages readers to contrast the present book with the children's literature that they already know. Nowhere is the parody more apparent than in the contortions through which Carroll puts the scientific dialogue: a favorite literary form for communicating natural theology to children. In his essay "Science for Women and Children"

(1989), Greg Myers explains that the nineteenth-century scientific dialogue usually presents a child who asks questions about natural history and an adult who supplies complete and elucidating answers. For instance, Fanny Umphelby's popular *The Child's Guide to Knowledge* (1825), reissued multiple times, opens with, "QUESTION. What is the world? ANSWER. The earth we live on. Q. Who made it? A. The great and good God."[45] For Myers, dialogues like Umphelby's "depend on the symmetry of questions and answers, on the asking of questions of the right kind in the right order."[46] The genre perfectly fits natural theology because the reciprocity between question and answer is intended to instill in the child reader a reverence for the reciprocity between natural fact and human need.

Myers uses *Wonderland*'s "Mad Tea-Party" to illustrate Carroll's mockery of the scientific dialogue and his challenge to the symmetry that carried epistemological value. Here, the Mad Hatter famously asks Alice the riddle without an answer: "Why is a raven like a writing-desk?" (60). Myers writes, "instead of the symmetry of questions and answers" conventionally found in scientific dialogues, "we have the Mad Hatter posing a riddle that turns out to have no answer," "Alice asks questions that lead to *non-sequiturs* or that are ignored," and ultimately, "with no answers available, all questions become equally valid."[47] The riddle without an answer, like the nature poem without a moral application, alerts the child readers – even readers with no expressed investment in the debate between natural theology and evolutionary theory – that the rules of *their* literature have been broken and that some other, related but not identical, version of children's fiction has taken its place. Though child readers may not be able to articulate what a parody is, much of the humor of *Wonderland* and *Looking-Glass* depends on their being able to recognize one when they see it. Something has changed, and in the new product, a version of the old product remains, draws attention to itself, and announces its readiness, and perhaps even need, for updating. Carroll's *Alice* books announce to young readers whose frame of reference is other children's literature that time has not stood still, that forms change – and change for the better – without losing their place in the familiar taxonomy of children's literature.

Within Carroll's tea party, then, we should not be surprised to find more sophisticated parodies lurking. "A Mad Tea-Party" also mocks natural theology's most famous symbol and most paradigmatic argument for design: Paley's watch. The opening of Paley's *Natural Theology* asks readers to imagine the nonsense that would ensue from his hypothetical watch being constructed on any plan other than the most intelligent premeditation. The watch's "several parts are framed and put together for a purpose,"

Paley writes, and if they were "placed after any other manner, or in any other order, than that in which they are placed, either no motion at all would have been carried on in the machine, or none which would have answered the use, that is now served by it."[48] The same, he claims, must be true of a stone we find on the heath; if we admit that we know instinctively that the watch was designed by a Watchmaker, then the stone must have been designed by a more primary Stone Maker. The watch also functions as a symbol for the solar system, the larger clock by which God keeps time and that, like the watch's perfect composition of wheels and springs, displays just the right arrangements of planets and regulated orbits. Even more importantly, according to Paley, this great celestial watch has been wound to accommodate man's life on earth: the revolution of the earth around the sun allows for growing seasons and regular tides, and even "the relation . . . of sleep to night, is the relation of the inhabitants of the earth to the rotation of their globe."[49] Cosmic time has been created for mankind by a beneficent God who alone could get all the parts running correctly. For Paley, a haphazard collection of wheels and springs might look like a watch and might tick like a watch, but it would not keep time in the manner intended by its Maker.

It is fitting, then, that Carroll gives us exactly this slapdash timepiece in *Wonderland*. The Hatter's broken watch purports to announce the day rather than the hour, though, in Carroll's further Wonderland twist, it reports the wrong day because the March Hare has filled it with butter. Although the Hare insists that "it was the *best* butter," the Hatter surmises that "some crumbs must have got in as well" (62). According to the Hatter's diagnosis, the problem is not misuse (treating the machinery with butter) but chance (the crumbs). And as Paley has predicted, the random addition – here of breadcrumbs – derails the watch's functioning and has made it "two days slow." When the Hatter admits that his riddle, "Why is a raven like a writing-desk?," has no answer, the scientific dialogue of natural theology has broken down. So too has the notion of anthropomorphic time. In a perfect world, he explains, time would operate in beneficent submission to human need, and he offers an anthropocentric fantasy that extends the claims of natural theology to the point of absurdity:

> Alice sighed wearily. "I think you might do something better with the time," she said, "than wasting it in asking riddles that have no answers."
>
> "If you knew Time as well as I do," said the Hatter, "you wouldn't talk about wasting *it*. It's *him*."
>
> "I don't know what you mean," said Alice.

"Of course you don't!" the Hatter said, tossing his head contemptuously. "I dare say you never even spoke to Time!"

"Perhaps not," Alice cautiously replied; "but I know I have to beat time when I learn music."

"Ah! That accounts for it," said the Hatter. "He wo'n't stand beating. Now, if you only kept on good terms with him, he'd do almost anything you liked with the clock. For instance, suppose it were nine o'clock in the morning, just in time to begin lessons: you'd only have to whisper a hint to Time, and round goes the clock in a twinkling! Half-past one, time for dinner!" (62–63)

In the Hatter's description of what could be or was before his argument with Time, Time is no abstract product of the impersonal orbits and rotations of celestial objects. Rather it is a being who controls the length of hours and days for our continued existence and who is more than willing to bend the rules for our gastronomical pleasure. Certainly, Paley never promised such individual attention from God, but the Hatter's portrait of time depends on the same principles at work in natural theology: a personal Time, who cares not only for our survival but for our happiness, and a temporal system based on our need to eat, to rest, and to enjoy ourselves. But, in Carroll's parodic exaggeration of natural theology's central metaphor, it is the design argument – and not the absence of design – that looks like nonsense.

At the tea party, parody has produced parody. Time no longer serves either the hosts or the guests because, according to the back story he tells Alice, the Hatter "murdered" the time while singing a particularly off-tempo version of "Twinkle, twinkle, little bat" (63). Replacing "star" with "bat," the Hatter turns the celestial subject of the original poem – a synecdoche for the solar system – into a bat – a taxonomic oddity seemingly stranded between mammal and bird. Without the "little star" of the original song or a beneficent Time, the Hatter and his guests are condemned to an eternal tea party, ceaselessly moving around the table because "we've no time to wash the things between whiles" and presumably no time for the acquisition and preparation of more food. A reversal of providential nature, the parodic time at the tea party explicitly fails to provide for those caught in it. Since no items appear on the dirty dishes, the last food available to the party seems to have been the butter that worried the watch's functioning and threw it off by two days. The Hatter does not reveal whether the butter moved the date forward or back, but it is significant that the watch does not read the same day the story began: the fourth of May, Alice Liddell's actual birthday. This means that Alice's birthday has been either annulled or eclipsed, another understated threat to her identity, indeed her very existence. The watch, then, that would in Paley's formulation provide the child with an illustration of a universe created for her instead offers her a glimpse into a universe created without her, menacing her ability to grow up.

Cyclical time, as demonstrated by the Mad Tea-Party, is not Darwinian; evolution depends on linear gradualism. But the idea of cyclical time was, recently for Carroll, part of Charles Lyell's theory of geological history and perhaps apropos to Carroll's "wonder"-ful title. In *Principles of Geology* (1830–1833), Lyell imagines geologic time analogous to a cyclical "great year," and he speculates that a future return to a tropical summer might bring a renaissance of extinct creatures: "the huge iguanodon might reappear in the woods, and the ichthyosaur in the sea, while the pterodactyl might flit again through umbrageous groves of tree-ferns."[50] Lyell's claim sounded like nonsense to many of his contemporaries, including the geologist and paleontologist Henry De la Beche. De la Beche's caricature, "Awful Changes: Man Found Only in a Fossil State – Reappearance of Ichthyosaur" (1830), depicts this imagined future in which "Professor Ichthyosaur" lectures to a dinosaur audience about now extinct humans [Figure 9]. As in the Mad Tea-Party's renegotiation of time operating without regard for (or antagonistic to) its guests, man is no longer central to this view of natural history. This perspectival shift in which animals rise to observe and to study man also resembles, in *Wonderland*, the Pigeon's classification of Alice as a serpent and, more closely in visual detail, the Dodo's passing out prizes following the Caucus-race [Figure 10]. Tenniel's illustration of the notoriously extinct Dodo, who hands Alice comfits so that she can then pass them out to all the runners, may only coincidentally mimic De la Beche's unearthed academic, but the similarities in their profiles and positions fancifully forge a connection. Carroll's Dodo has also returned from the dead to judge man, as a competitor in the Caucus-race, but instead of awarding a winner, he asserts that "*Everybody* has won" because the race course itself has neither a beginning nor an end (26). It is just a potentially infinitely recurring loop.

The seeming opposite of cyclicality, rupture, also dominates Alice's experience at the tea table and, indeed, throughout *Wonderland*. When Alice asks her reluctant hosts eternally circling the table, "what happens when you come to the beginning again?," the March Hare curtly "interrupted," saying "Suppose we change the subject ... I vote the young lady tells us a story" (64). This rupture in the conversation echoes the first rupture when the Hatter cut into the debate about whether or not it is

AWFUL CHANGES.
MAN FOUND ONLY IN A FOSSIL STATE———REAPPEARANCE OF ICHTHYOSAURA.

A Lecture.—"You will at once perceive," continued PROFESSOR ICHTHYOSAURUS, "that the skull before us belonged to some of the lower order of animals; the teeth are very insignificant, the power of the jaws trifling, and altogether it seems wonderful how the creature could have procured food."

Figure 9   Henry De la Beche, "Awful Changes: Man Found Only in a Fossil State – Reappearance of Ichthyosaur," 1830. From Francis T. Buckland, *Curiosities of Natural History* (New York: Follett, Foster and Company, 1864), Frontispiece.

polite for Alice to seat herself at the table with his unanswerable riddle. And the riddle itself – "Why is a raven like a writing-desk?" – foregrounds rupture since it is only half a riddle, a question for which Carroll famously provided no answer in the original edition of *Wonderland*. The Hatter's riddle is a linguistic version of his broken watch, for a riddle without an answer is like a *tick* without the complementary *tock*. This ruptured temporality abruptly shifts the conversational landscape, and Alice is forced to reorient herself to the new terrain. If we continue with the geological metaphor suggested by "Wonderland," then the interruptions and reorientations of the underground dialogue might suggest something like the intermittent global catastrophes posited by geologist William Buckley in the 1830s, whereby sudden environmental changes (like the Biblical flood) lead both to extinctions and to new moments of divine creation.[51] Of course, Alice's creation consists entirely of language. Parody,

Figure 10 From Lewis Carroll, *Alice's Adventures in Wonderland*, illustrated by John
Tenniel, 1865 (London: Macmillan and Company, 1866), 35.

by connecting the past and the present, offers an antidote to the rupture of
modern geological theory and allows for different ways of being in time.

Evolutionary theory, geologic cyclicality, and rupture seemed to deny
human centrality to global processes. In the midst of this scientifically
derived destabilization, *Wonderland* seeks a linguistic solution that puts
human agency back in the picture. As much as it highlights the author's
dependence on existing literary forms, parody celebrates authorial intention; the parody only works as a parody if the reader appreciates the
author's purposeful refunctioning of the previous text. Discussing

nonsense and parody, Terry Caesar explains, "parody is almost by definition alert to the human presence in the work, which is to say the authorial
presence, putative or otherwise."[52] In *Darwin and the Novelists: Patterns of
Science in Victorian Fiction* (1988), George Levine claims that, with the
retreat of natural theology in the second half of the nineteenth century and
the prominence of evolutionary theory in its stead, "the center of value
must shift from the divine creator to the human sharer."[53] Though the
retreat of a personalized Time traps the tea party guests in an endless
circularity, Alice breaks free by asserting herself as the center of value and
law. Getting up from the table, she pronounces the gathering "the stupid-
est tea-party I ever was at" and says "enough" (67). Stewart calls this kind of
abrupt closing of an infinite loop a "stop rule."[54] By enacting a stop rule,
Alice is able to withdraw from the nonsense and live by rules that make
sense to her. She uses the same strategy at the trial, when she cries, "Who
cares for *you*? ... You're nothing but a pack of cards," allowing her to exit
the dream and return aboveground (108). The stop rule trades infinite
cyclicality for rupture, while parody (I would argue, the *Alice* books'
preferred strategy) reasserts continuity, transforming flux into manageable
and creative continuity.

Carroll added "Pig and Pepper" and "A Mad Tea-Party" when his
original gift-book to Alice Liddell, *Alice's Adventures under Ground*
(1864), became *Alice's Adventures in Wonderland*. In *under Ground*,
Alice's concern about her identity and the radical changes in size that she
experiences down the rabbit hole seems largely resolved once she leaves the
Caterpillar and the Pigeon. She takes comfort in the fact that "I've got to
my right size again," and shifts her attention "to get[ting] into that
beautiful garden."[55] Immediately, in *under Ground*, a doorway opens in
the trunk of a nearby tree, and confident that she can "manage better this
time," Alice soon finds "herself at last in the beautiful garden, among the
bright flowerbeds and the cool fountains." At the croquet game, she meets
the Queen's question, "what is your name?" with the self-assured
"My name is Alice, so please your Majesty."[56] Now knowing how to
identify herself with a name, the fluctuations of her body and concerns
about her identity seem to be behind her. But *Wonderland* is not quite the
same story as *under Ground*; indeed, some of the episodes have been
altered. Now in "Pig and Pepper," a baby boy whom Alice tries to save
from abuse in the Duchess's chaotic home devolves into a pig, and Alice is
confronted with the Hatter's broken watch and its permutation of providential time. Though both these episodes are entertaining for a multitude
of reasons, the inclusion of two new jokes on evolution and natural

theology significantly constitutes Carroll's second look at his fantasy for children.

Despite the changes from *under Ground* to *Wonderland*, *Looking-Glass* does not feature Alice's contortions of familiar verse. Though the White Knight provides a parody of Wordsworth's "Resolution and Independence," when Alice wants to repeat the poetry that she has learned from previous children's literature, she does so without any of the hiccups in recitation that she had experienced in the earlier book. The verse she repeats about Humpty Dumpty's fall, for example, mostly remains faithful to the nursery rhyme as it appears in *Halliwell's Nursery Rhymes of England* (1846), and her recitation about Tweedledum's and Tweedledee's battle likewise replicates another rhyme found in *Original Ditties for the Nursery* (1805) and *The Nursery Rhymes of England* (1853).[57] But her ability to recite the poems almost verbatim is not the boon that Alice thought it should be in *Wonderland*. In fact, her unaltered repetitions prove damaging, even deadly, to the characters in each of the rhymes. Humpty Dumpty, like his literary namesake, crashes to the ground, shatters into unredeemable pieces, and is never heard from again. The Tweedles, though not crushed by their nursery rhyme, engage in a battle that they seemingly have no power to avoid and no agency in carrying it out. Explaining the "rules" of their battle, Tweedledee proudly tells Alice, "I generally hit every thing I can see – when I get really excited," and his brother chimes in, "And *I* hit every thing within reach... whether I can see it or not!" (168). Though Tweedledee may practice willed moves, Tweedledum admits that he hits things simply because they lie in the path of his swing. Fighting their interminable battle without even the benefit of a conscious strategy, the Tweedles are slaves to both literary repetition and physical law. They are not "human sharers" of meaning production.

The rote memorization and automatic repetition of past literary forms that Arnold celebrated as a counter to scientific instruction rob the poems' subjects of agency. For Carroll, in contrast, the transformation of previous literary works into parody signals, or stands in for, the ability for human agency outside of physical laws: the ability to direct one's own growth, movement, actions, and creative output. *Wonderland* thus offers Alice a literary power that is also a physical power, and one largely lost by *Looking-Glass*. Perhaps because parody demands a knowingness on the part of the reader, literary critics eager to maintain the innocence of child characters and readers in Golden Age fiction have either said nothing about parody or expelled parody to the "adult" portion of Carroll's texts. But, I am arguing, through Carroll's parodies and Tenniel's illustrations depicting what parody does, *Wonderland* not only shows that change can be tamed and identity secured but that it is linguistic agency alone that exerts this power. In a new environment that compromises her sense of herself, surrounded by animals that deny the specialness of humanity, and searching for a way to change and yet to maintain a unified identity, Alice confronts the central anxieties associated with Darwinian evolution without entering into a Darwinian allegory. The *Alice* books are, instead, a funhouse distortion of the patterns taking place in contemporary children's works and in critical discussions of elementary education. Being human means being able to manipulate language and to make literary forms evolve; this linguistic power then engenders our capacity to imagine how we ourselves can evolve without radically changing who we are.

The success of *Wonderland* spawned numerous imitations, which either employ nonsense in order to venerate sense (like Hood's and the Gresswells' texts) or, erring in the opposite direction, so scramble the works they borrow that they dissolve parody's unifying potential. In G. E. Farrow's *Wonderland*-inspired *The Wallypug of Why* (1895), for instance, the protagonist Girlie enters the Land of Why, where the King's Minstrel sings, "Four and twenty blackbirds baked in a pie./ Gin a body, kiss a body, need a body cry./ Humpty-dumpty sat on a wall./ And if I don't hurt her she'll do me no harm," which Farrow's heroine rightly characterizes as "just a lot of separate lines from nursery rhymes all strung together."[58] Such cacophony offers no palliative for the protagonist's confusion, merely serving as a weaker Carroll-like echo. In contrast, Juliana Horatia Ewing's "Amelia and the Dwarfs" (1870) and Christina Rossetti's *Speaking Likenesses* (1874) play with doubling in ways that fruitfully nod to both Carroll and Darwin. Ewing's Amelia learns to behave after seeing an effigy in her clothes, but "with a face like the oldest and most grotesque of apes."[59] Rossetti's protagonist, Flora, is similarly reformed after playing party-games tinged with Darwinian horror: boys with hooks and quills and girls sticky with slime warring with each other for physical dominance. She sees her own "fifty million-fold face" in an infinite regress of mirrors that produce "not merely simple reflections, but reflections of reflections, and reflections of reflections of reflections."[60] Me and not me, likeness and difference, old and new, original and parody, are thematized by both the female characters and the self-consciously referential texts – parodies of a sort – in which they appear.

Today, nonsense and parody are staples of the children's literature market. Scholars praise the genre's adoption of such irreverent modes for recognizing that children are sophisticated readers who revel in unorthodox inversions and satirical adaptations of the well-worn classics.[61] But Carroll, facing the flux of evolutionary biology, saw in parody a way to show his readers how to take control of that flux and to impose direction onto the seeming inevitability of change. Arnold, in "Literature and Science," singled out Darwinism as the scientific turn that made humanist education all the more necessary; quoting Darwin's *The Descent of Man, and Selection in Relation to Sex* (1871), Arnold says, "the 'hairy quadruped furnished with a tail and pointed ears, probably arboreal in his habits,' this good fellow carried hidden in his nature, apparently, something destined to develop into a necessity for humane letters."[62] For Arnold, the humanist tradition should be preserved because it alone allows us to relate scientific fact "to our sense for conduct, to our sense for beauty."[63] For Carroll, the literary canon provides material for our creative manipulation because it appeals to our sense for play, which is just as essential to human nature. Parody manifests our desire for both tradition and novelty and, most of all, for seeing the power of our own hand (apart from God's or nature's) in turning A-P-E into M-A-N.

CHAPTER 4

The cure of the wild
Rudyard Kipling and evolutionary adolescence at home and abroad

The 1870 Elementary Education Act did not transform the Victorian education system overnight. Not until the first decade of the twentieth century was mandatory, universal education systematically enforced and local school boards centralized under a national agency.[1] While Thomas H. Huxley's and Matthew Arnold's famous exchange about the relative merits of the natural sciences and the humanities crystallized the stakes of the debate for higher education, in elementary schools, scientific subjects were embraced without ousting reading lessons from the curriculum.[2] By the end of the century, the concern about what pupils were learning in their classes also now included what they were doing in their leisure time. Rudyard Kipling's series of anti-school-story school stories, collected together as *The Complete Stalky & Co.* (1899–1926), for instance, chronicles the exploits of three boys (one of whom he modeled on himself) who shirk their classes, trespass outside school grounds, swindle their fellow students, and defile school property with the aid of a dead cat. Yet, while disobeying all the school rules, they nevertheless imbibe all the school values. After leaving Kipling's fictional version of the United Services College at Westward Ho!, the eponymous Stalky – who has learned to sneak without being caught, to fight without being beaten, and to best others at their own games – becomes a military hero in the colonies. As a legend to the younger classes, Stalky is hailed as "the great man of his Century."[3]

The question of how education could spread English culture across social classes (Charles Kingsley's Christianity, Arnold's humanism, etc.) had become the question of how education could retain British dominance across the Empire. Anxiety about Britain's waning military supremacy revived popular interest not only in education but also in evolutionary theory. At midcentury, the hierarchy of animals and races suggested by Jean-Baptiste Lamarck's "transmutation" hypothesis seemed to justify the acculturating program of imperialism. Colonization was interpreted as a kind of stewardship: the advanced races helping those stuck in lower levels of atavism to evolve. But this paradigm jarringly suggested that what goes up can come down and that perhaps British civilization was not the highest point yet reached on an ever-climbing vector but rather the apex on a curve, tottering on the edge of decline. The working class, immigrants, homosexuals, and criminals had each taken turns as representatives of cultural degeneration, but as the British Empire felt increasingly less secure at the end of the century, many Victorians worried that the malady was more widespread.[4] Biologist E. Ray Lankester defined degeneration as "a gradual change of the structure in which the organism becomes adapted to *less* varied and *less* complex conditions of life"; "the cessation of work" in one or more body parts leads to atrophy, and the whole organism is henceforth "fitted to less complex action and reaction in regard to its surroundings, than was the ancestral form."[5] If the evolution of species is analogous to the life span of an individual, then species – and nations – also have old ages. In the early 1890s, Kipling diagnosed Britain with a strain of phylogenic senility characterized by the loss of activity and versatility. In "One View of the Question" (1893), a fictionalized account of the humbling 1857 Indian Mutiny, he calls out the British for having been spoiled by "soft-living" and "long idleness"; "the fountain-head of power," he writes, "is putrid with long standing still."[6]

In the same year that he complained of Britain's evolutionary old age, Kipling composed a tale celebrating an image of evolutionary youth. "In the Rukh" (1893) introduces Kipling's man-cub Mowgli one year before *The Jungle Book* (1894). Here, in his early appearance, Mowgli is a seventeen-year-old Indian orphan raised by wolves, discovered by a British officer, and hired to oversee local natives. In contrast to the Victorians' "soft-living," Mowgli's jungle upbringing has given him the youthful, animal, and savage virility necessary for the work of the Empire; he is an "ideal ranger and forest-guard" because he has not been subject to the late stages of human (European) evolution.[7] The German camp supervisor says that Mowgli "is an anachronism, for he is before der Iron Age, and der Stone Age ... he is at der beginnings of der history of man."[8] Mowgli is more accurately man on an upward evolutionary climb, when animal strength and cunning are just beginning to give rise to human intellect but before overcivilization leads to atrophy and degeneration. Immediately after writing "In the Rukh," Kipling began contemplating what kind of upbringing and education this Mowgli might have had among the wild beasts of the Indian jungle. When the ten-year-old Mowgli learns the Law of the Jungle and the Master Words, Kipling's *Jungle Book* merges primitivistic romance and the Victorian school story into a recapitulative fantasy for an imperial age. Mowgli absorbs the lessons of each of the jungle's species as he ascends from being "Mowgli the frog" to becoming "the Master of the Jungle."[9] But, as with Stalky, it is how Mowgli manifests the fruits of his lessons outside the classroom – even the jungle classroom – that demonstrates his superiority.

The Jungle Book and *The Second Jungle Book* (1895), thus, mark a significant shift in the narrative of recapitulation and its proffered correction to British education. Because the goal of the civilizing process was now the imperial soldier rather than the Christian gentleman, survivalist instincts best not be expunged; because pupils were meant to export their skills outside England into the colonies, extracurricular education mattered more than the classroom; and because the midpoint between animal savagery and civilized softness was deemed mankind's most potent evolutionary stage, its recapitulative equivalent – adolescence – now commanded critical attention. In capturing the essence of this cultural turn, Kipling's story of a boy raised by wolves who learns to become a man inspired the foundation of boys' organizations, like Sir Robert Baden-Powell's Boy Scouts, the theories of American psychologists and pedagogues, like G. Stanley Hall and John Dewey, and a trans-Atlantic reconsideration of the place of the other "Indians" – Native Americans – in boys' literature. The early-twentieth-century discourse about boys used the narrative of recapitulation to solve the perceived problem of degeneration; each generation renewed the primal masculinity of the race, which offered an opportunity to recapture what modern civilization had lost. But in contrast to the theories of evolution it absorbed, the encomium to imperialism it implies, and the discourse of adolescence it inspired, Kipling's account of his man-cub challenges the very Victorian ideas about progress that generated the theory of recapitulation, and its imperialist extrapolation, in the first place. Through their literary style, which is not reducible to their mere recapitulative plotting, *The Jungle Books* offer a unique evolutionary fantasy that newly contours childhood and adolescence and gives shape to the twentieth-century boy.

Managing the middle

"In the Rukh" presents a teenager precariously positioned between childhood and adulthood, a feral adoptee fantastically situated between animal and man, and a native son politically stationed between Britain and India. *The Jungle Books*, written over the next two years, further exploit Mowgli's intermediacy: at the end of "Tiger-Tiger!," the story that closes the Mowgli sequence in the first book, Kipling's liminal hero sings, "the Jungle is shut to me and the village gates are shut . . . As Mang [the bat] flies between the beasts and birds so fly I between the village and the Jungle" (97). Mowgli's complaint has resonated with literary scholars who allegorize Mowgli's dually constituted identity of "man-cub" as a particular effect of British imperialism. Literary critic Zohreh Sullivan, for instance, characterizes Mowgli as "the quintessentially divided imperial subject," desiring to be "brother" to the wolves and "master of the jungle" in a fantasy of simultaneous fellowship and domination.[10] Jane Hotchkiss agrees that Mowgli expresses an uneasy "colonial self, born between two worlds."[11] Don Randall's *Kipling's Imperial Boy: Adolescence and Cultural Hybridity* (2000) extends this analysis to all of Kipling's adolescent protagonists, who are, he argues, "figures set upon the thresholds . . . between animal and human, early childhood and full adulthood, between nature and culture, barbary and civilization, between white and dark, East and West, colonizer and colonized."[12] According to this critical tradition, the man-cub's hybridity, divided between the scene of his childhood and the seat of his heredity, represents a new population of displaced imperialists, Kipling among them.

Randall's postcolonial reading, to which the past decade and a half of Kipling criticism defers, resolves Mowgli's intermediacy by making "In the Rukh," and his ultimate service to the British Empire that concludes that story, the proleptic coda to Mowgli's narrative.[13] For Randall, all of the subsequently written adventures become mere preludes to the "comedic, empire-affirming, dénouement of an as yet untold story."[14] Aiming to show that "Mowgli's jungle history repeats, in ideal form, the history of the British presence in India," Randall marshals particular stages of the "man-cub's" story: Mowgli is the pushy newcomer in "Mowgli's Brothers"; he is educated in imperial codes in "Kaa's Hunting"; he defeats the native adversary when he kills Shere Khan in "Tiger-Tiger!"; and he, finally and fittingly, consolidates his identity as part of the colonial workforce in "In the Rukh."[15] This retelling neatly fits Randall's allegorical reading, but only, I am arguing, by reconstituting the elements of *The Jungle Books* into the *Bildungsroman* it never was. Randall extracts the three Mowgli stories from the first *Jungle Book*, jettisons all the stories that do not include Mowgli, virtually ignores the five additional Mowgli stories from *The Second Jungle Book*, and turns "In the Rukh" into the fourth and final chapter of a now coherent novelized version of Mowgli's story.[16] While Randall's reading is supported by the fact that at least two nineteenth-century editions of *The Jungle Books* did, in fact, package all the Mowgli stories, including "In the Rukh," in one volume, saving the non-Mowgli tales for the second volume, the sequence most read by child readers and authorized by Kipling's first publication splits the Mowgli stories, intersperses them with tales of other characters, and completely excludes "In the Rukh."[17]

This two-volume series, with three Mowgli tales in the first, five Mowgli tales in the second, both including the stories of other animals like "Rikki-Tikki-Tavi" and "The White Seal," and excluding the account of Mowgli's dawning adulthood presented in "In the Rukh," is what this chapter takes to be the children's version of *The Jungle Books*. This assemblage of the stories complicates the insistence on Mowgli's hybridity (child/adult, animal/man, and Indian/British) and the inexorable teleology of his progress from one part of the binary to the other. Rather, the convoluted contrasts between jungle and village, the multitude of animals that are juxtaposed with "man," the murky chronology of Mowgli's biography that is also interrupted by glimpses into the lives of other animal characters, and the poetic interludes bookending each narrative chapter challenge both the assertion of any simple dichotomy at work in *The Jungle Books* and the confidence on the linearity necessary for teleological unfolding. No single-minded climber along a Lamarckian ladder of monodirectional advancement, in the child's version of *The Jungle Books*, Mowgli is dizzyingly buffeted back and forth along a nonprogressive narrative that Kipling, looping into Mowgli's youth for the first *Jungle Book* and then looping back a year later for the *Second*, seems reluctant to end. The middle ground that Mowgli occupies is one that can be endlessly filled, and is thus far more prolific than the positions on either side of him. Heterogeneity, not hybridity, characterizes Mowgli's dilemma as well as his evolutionary achievement.

Though Mowgli's parting cry that both the jungle and village gates are shut to him, at the end of "Tiger-Tiger!", advances a straightforward binary, these two locales never serve as analogies for primitive/civilized or child/adult in *The Jungle Books*. The jungle "beasts" possess language, laws, rituals, and manners; they address each other with formalized salutations and valedictions, like "good luck go with you" (35). If this is wildness, what could possibly constitute civilization? If this exchange represents a phylogenic childhood, what advance could adulthood offer? Answers to these questions are not provided by the human villagers. When Mowgli encounters them in "Tiger-Tiger!," they either repeat the actions of the jungle animals – looking him over "like another looking over by the Pack" (81) – or show themselves to be far more depraved – greeting him with "a shower of stones" (93). The villagers domesticate animals, they make fire, they have marriage and language, they exchange money, they wear clothes, and they cultivate the land. Yet despite this, the village is a paltry exemplar of humanity or civilization. Mowgli's position between jungle and village cannot, on its own, represent a dual Anglo-Indian (or even animal-man) identity. To work, the imperial allegory assumed and repeated by literary critics needs Mowgli's exercise of occupational loyalty to the British Empire that occurs in "In the Rukh." *The Second Jungle Book* mentions the English only twice, as people who "would not let honest farmers kill witches in peace" (213) and "do not suffer people to burn or beat each other without witnesses" (219). Though Kipling's Anglo-centric bigotry is clear, these mentions are not enough to establish British-ness as the goal of Mowgli's development in *The Jungle Books*. We must look elsewhere for the route that Mowgli's *Bildung* takes.

Just as jungle and village fail to provide a neat dichotomy in the children's series, so too do animal and man. "Man-cub" (51), as the wolves call Mowgli, and its obverse "wolf-child" (81), as he is known in the human village, are only two of the multiple names used to describe the boy. He is called "Mowgli the frog" by his wolf foster mother (40), "Little Brother" by the panther Bagheera (52), "blood-brother" by the simian Bandar-log (58), "Man with the snake's tongue" by the White Cobra (262), "Ape with a wolf's tongue" by the red dog (313), and finally "Master of the Jungle" by all the jungle beasts (256). This assortment of names belies the impulse to understand him as a split subject situated on the threshold between only two discrete identities. That kind of no-man's-land is represented by the Bandar-log, the "monkey-people" stranded at an evolutionary threshold they cannot cross and who, according to the brown bear Baloo, are "without a Law" (58) and "have no speech of their own" (59). Mowgli, in contrast, learns the "Master Words" of each jungle species and all "the Wood and Water Laws" (55). Baloo explains to Bagheera (his teacher's helper) that, "a man's cub is a man's cub, and he must learn *all* the Law of the Jungle" (56). This variety of animal potentialities – identities Mowgli assumes, language he masters, and laws he obeys (and breaks) – means that "animal" is not a monolithic class to be facilely contrasted with "man." The violence, indeed beastliness, of the villagers further suggests that man (or at least "village man") is simply one more animal, given equal weight within a diverse population of wolf, bat, frog, and panther. Though Baloo asserts the duality of the "man's cub" when he says how much his pupil has to learn, the bear imagines Mowgli inhabiting an intermediate position that is not the same as the Bandar-log and moving toward a humanity that is not the same as the villagers, or even the English. Rather, Baloo gestures toward a humanity that will be the all-inclusive culmination of Mowgli's jungle training, not its contradiction.

Throughout *The Second Jungle Book* but especially in "The Red Dog," the penultimate story of the collection, Mowgli illustrates the fruits of his panzooic education. By now an adept mimic of animal manners, he deftly synthesizes the bestial behaviors he has learned in order to exterminate "the *dhole* of the *Dekkan*," the canine marauders that are the latest threat to the jungle. He taunts the swarming pack by "imitat[ing] perfectly the sharp chitter-chatter of Chikai, the leaping rat of the Dekkan" (311) and enrages them further when his "hand shot out like the head of a tree snake" to sever their leader's tail (312). Certain that the dogs will chase him into the trap he has preconceived for them, "he moved monkey-fashion, into the next tree" (313) toward the hives of the wild bees that he studied in childhood. Agitating these tiny killers to attack, Mowgli "dived forward [into the river] like an otter," leaving the *dhole* behind to receive their deadly stings (315). In an exultant shout as he begins his final attack upon the red dogs, Mowgli proclaims his eclectic collection of bestial identities: "'Mowgli the Frog have I been,' said he to himself, 'Mowgli the Wolf have I said that I am. Now Mowgli the Ape must I be before I am Mowgli the Buck. At the end I shall be Mowgli the Man. Ho!'" (310–311). Mobilizing the survivalist behaviors that have constituted his jungle training and using them "out of school," so to speak, the Mowgli of "The Red Dog" systematically recapitulates *The Jungle Books* as a whole and his education within them.

Anatomically, Mowgli is always human, but here recapitulation is not a morphological process. Rather, *The Jungle Books* redefines the "animal" – and the "animal stages" through which Mowgli passes – as a multiplicity of behaviors and survival strategies. In *Adolescence: Its Psychology and its Relations to Physiology, Anthropology, Sociology, Sex, Crime, Religion and Education* (1904), a two-volume compendium of clinical observation and survey data, Hall reiterates the concerns that Kipling articulated in "One View of the Question." "Modern man," Hall writes, "has lost much keenness of sense and his motor life tends to caducity. His muscles are flabby from disuse, and efferent stimuli are long-circulated to cerebral activities instead of being reflected at once into motion."[18] In a series of discordant metaphors, he stresses that elementary education must do all it can to stave off "our urbanized hothouse life, that tends to ripen everything before its time" and to rectify "the old error of amputating the tadpole's tail rather than letting it be absorbed to develop the legs that make a higher life on land possible."[19] Both horticultural and zoological metaphors are calls to recover, in adolescence, the bestial behaviors that civilization fast-forwards to its own detriment. Hall channels Kipling's definition of the animal: "each animal group may represent some one quality in great excess, the high selective value of which made possible the development and survival of a species, genus, or group"; in short, "each species is a set of reactions and adaptations to a certain environment."[20] Here is Aesop with a Darwinian twist; the peacock's pride and the fox's cunning are replaced with strategies for eluding predators, capturing prey, and enticing mates.[21] Learning all the "Laws of the Jungle" and acing the final exam in "The Red Dog," Mowgli triumphantly recovers the multivalent voice of our bestial past, and what Hall calls "the far-off dying echo of what was once the voice of a great multitude" becomes Mowgli's victory cry.[22]

Mowgli's success is the result not of his hybridity (poised between binaries) but of his privileged heterogeneity: as an encyclopedia of the entire animal kingdom, he can be every animal at once. Of course, this revision of recapitulation's sequential stages into a fantasy of simultaneous totality is not countenanced by Darwinism. In *Adolescence*, Hall wants modern manhood to maintain animal cunning and strength, but he knows that recapitulation – even if it could be activated in this way – would recover *man's* line of descent only. He admits that Charles Darwin's branching tree, rather than Lamarck's monodirectional ladder, means that "our line of descent is restricted, and if we had all that our heredity could possibly bestow, we should be but specialized and partial beings."[23] Mowgli's ebullient cry at the end of "The Red Dog" that he is all of the animals at once, thus, suggests to Allen MacDuffie that literary critics like Hotchkiss and Seth Lerer are wrong in seeing *The Jungle Books* as Darwinian.[24] In "*The Jungle Books*: Rudyard Kipling's Lamarckian Fantasy" (2014), MacDuffie argues that the deployment of hierarchy and teleology in Mowgli's movement from animal to "Master of the Jungle" depends on "Lamarckian fantasies of converting experience into instinct and tracing humankind's path to becoming the culminating figure of the evolutionary process."[25] That Mowgli's development is not simple Darwinism seems clear, but the claim that it is Lamarckian is still only partially right. Mowgli's cry at the end of "Red Dog" – "Mowgli the Wolf have I said that I am. Now Mowgli the Ape must I be before I am Mowgli the Buck. At the end I shall be Mowgli the Man" – perplexingly places "buck" between "ape" and "man." This procession disrupts the ordering of species constitutive of the Lamarckian hierarchy. Kipling's *Just So Stories* (1902) parodies Lamarck's theory of willed adaptations, and *The Jungle Books* may be already looking elsewhere for a more powerful recapitulative paradigm.[26]

Since *The Jungle Books* are children's fantasy, they need not rigorously employ any scientific rationale. But Kipling's texts offer a surprisingly savvy intersession into evolutionary theory. In "Progress: Its Law and Cause" (1857), Herbert Spencer characterized evolution as the progress from homogeneity to heterogeneity; man occupies the supreme position because he is "the latest and most heterogeneous creature" in the world.[27] Given Mowgli's accumulation of animal identities, we might think that *The Jungle Books* – perhaps even more than Charles Kingsley's *The Water-Babies: A Fairy Tale for a Land-Baby* (1863) – illustrates Spencer's ideal heterogeneity. Baloo's insistence that "a man's cub is a man's cub, and he must learn *all* the Law of the Jungle" suggests that Mowgli surpasses the necessarily limited existences of his jungle peers to encompass the heterogeneous strategies of the jungle as a whole. But by heterogeneity, Spencer does not mean this animal totality. Rather, humans are uniquely heterogeneous, according to Spencer, because both our anatomy and our societies exhibit admirable divisions of labor: our hands and feet perform different functions unlike our quadruped relations, and our workforce is constituted by discrete classes. Spencer's heterogeneity, then, is simply another word for specialization. The humans in *The Jungle Books* fail by this measure of success. From Mowgli's point of view, the human villagers represent a stifling homogeny: they are described as a "crowd" (81), with "the gray-beards nodding together" at Buldeo's specious tales (85). Mowgli explains their undifferentiated behavior by saying "they are all mad together" (213).

Surely, fitting into this monotony is not the goal of Mowgli's development, but neither is achieving the specialization that Spencer admires. In contrast, *The Jungle Books* aim for a heterogeneity that is lost, rather than gained, as species and individuals advance. Spencer's concept of heterogeneity originated with one of recapitulation's early detractors, German anatomist Karl Ernst von Baer, who said in 1828 that each embryo sequentially diverges from a purely germinal similarity (homogeneity) to a unique complexity (heterogeneity) that determines species.[28] Within von Baer's formulation, the undifferentiated embryo's homogeny contains within it the *potential* to become multiple organisms, which the specialized adult forfeits. In other words, the embryo's generality still maintains heterogeneity. American zoologist and anatomist Edward Drinker Cope carried this suggestion further, arguing that specialization – far from being the goal of evolution – in fact, heralds extinction. Most famous for his role in the "Bone Wars" – the race to unearth dinosaur fossils in the American West – Cope argued that morphological specialization, though advantageous when environmental conditions are stable, is disastrous during climate fluctuations and geological disruptions. While overspecialized organisms (like dinosaurs) cannot adapt easily or quickly to changed conditions, those organisms (like our small mammalian ancestors) that have not narrowed their niches, diets, or skills survive. In *The Primary Factors of Organic Evolution* (1896), Cope codifies this "evolutionary law" as the "Doctrine of the Unspecialized" and gives it clear expression:

> [T]he "Doctrine of the Unspecialized" . . . describes the fact that the highly developed, or specialized types of one geologic period have not been the parents of the types of succeeding periods, but that the descent has been derived from the less specialized of preceding ages. No better example of this law can be found than man himself, who preserves in his general structure the type that was prevalent during the Eocene period, adding thereto his superior brain-structure.[29]

Cope was a Lamarckian, and he says in the preface to *Primary Factors* that he is defending American Neo-Lamarckism against its British detractors.[30] But the idea that evolutionary "progress" depends upon the benefits of the not yet "progressed" is a departure from orthodox Lamarckism. In the moment when Mowgli knows all the jungle laws and embodies all the animal strategies for self-preservation and predatory success, the "man-cub" is an extrapolated version of von Baer's still undifferentiated embryo and an expression of Cope's "unspecialized." For Kipling, by checking his development while he is still not-yet specialized, the boy retains an adolescence that is also a perfect heterogeneity, possessing the potential to become the entire animal kingdom.

At the end of *The Second Jungle Book*, Mowgli leaves the jungle ostensibly because he has reached sexual maturity and must find a species-suitable mate. But Mowgli must depart also because he now embodies the jungle in its totality. "The Spring Running," the final story, takes place in the mating season, and because the jungle has no companion for him, he must take his place among humans. But Kipling gives this romantic plot – the expected end of a *Bildungsroman* – the attention of only one paragraph. He, instead, dedicates the majority of this last tale to Mowgli's reenactment of the jungle's origin myth that Hathi the elephant tells in "How Fear Came," the first story of *The Second Jungle Book*. According to the elephant's tale, all the jungle animals used to live in vegetarian bliss until the First of the Tigers and the Gray Ape brought about a Fall. The First of the Tigers intruded into a dispute between two bucks, breaking one of their necks, and therefore brought "Death into the Jungle" (183). The Gray Ape, "hanging, head down, from a bough, mocking those who stood below," magnified the defilement of death with the indecency of shame (183). In "The Spring Running," Mowgli replicates these feline and simian violations; he disregards the Jungle Law by first intruding in a wolf fight, as the First of the Tigers had done, and then, like the Gray Ape, shames Mysa, the buffalo for once being a domesticated pack animal. As the disturbing combination of all the animal behaviors and the simultaneity of the jungle's past and present, Mowgli must be excised. He, thus, recapitulates twice over, and is now a man because he embodies the entirety of both the jungle's strategies and its temporalities.

Kipling's fantasy of a vigorous boyhood that hungrily accumulates animal skills and identities into an impregnable whole presents an even more powerful metaphor for global imperialism than the one commonly provided by postcolonial critics. Mowgli is the ideal imperialist not because he sits *between* animal and human, child and adult, and jungle and village, but because he holds all possibilities *simultaneously* within himself. My reading of Mowgli recalls the eponymous hero of Kipling's *Kim* (1901).[31] According to Randall, because Kim never chooses between serving the British Empire or following the Buddhist monk, "Kim's truncated *Bildung*, his insuperable adolescence, mirrors the problem of imperial consolidation, the problem of an empire that has not discovered – that may never discover – its appropriate coming of age."[32] Six years earlier, *The Jungle Books* had already rejected the "coming of age" script and its evolutionary overlay. Adolescence, for Kipling, is not a threshold, but a multifaceted wholeness. Thus, Mowgli might symbolize an ideal vision of the Empire, but as a composite middle rather than an ossified end, he does not represent Britishness. *Kim*, because it is not "just" a children's book, has received more credit for exploring this complexity. In "Drawing the Color Line" (1991), Satya P. Mohanty recognizes in Kim "a mode of perception that suspends social codings and even intellectual categories in order to reveal the pure energy of movement and diversity . . . Kipling's profoundly renewed and vital perception almost veers into a utopian assertion of pure *becoming*."[33] About Mowgli, we might say "mode of action" rather than perception, but the result is still the sense that *becoming* is more powerful than what has already become. *The Jungle Books* suspend the boy, the species, and perhaps the British Empire in eternal, unspecialized, heterogeneous, and infinitely powerful adolescence.

Pressing pause

Everywhere, *The Jungle Books* maintain multiplicity, avert manhood, and avoid being "In the Rukh." For Hall, bestial and savage adolescence was to be indulged, but eventually overcome; it was a period to exercise and thereby to inoculate oneself against the lower instincts, which if "suppressed, perverted, or delayed" would "crop out in menacing forms later."[34] But unlike Hall and many of his contemporaries, Kipling celebrates adolescence as its own end. He reconfigures the theory of recapitulation to invent an alternate mode of development that accumulates without accreting and adds without adding up. Just as importantly, he fashions a story that performs its own rejection of progress. The nonchronological ordering of Mowgli's plot and the alteration of the Mowgli tales with accounts of other characters are but two of the ways that *The Jungle Books* force their readers out of the habit of reading forward, from beginning to end, in a neat, Lamarckian-style trajectory. In *The Jungle Books*, Kipling takes advantage of the malleability of children's literature, inventing multivalent aesthetic elements that delay, prolong, and distort the forward-looking narrative time on which recapitulation, imperialism, and the *Bildungsroman* depend. The narrative and lyrical textures of *The Jungle Books*, I am arguing, enact Kipling's manipulations of the recapitulative plot, expanding his protagonist's youth and generating a similarly elastic experience for his readers. Through their use of language, song, and play, the Mowgli stories present a literary style dedicated not to progress but to pause.

The jungle and village defy our interpretation of these two locales as sequential points on an evolutionary progression. Even more resistant to this straightforward allegorical reading is the jungle language. Kipling's beasts have codified rules about who can speak, when, and in what order. All Kipling's jungle animals communicate in archaic English, with phrases like "we be of one blood, ye and I" (57) and "thou art the master" (51). They indulge in nicknames and metaphors; Bagheera calls the brown bear Baloo "old Iron-feet" (56), and he tells the python Kaa that the *Bandar-log* call him "footless, yellow earth-worm" (64). Their lexicon also employs metaphorical substitutions to describe human inventions; "Red Flower," for example, stands in for "fire" because "no creature in the jungle will call fire by its proper name. Every beast lives in deadly fear of it, and invents a hundred ways of describing it" (47). Kipling peppers *The Jungle Books* with Hindustani words: *hugas* for water pipes (84), *mohwa* for timber tree (174), *machans* for platforms (229), *dhole* for wild dog (300), and *pheeal* for the jackal's shriek (300), as well as the names of the jungle animals themselves. The jungle language is so nuanced that, Kipling's narrator tells us, it would be inaccessible to readers without his intercession as translator: "the Law of the Jungle," he says, is "translated into verse" so that we can understand it (189).

Many scholars have noted the strangeness of the beasts' language, though few read these linguistic idiosyncrasies as relevant to Kipling's twist on Mowgli's *Bildung*. In *Talking Animals in British Children's Fiction, 1786–1914* (2006), Tess Cosslett argues that the jungle language is consistent with *The Jungle Books'* imperial allegory. She also argues that Kipling's translator, who converts mysterious speech into legible text "treat[s] the animal language as if it were a 'native' dialect, translated by a Western scholar."[35] For Cosslett, the jungle language represents an earlier linguistic moment in human evolution: the animals' archaisms, the sprinkling of native words, and the fact that they have "no words for the man-made" are evidence of their "primitive, poetic status."[36] But because the animals' "low" linguistic register also contains elements of "high" (Bagheera's irony, for instance), Cosslett concludes that the jungle talk is a primitive/civilized hybrid, perfectly suited to the hybrid boy at the books' center.[37] In *Kipling's Children's Literature: Language, Identity, and Constructions of Childhood* (2010), Sue Walsh contests reading the animal language as primitive as well as the imperial allegory that it reinforces; she says, "the text no more produces the animal free of cultural contamination, than it constructs the human without recourse to the (repressed) animal that is nevertheless there. This has significant implications if the text is to be read as an allegory of colonialism."[38] Walsh rejects the idea that Mowgli is ever *between* two juxtaposed categories and claims that the indistinctness of jungle and village challenges all the supposed binaries of postcolonialism. While Walsh's analysis ends with this dissolution of the duality into sameness, I want to argue instead that Kipling's use of language explodes the duality into multiplicity. More than a celebration of heterogeneity, however, language in *The Jungle Books* also enables the man-cub's perpetual, anti-progressive, and lyrical adolescence that need not move forward into formalized notions of white, Western manhood.

"The King's Ankus," the fifth tale in *The Second Jungle Book*, illustrates the jungle language's resistance to Victorian narratives of human progress. Mowgli and Kaa stumble upon an ancient underground cavern filled with treasure and guarded by a White Cobra, so old he does not know that there is no longer a human settlement above him. The Cobra tells his visitors that "Salomdhi, son of Chandrabija, son of Viyeja, son of Yegasuri, built [the lair] in the days of Bappa Rawal" (261). Entirely ignorant of and uninterested in this catalog of patriarchal lineage, generational descent, and inheritance, Mowgli dismissively says, "I know not his talk." The Cobra's ventriloquization of language rooted in human ideas about manhood and material wealth makes no sense to either the python or the boy.

The ankus – the elephant goad for which the story is named – likewise conveys lessons in conquest, possession, patriarchy, and imperialism, but Mowgli likes it only because its engraving of an elephant reminds him of his friend Hathi. He prefers pictures to text and resemblance to hierarchy. Indifferent to both its material worth and its intended purpose to bend animals' will, Mowgli eventually returns the ankus to the lair. The ankus is meaningless in the jungle language precisely because it represents a distinctly human symbolic order of inheritance and possession that Mowgli refuses to enter. In rejecting the man-made symbol, he rejects the progress to manhood that its acceptance would entail and instead responds to what he understands as the Cobra's nonsensical talk with an oft-repeated jungle metaphor: "it is a lost trail" (261).

While stories like "The King's Ankus" show Mowgli's dismissal of human symbolic systems, *The Jungle Books'* principal examples of animal language occur not within the stories but in the poems that border them. Each tale in *The Jungle Books* begins with a poetic epigraph and concludes with a song usually in the voice of one of the books' animal denizens: after "Mowgli's Brothers" is "*Hunting-Song of the Seeonee Pack*"; "Kaa's Hunting" closes with "*Road-Song of the* Bandar-log"; an elephant's serenade follows "Toomai of the Elephants"; "The White Seal" begins with a "seal lullaby"; and so on. Though *The Jungle Books'* songs have inspired at least one orchestral cycle (by Charles Koechlin, 1899), one extensive composition (by Percy Gainger, 1898–1947), and one opera (by Michael Berkeley and David Malouf, 1993), literary scholars have had little to say about them, ostensibly seeing them as afterthoughts to the real stuff of the prose.[39] This oversight – especially in criticism invested in Mowgli's hybridity – surprisingly ignores the other half of the "mixed form" that T. S. Eliot praised Kipling for inventing.[40] In "Kipling's Singing Voice: Setting the *Jungle Books*" (2001), an analysis of Berkeley and Malouf's opera, Stephen Benson draws our attention to "those moments when the text breaks out in song" and then rightly corrects himself: "to say the text breaks into song is not quite true, for the [*Jungle*] *Book* commences with song before breaking into prose."[41] Since "*Night-Song in the Jungle*" precedes the first story, it is impossible to say which literary mode is primary and which secondary. Benson writes that, in song, "the voice is felt as being most resonant, *present*, in the sheer materiality of sound."[42] With no accompanying musical score, the lyrics of *The Jungle Books'* "songs" that we read on the page do not express the "sheer materiality of sound," but they do interrupt the monolithic human narrator of the prose with a plethora of imagined animal voices, and they likewise disrupt the forward thrust of narrative time.

As an anthology of animal songs – where a wolf, monkey, seal, grass-hopper, horse, camel, elephant, and kite enjoy extended solos – *The Jungle Books* textually replicate Mowgli's own cumulative recapitulation of animal identities. Fittingly, in contrast to the prose narratives that formally project (even if they forestall) beginning, middle, and end, the poetic interludes are immune to the demands of linear progress. In *Narrative Means, Lyric Ends: Temporality in the Nineteenth-Century British Long Poem* (2009), Monique Morgan argues, "whereas narrative requires temporal progression and sequentiality, lyric is a suspended moment that stops the time of narrative and focuses instead on the 'now' of composition and reception."[43] Mowgli's songs do the opposite work of Lewis Carroll's parodies in *Alice's Adventures in Wonderland* (1865). Whereas the tension between the original and the parody serves to model a willed change in Carroll's work, Mowgli's songs present the possibility of preserving the present just as it is. Alternating with the prose in Kipling's text, the songs pause narrative time and suggest modes of being that have nothing to do with progression and sequence. Much of *The Jungle Books'* verses are lullabies, anthems, and hunting songs designed for ritualized repetition. They thematize their suspended temporality in contrast with the prose tales. The story "Mowgli's Brothers," for example, opens with, "it was seven o'clock" (35), establishing that prose occurs within quantifiable time. But each verse in "*Hunting-Song of the Seeonee Pack*," that follows the story, twice repeats the refrain, "Once, twice and again!" (54); the song is meant to go on cyclically. The non-Mowgli stories and their adjacent songs also reveal this contrast: the elephants' chant that begins "Toomai of the Elephants" says, "I will remember what I was," "I will forget my ankle-ring," and "I will revisit my lost loves" (133), resisting the movement toward domestication and the work of the Empire that occur inside its companion story. In their content and in their formally inscribed repetitions and remembrances, the songs defer resolution.

Both of the songs sung by Mowgli, one after "Tiger-Tiger!" and another after "Letting in the Jungle," convey his animosity toward man, and each provides a literary interlude that defies the temporal sequencing on which his development toward manhood would depend. "Tiger-Tiger!" ends with a promise of narrative resolution: "So Mowgli went away and hunted with the four cubs in the jungle from that day on. But he was not always alone, because, years afterward, he became a man and married. But that is a story for grown-ups" (95). The status of this statement as a resolution is conflicted: the sense of community (being with the cubs) and permanence ("from that day on") is undercut by the shift in the second sentence that offers a new end in marriage "years afterward." This sentence employs an odd tense only available in prose fiction, projecting a human future though narrated in the past tense. In contrast, the song that follows emphasizes the simple, uniform present tense: "The Song of Mowgli" begins with, "I, Mowgli am singing" (96). Mowgli's song continues to stress his material and bodily presence through first-person, present-tense declarative statements unspeakable in prose: "Here come I," "Here is meat," "I am naked," "My mouth is bleeding," and "I dance on the hide of Shere Khan" (96–97). The immediacy of Mowgli's voice and body rendered by these lyrics suggests an eternally present moment, in which actions have neither beginning nor end. "Here," naked and dancing, the singer conveys the "pure energy of movement" that Mohanty identifies as "pure *becoming*" in *Kim*. After Mowgli commands the destruction of the village in "Letting in the Jungle," "Mowgli's Song against People" shifts away from the eternal present of his first song into future tense: "I will let loose against you the fleet-footed vines" and "I will reap your fields before you" (233). The future promise of this song, like the present movement of the previous one, refuses to put Mowgli's bestiality into the past.

Rejecting the *Bildungsroman*'s movement toward closure, Kipling's "mixed form" might seem to mimic the hybridity of the "man-cub." But Mowgli's songs fuse singer and song within a present moment that is whole unto itself. Though "Mowgli's Song" contains the line, "I am two Mowglis," the full lyrics invoke the multiple animal identities that he simultaneously inhabits: he compares himself to the bat, calls himself a frog, dons Shere Khan's coat, and recalls the bull that Bagheera exchanged for his life (96–97). The song does not move forward into manhood but expands outward along a spectrum of identifications that keeps Mowgli heterogeneous and unspecialized. Mowgli's development also resonates with what Kathryn Bond Stockton more recently calls "growing sideways." In *The Queer Child; or Growing Sideways in the Twentieth Century* (2009), Stockton argues that queer children do not grow "up" according to the conventional narrative of heterosexual union and normative adulthood; they occupy instead "queer temporalities" through their associations with animals, and they exist in a "moving suspension" created by metaphor that allows them to "hang in delay" between vehicle and tenor.[44] Mowgli grows "sideways" rather than "up," and the songs that sit next to the stories provide a space for this lateral, rather than linear, movement. Intriguingly, in *Stalky & Co.*, one of the masters refers to one of the pupils as an "animal boy"; in his analysis of *Stalky*, Neil Cocks translates this euphemism as "homosexual."[45] Mowgli is not homosexual, but he is queer, and *The Jungle Books* are queer texts that recognize the normative path to manhood and marriage, but dwell in rhetorical and stylistic alternatives to that prescriptive future.

Songs and metaphors constitute Kipling's literary strategy to resist the expected evolutionary advancement toward Western Manhood, and they are not the only sources for pause in *The Jungle Books*. In "Letting in the Jungle," for instance, the wolf pack sings in the middle of the story, and before he prints the lyrics, the narrator admits that "they are a rough rendering of the song, but you must imagine what it sounds like when it breaks the afternoon hush of the Jungle" (214). Paradoxically, the absence of an accompanying musical score offers readers an unusual opportunity to "imagine what it sounds like": to compose the music and sing the song themselves. *The Jungle Books* repeatedly invite readers to fill in these textual lapses. In the middle of "Mowgli's Brothers," the narrator says, "now you must be content to skip ten or eleven whole years, and only guess at all the wonderful life that Mowgli led among the wolves, because if it were written out it would fill ever so many books" (43), and later the "editor" of "The Law of the Jungle" (the song following "How Fear Came") writes, "just to give you an idea of the immense variety of the Jungle Law, I have translated into verse (Baloo always recited them in a sort of sing-song) a few of the laws that apply to the Wolves. There are, of course, hundreds and hundreds more" (189). Both passages communicate what I have been arguing is the central message of *The Jungle Books*: that they could go on forever and, indeed, that readers should imagine them doing just that. They prompt the readers to make up for themselves "all the wonderful life" and even the "hundreds and hundreds more" laws to which the books gesture but that they cannot contain.

The most extended invitation for the reader to continue writing new adventures for Mowgli occurs at the beginning of "The Red Dog," the story that emphatically rewrites recapitulation as a cumulative rather than accretive process. After Mowgli destroys the village in "Letting in the Jungle," and returns to the wild seat of his childhood, the narrator tells us:

> The things that he did and saw and heard when he was wandering from one people to another, with or without his four companions, would make many, many stories, each as long as this one. So you will never be told how he met and escaped from the Mad Elephant of Mandla, who killed two-and-twenty bullocks drawing eleven carts of coined silver to the Government Treasury, and scattered the shiny rupees in the dust; how he fought Jacala, the Crocodile, all one long night in the Marshes of the North, and broke his skinning-knife on the brute's backplates; how he found a new and longer

knife round the neck of a man who had been killed by a wild boar, and how he tracked that boar and killed him as a fair price for the knife; how he was caught up in the Great Famine by the moving of the deer, and nearly crushed to death in the swaying hot herds; how he saved Hathi the Silent from being caught in a pit with a stake at the bottom, and how the next day he himself fell into a very cunning leopard-trap, and how Hathi broke the thick wooden bars to pieces about him; how he milked the wild buffaloes in the swamp, and how –

But we must tell one tale at a time. (298–299)

Reflecting the multispecies potential available in Mowgli's narrative suspension, these six embryonic adventures suggest limitless varieties – as many adventures as there are animals, weapons, traps, and settings in the jungle – and Kipling encourages readers to write them all. In fact, it is story-telling itself that Kipling offers as the means for the child reader to direct the possibilities of his own evolution. The reader is presented with an array of animal possibilities that exist alongside, and are disruptive of, his reading of the prescribed text. Kipling's call for the reader's collaboration is not unique to *The Jungle Books*. In *Artful Dodgers: Reconceiving the Golden Age of Children's Literature* (2009), Marah Gubar looks at other nineteenth-century children's books that ask readers to complete the stories begun by the authors, and she argues that these invitations open up the text as "a shared field of play."[46] Kipling similarly invites readers to create their own Mowgli adventures and to project themselves into the role. But in *The Jungle Books*, the goal of the reader's involvement is to defer indefinitely the completion of the story: to extend its possibilities out rather than forward.

In *Education: Intellectual, Moral, and Physical* (1860), Spencer argued that elementary education must be modeled on play because play is nature's teacher. He says, "what was once thought mere purposeless action, or play, or mischief, as the case might be, is now recognised as the process of acquiring a knowledge on which all after-knowledge is based."[47] Four decades later, Hall reiterated the importance of play, taking issue with psychologist and evolutionist Karl Groos, who argued that play is preparation for later life.[48] In contrast to Groos's preparation thesis and Spencer's idea of play as a building-block for after-knowledge, Hall argues that play does not train us for the future, but rather reiterates "the motor tendencies and the psycho motives bequeathed to us from the past."[49] Like the wildness that all children inherit along with their bestial past, play rehearses rather than predicts. Mowgli's play in *The Jungle Books* reconstructs and improves upon previous animal action; more importantly, play keeps his strategies supple and staves off the specialization that heralds an injurious recalcitrance. In "The Red Dog," Mowgli pretends to be a deer, wolf, otter, and ape, but rather than fighting for his life as these animals must, Mowgli only "pull[s] the whiskers of Death" as if in a game (310). He wins because, unlike the other animals, he is only playing. For Kipling's reader, the opportunities to play are similarly recuperative rather than progressive, encouraging narrative flexibility rather than promising conclusion. Through their lyrical suspensions and narrative pauses, *The Jungle Books* fashions children's literature as an invitation to the reader to play at being Mowgli and to keep the boundless boyhoods of both the character and the reader going without the need to finish the book or to grow up.

Resuming play

Since the publication of *The Jungle Books*, countless children have played at being Mowgli, not least of all because Kipling's man-cub became a prototype for General Robert-Powell's Boy and Cub Scouts. Baden-Powell established the Scouts after serving in the Boer Wars, military embarrassments for the British that intensified popular fears about national decline. To market this extracurricular project of fostering the natural vitality of boyhood, he lifted episodes from Kipling's *Kim* for his *Scouting for Boys* (1908) and likewise from *The Jungle Books* for *The Wolf Cub's Handbook* (1916), a branch of the Scouts for younger boys seven to eleven years old.[50] Despite its very British inception, the desire to recover a primitive past in order to safeguard an imperial future found a receptive home across the Atlantic as well. In fact, aspects of *The Jungle Books* ethos were already at work in the United States and Canada, where Kipling's characterization of Indians ran parallel to North America's lore about its so-called Indian. American anxieties about cultural degeneration due to urbanization, immigration, feminization, and the loss of the pioneering spirit that had defined manhood led pedagogues, authors, and youth organizers to seek a space outside of school and society where boys could recover their savage past by alternatively playing Indian and playing pioneer. Mowgli's adoption by the Boy Scouts, his move to North America, and his ethnic makeover in youth organization and boys' literature illustrate the prevalence of this new recapitulative model and reveal the distinct national flavors of its trans-Atlantic adaptations.

One of the few celebrated heroes from the Boer War, Baden-Powell founded the Scouts to remasculinize the Edwardian boy. In *Sons of the Empire: The Frontier and the Boy Scout Movement, 1890–1918* (1993), Robert

H. MacDonald says that boys were "trained to duplicate the savage life" in order to regain "everything that the savage had not yet lost – virility, hardiness, martial spirit."[51] Appropriately, Baden-Powell's dedication of *The Wolf Cub's Handbook* praises Kipling for having "done so much to put the right spirit into our rising manhood."[52] The *Handbook* handily transforms *The Jungle Books* into rituals for the boys to perform. Because "when Akela, the old wolf, the head of the pack," in Kipling's stories, "took his place on the rock [the wolves] all threw up their heads and howled their welcome to him," the Cub Scouts should behave likewise: "when your Old Wolf, Akela – that is your Cubmaster or other Scouter – comes to your meeting you salute him by squatting round in a circle as young wolves do, and giving him the Wolf Cub Grand Howl."[53] Drawing episodes from *The Jungle Books*, Baden-Powell encourages the Cub Scouts' wildness, but only, it seems, to tame them all the more thoroughly. During "The Dance of the Death of Shere Khan," the Cubs chant the tiger's funeral dirge while making stabbing motions and letting their growls increase "gradually in noise and anger," until they throw themselves to the floor and play dead.[54] The bestial performance, casting the Cubs as both the slayer and the slain, might recollect the heterogeneous spirit of Kipling's text, but the dance is then framed by the avuncular suggestion that "if you want to entertain your fathers and mothers and friends, it is good to do ... the Dance of Shere Khan's Death."[55] Likewise "The Bagheera Dance," in which the pretend-panthers "all spring forward on to the imaginary deer with a yell, seize him and tear him to pieces," is immediately followed by the taming of another activity called "Mothering Day," which directs them to "try to do things that will make [your mother] feel proud that you are her son, and never do anything that would cause her to feel grieved or ashamed."[56]

In reveling in and subsequently curbing boys' wildness, Baden-Powell's *Wolf-Cub's Handbook* seems to carry out a mission closer to Hall's than to Kipling's. For Hall, the "rudimentary organs of the soul" should be "developed in their season so that we should be immune to them in mature years."[57] The goal of letting such wildness out was to reach a healthy manhood freshly inoculated. Baden-Powell likewise said in a newspaper interview in 1910 that the goal of Scouting was "to put some of the wild man back into" the boys, but not too much; if they "get too wild," he continued, "they lack courtesy and deference to the weak and helpless."[58] For all his praise of Kipling in his dedication, Baden-Powell's use of *The Jungle Books* is highly selective; in fact, his version of *The Jungle Books* looks very similar to Randall's. *The Wolf Cub's Handbook* only includes episodes from the first *Jungle Book* (ending with the death of

Shere Khan) and augments them with an imperial mission that recalls "In the Rukh"; Baden-Powell writes, "our object in taking up the training of the Wolf Cubs is not merely to devise a pleasant pastime for the Cubmasters or for the boys, but to improve the efficiency of the future citizens of our Empire."[59] Baden-Powell, then, turns *The Jungle Books* into the same progressive and imperial *Bildungsroman* that postcolonial literary criticism does, and the effect is a similarly restricted version of Mowgli's play. Consider the difference between Kipling's songs that maintain a lyrical sense of presence and the war cry that punctuates Shere Khan's death in *The Wolf-Cub's Handbook* (bafflingly to the tune of "Frère Jacques"): "Mowgli's hunting/ Mowgli's hunting/ Killed Shere Khan/ Killed Shere Khan/ Skinned the Cattle-eater/ Skinned the Cattle-eater/ (Yell) *Rah-rah-rah!/ Rah-rah-rah!*".[60] Except for its first two lines of repeated participial phrase, the song celebrates finitude. Upon the completion of the song, the boys are directed to cry "Dead – dead –dead!." What dies here is not only Mowgli's feline nemesis but also the beast within the boys, exorcized by the song's temporary and controlled excursion into the savage past.

Baden-Powell's and Hall's cultural fantasy of recovering man's primitive vigor without sacrificing any of his acculturated civility found its most pristine expression not in *The Jungle Books* but in Edgar Rice Burroughs's *Tarzan of the Apes* (1914). While Mowgli occupies an evolutionary middle, Tarzan is a proper hybridization of two evolutionary poles. In Burroughs's novel, Tarzan's bestial childhood makes him the "embodiment of physical perfection and giant strength," but he is simultaneously graced with "an hereditary instinct of graciousness which a lifetime of uncouth and savage training and environment could not eradicate."[61] It is Tarzan, rather than Mowgli, who can murder tigers and Africans and return home just in time to perform gallant rescues of damsels in distress. Dana Seitler's *Atavistic Tendencies: The Culture of Science in American Modernity* (2008) argues that *Tarzan*'s serialization demanded that the ape-man continually return to the jungle and thus remain engaged in "a dialectic between progress and regress, linearity and recursivity."[62] But this hybridity is also written into Tarzan's unique evolution. Both Seitler and Gail Bederman see *Tarzan*'s appeal in terms of the U. S. imperialism influenced by Theodore Roosevelt at the turn of the century. "A manly advocate of a virile imperialism," according to Bederman's *Manliness & Civilization: A Cultural History of Gender and Race in the United States, 1880–1917* (1995), Roosevelt self-consciously reformed his image "from effeminate dude to masculine cowboy" and sought to transform the United States in his own made-over image.[63] The refined, urbane capitalist working in the Northeastern centers of commerce was balanced against the hypermasculinized, rough and tumble, frontiersman of the West to make up a hybrid image of America. The Scouts' instructions on how to best a Zulu warrior and then to escort one's mother to tea, though forged in England, already contained the duality of this particular American masculinity.

Tarzan's language acquisition demonstrates the dichotomy that constitutes his manhood and makes Burroughs's ape-man more representative of both Baden-Powell's Scouting philosophy and Randall's imperial allegory than is Mowgli. Burroughs describes Tarzan's learning to read as a recapitulation: "Tarzan of the apes, little primitive man, presented a picture filled, at once, with pathos and with promise – an allegorical figure of the primordial groping through the black night of ignorance toward the light of learning."[64] But, in fact, Tarzan is like Daniel Defoe's Robinson Crusoe, whom Jean-Jacques Rousseau celebrated as the "natural man" but who, as Karl Marx pointed out, relies on the debris of civilization gathered from the wrecked ships.[65] Reading primers fortuitously found in his dead parents' cabin, Tarzan sees the word "BOY" under a picture of a boy, and thus reading propels Tarzan simultaneously into language and a sense of his own masculine humanity. Language, he learns, conveys mastery and confers possession. When he leaves his first-ever written note for the party of marooned travelers, it reads, "THIS IS THE HOUSE OF TARZAN, THE KILLER OF BEASTS AND MANY BLACK MEN. DO NOT HARM THE THINGS WHICH ARE TARZAN'S. TARZAN WATCHES. TARZAN OF THE APES."[66] The "love letter" that Tarzan later writes to Jane likewise insists, "I am yours. You are mine," including woman among the "things" others must be warned not to "harm."[67] White manhood requires identifying oneself with the word of the father in order to befriend white men, to kill beasts and black men, and to seize everything else. But entering into language comes with Lacanian self-division: discovering Tarzan's note, the marooned party assumes that the "Tarzan" who signed it cannot be the speechless ape-man they have seen fighting lions on their behalf. However, this split is not disorienting but empowering, allowing hybrid Tarzan to be simultaneously "King of the Jungle" and "Lord Greystoke." But unlike Mowgli's speech and song, Tarzan's language does not suspend an eternal presence of lyric. Rather, his mastery of the written word solidifies his access to the evolutionary end point: male dominance and possession.

In conquering wild spaces and claiming them for himself, Burroughs's ape-man perfectly performs the fantasy of the pioneer, which like Spencer's animal child in England, was becoming the figural center of a newly compulsory educational system in the United States. In the second half of the nineteenth century, the United States was also beginning to mandate elementary education, beginning in Massachusetts in 1852 and ending with Mississippi in 1918.[68] In 1901, Hall devised an "Ideal School" based on the child's slow development out of his originary proto-humanity and stressing self-directed activities and play.[69] Influencing the training of kindergarten teachers attending Clark University, where he served as President, Hall helped to reshape Friedrich Froebel's pedagogy according to recapitulative principles.[70] Hall's theories were even more important to Dewey, a fellow psychologist. Perhaps fueled by the particular form that Neo-Lamarckism took in the United States, Dewey also saw in recapitulation a coherent principle for curricular reform. In *The School and Society* (1899), he notes a "natural recurrence of the child mind to the typical activities of primitive peoples; witness the hut which the boy likes to build in the yard, playing hunt with bows, arrows, spears."[71] Lessons should retrace technological progress from its rude beginnings in a rehearsal of the history of American pioneering. To learn about fabric-making, for instance,

> [T]he children are first given the raw material – the flax, the cotton plant, the wool as it comes from the back of the sheep . . . Then a study is made of these materials from the standpoint of their adaptation to the uses to which they may be put . . . They then followed the processes necessary for working the fibers up into cloth. They re-invented the first frame for carding the wool . . . They re-devised the simplest process for spinning the wool . . . Then the children are introduced to the invention next in historic order, working it out experimentally . . . You can concentrate the history of all mankind into the evolution of the flax, cotton, and wool fibers into clothing.[72]

In this process, according to Dewey, "the historic development of man is recapitulated." As the iconic one-room schoolhouse was succeeded by classrooms graduated by age and divided by gender, Dewey's recapitulative curriculum offered a rational structure and starred the pioneer as the child's vigorous and lively historical counterpart.

The conceit of the pioneer was created in tandem with its counterpart on the Western frontier: the Indian. In the popular imagination of American colonialists, the Indians of James Fennimore Cooper's *Leatherstocking Tales* (1827–1841) were more exciting than the sundry colonial subjects and adversaries of, for instance, George Alfred Henty's imperialist adventures for British boys. According to Lora Romero's critical study *Home Fronts: Domesticity and Its Critics in the Antebellum United States* (1997), Cooper's early nineteenth-century fiction had already turned

aboriginals into "an earlier and now irretrievable lost version of the self . . .
a *phase* that the human race goes through but which must inevitably *get
over*."[73] The American Indian constituted an evolutionary middle. Within
the neo-Lamarckism of late nineteenth- and early-twentieth-century
America, the figure of the Indian was already available and thereby easily
co-opted to represent the crucial intermediary evolutionary stage for the
white boy's ontogenic development. Kenneth B. Kidd argues in *Making
American Boys: Boyology and the Feral Tale* (2004) that "even before the
official introduction of evolutionary science, boyhood was increasingly
constituted through a social biology – a nascent boyology – that designated
the racial other as irretrievably primitive."[74] If the pioneer was the starting
point for American education inside the official classroom, the Indian was
the featured analogue for the boy in his extracurricular adventures beyond
the school.

An important precursor to Baden-Powell and the Boy Scouts, Ernest
Thompson Seton – an England-born, Canada-bred, and United States-
residing naturalist – established in 1902 the League of Woodcraft Indians,
a Connecticut-based boys' organization featuring outdoor activities modeled on the supposed practices and lifestyle of the American Indian.
Initially finding much in common with Baden-Powell's project, Seton
headed the U.S. chapter of the Boy Scouts from 1910 to 1915, but differences between the British and American programs and the approach of
World War I put the two men at odds.[75] Seton was a pacifist and socialist
who revered the Native Americans' respect for nature and would, in
The Gospel of the Redman: An Indian Bible (1936), urge Americans of
European descent to adopt the community and spiritualism of the con-
tinent's first inhabitants; these elements of Seton's mythology held no
interest for Baden-Powell.[76] But the difference between the two men ran
deeper. Though Seton adopted the analogy between boy and "native," he
did not wish to encourage boys to pillage this presumed racial past only to
quickly surpass it in attaining a white manhood. Distinct from many of his
compatriots, Seton was not a neo-Lamarckian. For him, Indians were not
a way station en route to a higher humanity, but a noble branch on a
Darwinian tree that was sadly being hewn. Seton's first work of fiction,
a collection of animal tales called *Wild Animals I Have Known* (1898),
unambiguously draws its portrait of animal life from Darwin rather than
Lamarck: "the life of a wild animal," he claims in the Preface, "*always has
a tragic end*."[77] The extinction of the Native American way of life troubled
Seton far more than the worry that the white boy might get stuck in an
equivalent stage of atavism.

Perhaps because Seton feared that the United States' and Canada's internal imperialism was erasing the Indians, his book illustrating the ideals of the Woodcraft Indians registers the same desire to pause the individual and national *Bildungsroman* that we see in Kipling's *Jungle Books*. Appropriately, it was Kipling who dissuaded Seton from writing an encyclopedia on the movement and instead encouraged him to write a novel.[78] Seton's *Two Little Savages: Being the Adventures of Two Boys Who Lived as Indians and What They Learned* (1903) tells the story of Yan, a boy sent to work on a farm, who takes to the woods with his friend Sam to camp, to build forts, and to make weapons according to Indian methods and materials.[79] Not wholly freed from Seton's original plan for an encyclopedia, *Two Little Savages* is stuffed with step-by-step instructions on how to skin animals and detailed diagrams illustrating how to construct teepees; it is, as Daniel Francis remarks, "the only work of fiction I know that includes an index."[80] Seton gives readers a repository of an Indian culture on the verge of vanishing. Kidd draws parallels between *Two Little Savages* and Dakota Sioux writer Charles Alexander Eastman's autobiography *Indian Boyhood* (1902); in the preface to the latter work, Eastman admits to "put[ting] together these fragmentary recollections of my thrilling wild life expressly for the little son who came too late to behold for himself the drama of savage existence," as if the book was all that remained of a disappearing people.[81] Not surprisingly, Eastman joined Seton in establishing the Boy Scouts in the United States: an organization that sought to preserve the memory of what nonwhite culture was in order to give it to the white boy.

The awareness of loss and the preservative mission of children's literature make *Two Little Savages* less focused on moving through and getting over than in forestalling individual development and national history. Though Yan's and Sam's play usually involves the completion of discrete tasks – making bows, skinning animals, etc. – that have definite beginnings and ends, Seton also draws the reader's attention to the sounds of nature that exist outside human activity and technological progress. Early in his adventures, Yan hears the geese and thinks to himself:

> Oh! what a song the Wild Geese sang that year! How their trumpet clang went thrilling in his heart, to smite there new and hidden chords that stirred and sang response. Was there ever a nobler bird than that great black-necked Swan, that sings not at his death, but in his flood of life, a song of home and of peace – of stirring deeds and hunting in far-off climes – of hungerings and food, and raging thirsts to meet with cooling drink . . . Oh, what a song the

Wild Geese sang that year! And yet, was it a new song? No, the old, old song, but Yan heard it with new ears. He was learning to read its message.[82]

Though not rendered in verse like the songs that bracket *The Jungle Books'* chapters, the geese's song gestures toward eternal repetition, recovery, and pause. This is not a song of death and endings, like Baden-Powell's "Dance of the Death of Shere Khan," or the codification of masculine dominance and control in *Tarzan's* written texts. Rather, the goose sings like the animal inhabitants of *The Jungle Books*, "in the flood of his life." The song "that year" is the song sung every year. It is an "old, old song" but "new" in the ears of each new generation of boys who comes to the woods to hear it. Indian songs share this power of renewal, and when Yan and Sam sing "a little Indian war chant," "their savage instincts seemed to revive" and Yan's "whole nature seemed to respond: he felt himself a part of that dance."[83] It is a fitting consequence of Seton's literary translation of the disappearing past into an ever-renewed future that *Two Little Savages* also promotes the United States' burgeoning conservation movement. Yan plays Indian but better, according to Seton: "his ideal life" is "the life of an Indian with all that is bad and cruel left out . . . [H]e would show men how to live without cutting down all the trees, spoiling all the streams, and killing every living thing."[84] Passages like this remind us not to celebrate Seton's Indian-love without criticism, but *Two Little Savages*, nevertheless, invites the child reader into a way of being that is contrary, rather than simply preliminary, to the Western *Bildungsroman*.[85]

Though the Woodcraft Indians would lose out to the more popular Boy Scouts in the 1920s, Seton's and Kipling's influence can be seen in the development of the summer camp: perhaps the most long-lived cultural legacy of the theory of recapitulation.[86] Speaking to a group of camp directors in 1905, Hall praised the institution of the summer camp for its harmony with the theory of recapitulation and the child's natural atavism: "ought it not to be a rule," he said, "for children to go to the country – country for children, city for adults. City life in every race is developed much later than country life. Primitive man is essentially sylvan, not urban but rural."[87] Summer camps, which first started being founded in the United States in the 1870s, became widespread in the early decades of the twentieth century in coordination with compulsory schooling, in particular with the now regular summer vacation.[88] The camps' bucolic and secluded locales suggested space for children to relive their primitive past, but according to historian Leslie Paris, the experience was more touristy than authentic; in *Children's Nature: The Rise of the American*

Summer Camp (2008), she writes, "camps were hybrid cultural spaces, middle grounds where pioneer cabins sometimes coexisted with miniature golf courses, where children 'played Indian' one day and dressed as film stars the next."[89] This fusion of primitivism and modernity may turn the campers into Tarzans rather than Mowglis or even Yans. Unlike *The Jungle Books*, summer camp cannot last forever. But in this socially sanctioned retreat into wildness, Mowgli's effervescent and unending bestial play became entrenched in middle-class American culture, even though it had seasonal limits.

Kipling's *Land and Sea Tales for Scouts and Scout Masters* (1923), adventure stories featuring plucky boy heroes written explicitly for the Boy Scouts, concludes with an original adaptation of "Eeny, meeny, miny, moe": a children's rhyme used to count the players of various games and to choose who will be "it." Kipling's "A Counting-Out Song" presents the verse that we know as the chorus to a longer poem explaining the prehistoric origins of the child's rhyme:

> Eenee, Meenee, Mainee, and Mo
> Were the First Big Four of the Long Ago,
> When the Pole of the Earth sloped thirty degrees,
> And Central Europe began to freeze,
> And they needed Ambassadors staunch and stark
> To steady the tribes in the gathering dark:
> But the frost was fierce and flesh was frail,
> So they launched a Magic that could not fail.
>   (Singing)   *"Eenee, Meenee, Mainee, Mo!*
>   *Hear the wolves across the snow!*
>   *Someone has to kill 'em – so*
>   *Eenee, Meenee, Mainee, Mo*
>   *Make – you – It!"*[90]

In *Primitive Culture* (1871), Edward Burnett Tylor categorizes this kind of children's song or game as a "sportive survival": a remnant from ancient times that has "outlive[d] the serious practice of which it is an imitation."[91] After Tylor's work, counting-out rhymes were often understood as survivals. Henry Carrington Bolton argued that "European and American children engaged in 'counting out' for games are repeating in innocent ignorance the practices and language of a sorcerer of a dark age," and Alexander Chamberlain saw in them "the sortilegic formulae of past ages; children now select their leader or partner as once men selected victims for sacrifice."[92] In imagining that *"Eenee, Meenee, Mainee, Mo"* are the preserved names of prehistoric warrior-kings, Kipling's poem imaginatively returns the children's song to its ostensibly original context. Like Mowgli's songs in *The Jungle Books,* children's rhyming games so conceived are the opposite of the parodies explored in the last chapter; if parody is a literary model of evolution that demonstrates forms changing over time, the survival expresses the parts of human experience that refuse evolution and remain unchanged from prehistory to the present. The child, for Kipling and Seton, is such a survival, and therein lies his power. Literature must maintain this atavism rather than reform it.

The idea that children renew human prehistory or that this renewal was necessary for both Britain's and America's imperial futures was not Kipling's alone, but Kipling was unique in his skepticism about civilization and his desire to pause primitive boyhood without end. *The Jungle Books'* fantasy of indefinitely delayed maturation reappears in "A Counting-Out Song," where "Eenie," "Meenie," "Mainee," and "Mo" stand in for numbers that put the players in an order but do not convey values that can be added up to reach a mathematical totality or endpoint. Rather, the potentially endless sequence of "A Counting-Out Song" delights listeners with the joyously drawn out deferral of final choice of "it." Enjoying even more extensive delays and suspensions, *The Jungle Books* express a comprehensive evolutionary need for an expansive childhood, a prolonged adolescence, and a deferred adulthood. Kipling perceived that reforming the human condition required suspending development at its most plastic stage – adolescence – when the boy has full access to the species' heterogeneous animal potential but before a self-contained and specialized humanity eclipses this latent fantasy of becoming. The imperial allegory is still palpable, but Kipling's celebration of an evolutionary middle reappraises more familiar ideas about the species' ends. *The Jungle Books* devise a children's literature capable of providing a powerful alternative to Victorian narratives of progress and the speedy recapitulation that was adopted by schools in England and the United States and by extracurricular programs on both sides of the Atlantic. Kipling's Mowgli stories give us heterogeneity that is not simple duality, intermediacy that is not transitional, manhood that is not emptied of animality, play that is not preparation, survivals that do not need to be surpassed, and "growing" that is not "up."

CHAPTER 5

Home grown
Frances Hodgson Burnett and the cultivation
of female evolution

As the ready literary and cultural adoption of Rudyard Kipling's man-cub shows, recapitulation offered a developmental paradigm tailor-made for the imperial boy. Little girls had no place in these narratives of sequential or accretive animality; indeed, Victorians and Edwardians were loath to admit that girls underwent bestial stages at all. Psychologist G. Stanley Hall, largely responsible for transporting recapitulation theory to the United States, suggested in 1904 that, instead of animals, "flowers are the best expression nature affords of [the girl's] adolescence ... from the efflorescence of dawning puberty to full maturity she is a flower in bloom."[1] Hall's clumsy attempt to fashion a feminized recapitulation gathered few followers, but it points to the general problem of sexual difference within the individual/species analogy, evolutionary theory, and imperialist politics. If the species and the nation require brute strength to succeed in the struggle for existence, what function do girls serve in either the primitive past or the militarized present? This question follows from late-nineteenth-century anxieties about "the Women Question," a collection of uncertainties about women's role in society, her claims to education and work, the part she played in the human past, and her role in the future. "The Woman Question" spawned "the Girl Question" in the early twentieth-century, when compulsory elementary schooling for children of both sexes, rising numbers of female secondary students, and girls' demands for entrance into boys' organizations like the Boy Scouts sparked a search for the endemic nature of the younger members of this gendered demographic.

Evolutionary theory had little satisfactory to say about the female sex. The speculative histories of human ascent – those on which recapitulative theories about boys and twentieth-century conceptions of adolescence were based – seemed to unfold without female involvement. In "Have Only Men Evolved?" (1979), her censure of the androcentrism in evolutionary theory, Ruth Hubbard argues that Charles Darwin's accounts of human history rehearse a particularly "Victorian script" about male action and female passivity: "wherever you look among animals," she points out, "eagerly promiscuous males are pursuing females who peer from behind languidly drooping eyelids to discern the strongest and handsomest."[2] She points to Darwin's description in *The Descent of Man, and Selection in Relation to Sex* (1871), which describes "the male possessing certain organs of sense or locomotion, of which the female is quite destitute, or in having them more highly developed, in order that he may readily find or reach her; or again, in the male having special organs of prehension so as to hold her securely" and shows that here the male alone apprehends his world, both intellectually (through organs of sense) and physically (through limbs for grasping).[3] Hubbard recalls Elaine Morgan's "The Descent of Woman" (1973), which also reproaches the male evolutionists who "forget about [females] for most of the time. They drag her on stage rather suddenly for the obligatory chapter on Sex and Reproduction, and then say: 'All right, love, you can go now,' while they get on with the real meaty stuff about the Mighty Hunter with his lovely new weapons and his lovely new straight legs racing across the Pleistocene plains."[4] Nineteenth-century narratives of human evolution had a definite hero, and that hero was male.

Though Hubbard and Morgan made their charge in the 1970s, Victorian women educated in biology and evolutionary theory were well aware of the omission of the female and sought to correct it with alternate versions of human ascent. However, unlike their successors, they laid their claim to female influence almost entirely within what Morgan disparaged as "the obligatory chapter on Sex and Reproduction." Motherhood was hailed as the most important factor in the success or failure of species and, with an imperialistic twist, of nations. For some Victorian and Edwardian feminists, motherhood meant caring for children after birth; for others, it meant the female's considered selection of a mate, the promotion of advantageous traits, and the weeding out of undesirable ones according to the pseudoscience of eugenics. Thus, what was needed to prepare girls for motherhood implied contradictory pedagogical theories and practices. For the makers of the Victorian and Edwardian school's gendered curriculum, preparation for motherhood meant instituting "domestic economy" as a compulsory subject. For proponents of physical activity and youth organizations for girls modeled on the occupations of their brothers, motherhood demanded daily exercise to create strong bodies. For advocates of sexual purity and civic eugenics, being a good mother entailed being informed about when and how *not* to be a mother. These disparate and often clashing pedagogical goals made the girl's "natural" path to womanhood even thornier than the boy's. He lingered in a bestial boyhood readying him for military triumphs that would make him a hero, while she was fast-forwarded to reproductive maturity while paradoxically arrested by her strictly biological (animal) function.

Girls' literature at the turn of the century drew from both the prevalent motherhood ideal and the ambivalent directions that this ideal mapped out for the girl's development. Frances Hodgson Burnett's *The Secret Garden* (1911) – a novel that invites and frustrates feminist readings – incorporates Victorian evolutionary constructions of motherhood and early-twentieth-century eugenic dictates; it also intriguingly sketches out what female recapitulation might look like. Metaphorically linked to the flowers of the secret garden that constitutes the novel's most significant setting, Burnett's Mary Lennox might initially seem to exemplify Hall's flower girl, measuring her development according to vegetal phases. But Mary is a gardener, too, separating the weeds from the flowers and electing boy playmates, recalling the eugenic choice that real girls of her generation were being taught to make. And in her progression from a passive plant to a selective gardener, she is associated with a variety of animals that exhibit traits suggestive of an advancing scale of motherhood that Mary's growth recapitulates. The female empowerment figured by Burnett's novel is, no doubt, conflicted, but this chapter argues that Mary's story reflects the complex legacy of evolution and recapitulation for girls between the advent of the new century and the eve of the First World War. Transgendering Victorian recapitulation for the Edwardian girl, however, *The Secret Garden* finally rejects biology in favor of more flexible, aesthetic, and imaginative conceptions of girlhood and maternity.

Mommy fittest

The changing environment to which late-nineteenth-century and early-twentieth-century women and girls found themselves adapting seems Darwinian. Beginning with the United Kingdom's 1851 census reporting a surplus of women with no spouse to support them, women had to survive by finding new niches outside the home.[5] For Charlotte Perkins Gilman, the "new woman" who seeks her own sustenance is more evolutionarily viable than the "parasite mate" wholly dependent on her husband.[6] But Gilman's questioning of women's domestic role was not the only position taken by Victorian feminists, especially those who hoped that the story of human evolution would reveal strong female roles equal to the male warrior celebrated in Darwin's *Descent of Man*. Some speculative accounts of early human societies, like Otis Tufton Mason's *Woman's Share in*

Primitive Culture (1895), imagined women's contribution through the lens of a prehistoric gender division: "in contact with the animal world, and ever taking lessons from them, men watched the tiger, the bear, the fox, the falcon," Mason writes, "but women were instructed by the spiders, the nest builders, the storers of food and the workers in clay like the mud wasp and the termites."[7] By watching these diminutive animals just outside their homes, early women perfected domesticity and aided the species' evolution by doing the duties that Victorian society sanctioned for them: housework and motherhood. Late-nineteenth-century feminists with varied backgrounds and audiences, like Congregationalist minister Antoinette Brown Blackwell and secretary to Charles Lyell turned children's author Arabella Buckley, argued that evolution depended on mothers. Yet as restrictive as defining a whole sex's contribution to culture by that singular biological imperative may seem, this recognition of the importance of parenthood and family structure in the success of a species challenged the male evolutionists' myopic focus on the male individual. Likewise, by opening up evolutionary discourse to considerations of motherhood, Blackwell and Buckley, among others, initiated crucial changes in what it meant to be a girl.

Though Darwin came under fire from Hubbard and Morgan in the twentieth century, the male bias of Victorian biology and anthropology was hardly of his making alone. Herbert Spencer famously defended the "separate spheres" as the hallmark of a civilized society. In "Psychology of the Sexes" (1873), he asks, "are the mental natures of men and women the same?" and answers decidedly that they are not.[8] The difference is the result of their unique reproductive functions. According to Spencer, gestation and childbirth require so much energy that females are stunted by the expenditure. There exists, he writes, "a somewhat earlier arrest of individual evolution in women than in men, necessitated by the reservation of vital power to meet the needs of reproduction."[9] The female's "individual evolution" is halted by the toll maternity takes on her body, while male development surges ever onward. For this reason, the female always reverts to a childish or primitive stage. Even in her maternal duties, Spencer claims, she remains more egocentric than altruistic; she instinctively "responds to infantile helplessness," while the male "has a more generalized relation to all the relatively weak who are dependent on him." True morality, which self-consciously understands itself as moral, is for Spencer an exclusively male trait. As a picture of the species' mental and moral past, the female has little effect on the direction of future adaptations and evolution. This arrested development is pithily expressed in Hall's version of the female's floral recapitulation, or, similarly insulting, Thomas H. Huxley's quip that "five sixths of women will stop in the doll stage of evolution."[10] The female is not even animal, if she can be considered a volitional living being at all.

In *The Sexes Throughout Nature* (1875), Blackwell challenges this ostensible retardation in female development. She argues that Darwin's narrative of accreting masculine accomplishments "scientifically *adds to the male*" while Spencer's claim about energy lost in reproduction "scientifically *subtracts from the female*."[11] Offering instead "a new scientific estimate of feminine nature," *Sexes Throughout Nature* claims that though male and female organisms mature differently, they develop complementarily and on pace with each other.[12] Whatever vital power the female loses in reproduction and child-rearing, the male loses in hunting, fighting, and competing for female attention: the very pursuits celebrated by male evolutionists. Females, she writes, "bear and nourish their young children, at a cost of energy equal to the amount expended by [the male] as household provider."[13] Toppling Spencer's claim that females are more infantile than males, Blackwell goes as far as saying that the male who fights and struts is the more puerile, while "overburdened mothers have little energy to spare in becoming pugnacious ... or in growing worse than useless ornaments."[14] Because the energies of both sexes are equally taxed, they should balance each other at any comparable moment of development, but females have learned to be more frugal in the power they allow to dissipate. On the heels of the exclusion of women from scientific clubs like the Anthropological Society in 1871, Blackwell's argument is as politically provoked as it is biologically motivated. She seeks to convince her male contemporaries that, once the physical needs of reproduction and survival are met, women have even more energy for intellectual pursuits than do their fathers, brothers, and husbands.

Clear in her argument for women's education, Blackwell never questions women's seemingly inescapable domestication. For Blackwell, evolution is decided not on the battlefield but in the home, and thus the hero is not the soldier who fights for his brothers, but the mother who raises her children: "hence," she writes, "we find that among all higher animals it is the rule that the males shall expend the most energy in growth and locomotion, and shall be the active outside partners in every family firm," while "the females devote a corresponding larger share of direct force to social obligations, as more nutrition and care to the young, more skill, time, affection, and intellect to all direct family necessities."[15] By importing the commercial construction of the "family firm,"

Blackwell makes the unit of evolution not the individual, but the family. Her argument reverses Darwin's and Spencer's formulae: from the margins where male evolutionists had placed her, the female takes center stage in evolutionary processes – "no hereditary evolution is possible except through the prolonged maternal supervention" – while the male is only the "outside partner."[16] But as the outside partner, the male is the only one who exists on the outside. Evolution begins at home, but only the male has the ability to move out and to move on.

Blackwell's perpetuation of the "separate spheres" results from her reliance on Spencer's theory of heterogeneity. In "Progress: Its Law and Cause" (1857), Spencer argued that all progress is the "advance from homogeneity of structure to heterogeneity in structure," which he understands to include not merely the differentiation of cell structure in biological organisms but the division of classes and genders in advanced societies.[17] Blackwell rejects Spencer's diminution of female labor but still insists, "nature abhors a union too closely kindred."[18] Civilization, the ultimate goal of human evolution, needs femininity in juxtaposition to masculinity: the "beautiful instinctive love" that mothers feel for their children and "the deep, sisterly sympathy and aid" that they offer each other are the basis of our highest, civilizing feelings.[19] These "feminine" virtues appear even among animals: for example, the male lion is "the more fervid and more spirited," while the lioness is "the more constant and more maternal."[20] "Constant" and "maternal" are synonyms for Blackwell, and though she might mean only that mothers are less temperamental than their mates, her language suggests that, in contrast to the liveliness which makes the male lion successful, the female remains steady, passive, and unchanging. In Blackwell's scheme, maternal behavior is surprisingly uniform: female birds, lionesses, and women exhibit the same care, consistency, and empathetic impulses. In failing to make motherhood a variable quality, she denies Spencer's claim that females are ontogenically stunted only to affirm that they are phylogentically held back. Enabling evolution, motherhood is itself not a quality that evolves.

However, a new paradigm for a powerful and evolving motherhood appeared in a late Victorian natural history for children: Buckley's two-part series, *Life and Her Children: Glimpses of Animal Life from the Amœba to the Insects* (1880) and *The Winners in Life's Race; or, The Great Backboned Family* (1883).[21] At first glance, Buckley's work seems to offer a children's version of evolution inflected with stereotypical female virtue. The end of *Winners in Life's Race* asks readers to reevaluate their expectations that evolution "makes life a cruelty, and the world a battlefield" and to see instead in her portraits of animal life that "there is also love and gentleness, devotion and sacrifice for others, tender motherly and fatherly affection, true friendship, and a pleasure which consists in making others happy."[22] She says, "as strong, if not stronger, than the law of force and selfishness, *is that of mutual help and dependence.*" Writing about Buckley, Barbara T. Gates urges us to find more in her work than "Victorian sentimentality" emanating from "the female tradition of sympathy."[23] Instead, she places Buckley alongside well-known male evolutionists like Karl Kessler and Peter Kropotkin who were also trying to explain how human altruism could evolve out of brute nature.[24] For them, as for Buckley, the spontaneous acts of kindness and self-sacrifice among the social animals suggested an answer. But Buckley's contribution to the question of how morality evolved is even more singular and sophisticated than Gates claims. Whereas Kessler and Kropotkin focus on brotherly solidarity as the root of "mutual aid," Buckley not only argues that ethics is the out-growth of motherhood but also makes parental love a principle of evolution, thus going a step even beyond Blackwell.

Life and Her Children and *Winners in Life's Race* rely on a Lamarckian hierarchy of animals, but they innovatively rank species according to their commitment to parenting: from the insect who "has no interest in her children after they are born" and the fish guilty of "casting their eggs to the bottom of the sea" all the way up to the gestating mammalian mother who ensures that her unborn babies "go wherever she goes, the food which she takes feeds them, and they lie hidden, safe from danger, till they are born, perfectly formed, into the world."[25] Advances in motherhood drive animals up the evolutionary chain, but Buckley does not substantially differentiate animal mothers and fathers. She describes the elephant's trunk, with which the male "caresses those he loves, as gently as a mother strokes her child with her hand, or uses it to dash his enemy upon the ground, before he pierces him with his tusks or tramples him under foot," and the tiger's "soft paws in which the claws are hidden," that gently pat the little ones until "the claws are thrown forward, burying themselves in the flesh" of a rival or prey.[26] More than a half of a century later, Hubbard and Morgan would criticize Darwin for attributing organs of apprehension only to the male and those of reproduction only to the female, but Buckley was already insisting to her young readers that the appendages possessed by both sexes can sense, grasp, locomote, attack, and alternatively caress and protect. Buckley knows that "no tiger is so dangerous as is the mother tigress if any one approaches her young ones, or the lioness whose cubs are attacked," because the most advantageous adaptation is not the advance of military might but rather familial love.[27]

Despite the mammalian perfection of motherhood, however, birds are Buckley's featured players because they are nature's first parents. Their beaks and feet are designed for nest building, and those that make "the most perfect nests" rank as the highest types of birds.[28] Birds are distinguished from reptiles by their four-chambered hearts that pump warm blood. Buckley elides the anatomical condition of being warm-blooded and the metaphorically affective character of having a warm-heart, slyly melding morphology and morality into a single evolutionary leap: with birds, she says, "we find parental care beginning – the nest, the home, the feeding, the education in flying, in singing, in seeking food, the warm-hearted love which will risk death sooner than forsake the little ones."[29] Buckley's focus on nesting birds also allows her to break down further the presumed naturalness of the "separate spheres." Buckley's mother birds are not shut-ins, and her father birds are not deadbeat dads. The mother plover, perceiving a threat to her nestlings, for instance, will "move slowly away with a drooping wing as if wounded, hoping to make [the predator] follow her and pass by the little earthly hollow where her precious eggs are lying."[30] By moving away rather than staying at home, the plover protects its occupants. Nor is it the mother alone that guards the nest or even delivers the young. While ostrich "wives lay their eggs in a hole scooped in the sand," the fathers release the hatchlings from their shells: "pressing the large bare pad in front of his chest against each egg in turn," the male ostrich "breaks it, pulls out the membraneous bag with the young bird in it, shakes him out."[31] Parenting is an evolutionary imperative best shared.

Family care achieves its apotheosis in humans, not simply because we devote ourselves to our children as no other species does, but also because humanity, according to Buckley's texts, entails becoming a custodian to the entire natural world. Encouraging readers to see themselves as nature's parents is Buckley's pedagogical goal: *Life and Her Children* anticipates that the "glimpse of the labours of this great multitude," which it and its companion text provide, will help make readers "worthy to stand at the head of the vast family of Life's children."[32] Given the bird's pivotal role in the evolution of parenting, the final chapter of *Winners in Life's Race* is appropriately titled "A Bird's-Eye View of the Rise and Progress of Backboned Life." On the one hand, the chapter title is just a familiar metaphor connoting a wide lens view on the "panorama before us."[33] But, on the other hand, Buckley uses the metaphor literally: readers are meant to see with the caring and watchful eye of nature's first parent and protector. Not only do birds represent the first major step in the advance of "the tender love of mother for child," but the bird's eye view is also the watch of a sentinel safeguarding others: "many birds, such as rooks, starlings, wild geese, swans, and cranes, not only live in companies and exact obedience from their members, but even set sentinels to watch."[34] Thus, this "bird's eye view" at the end of *Winners in Life's Race* fulfills the promise at the beginning of *Life and Her Children*. This gathering of all life in one's visual scope resembles the colonizing stewardship that defined Kipling's masculine fantasy in *The Jungle Books*, but with this ethical distinction: unlike the imperialist, the consummate parent collects other beings only in her protective gaze, sympathizes with them, and sacrifices herself for them.

Motherhood, evolutionarily reinforced as female identity, dictated girls' education and extracurricular activities at the turn of the century, sometimes in Buckley's fashion of natural stewardship, but more often as a contradictory set of values and programs. Though the 1870 Elementary Education Act, establishing mandatory education in England and Wales, prompted questions about what kind of education could best serve all pupils from all social classes, the courses in which students were actually enrolled quickly split along gender lines. In Victorian England, the girls who did attend schools (though the percentage was small) received a practical education in homemaking: washing and cooking were the main staples of working-class girls' education in the 1870s and 1880s, while middle-class girls were compelled to take so much needlework that their coursework in mathematics was sometimes cut short.[35] Calls to expand female education still invoked motherhood as girls' principal destination, but new conceptions of what constituted a healthy female body sharply contrasted the Victorian ideal of "angelic" female fragility. Turn of the century school reformers, usually working in large girls' schools, argued that good mothers required fit bodies capable of gestating and delivering healthy children. Claudia Nelson's *Boys Will Be Girls: The Feminine Ethic and British Children's Fiction, 1857–1917* (1991) argues that attitudes toward girls' bodies shifted as concerns about a world war grew: "as fears about national decadence increased, ill health became unpatriotic, an indication that women were lax in not understanding that strong mothers bore strong soldiers."[36] In *The New Girl: Girls' Culture in England, 1880-1915* (1995), Sally Mitchell likewise says, "the medical awareness that exercise improved women's health and childbearing capacity contended ambivalently with fears of masculinization."[37] Despite this ambivalence, by the turn of the century, the pedagogy of motherhood was ironically starting to collapse the "separate spheres" of the school.

In youth organizations, this separation was even harder to maintain. Mitchell writes that within the first year of the Boy Scouts, six thousand or so girls had independently followed the Scouting rules, performed the tasks, and wrote to the headquarters requesting badges.[38] Like Buckley's fierce tigress, these girls did not seem worried that being physically capable would desex them. Partly to fend off the legions of girls asking to join the Scouts, Baden-Powell helped his sister Agnes Baden-Powell to form The Girl Guides in the United Kingdom and Juliette Low to establish The Girl Scouts in the United States. Now that exercise was a sanctioned preparation for motherhood, Agnes Baden-Powell's and Low's handbook for Guides and Girl Scouts could assert: "it is the duty of each one of us, both for our own sakes, and for the benefit of future generations, to perfect our physical frame."[39] Male evolutionists like Hall may have been uncomfortable with female recapitulation, but Scouting and kindred organizations were no less indebted to evolutionary thought when girls participated. Charlotte Gulick, who founded the Camp Fire Girls in 1910, said "if we go back as far as we possibly can in the life of the race, we come to a very primitive time when human life centered around the camp-fire."[40] In *Growing Girls: The Natural Origins of Girls' Organizations in America* (2007), Susan Miller shows that clubs like the Camp Fire Girls and the Girl Scouts recast camping as primitive housekeeping and rechristened nature study as sympathetic engagement.[41] At the heart of this new relationship between girls and nature was the broader conception of motherhood that Buckley identified as the "bird's eye view" by which Girl Scouts were to see themselves as the protectors of wildlife. Thus, in addition to "Athletics," girls were awarded merit badges for "Housekeeper," "Cook," "Child-Nurse," and "Birding" because, as their motto proudly claimed, "A Girl Scout is a Friend to Animals."[42]

Evolutionary theory and recapitulation, though primarily male-focused for Victorians, opened the door to new responsibilities and activities for girls in the next century. The need for strong mothers was a by-product of the perceived need for strong sons. The degeneration fears resulting from the Boer Wars, when so many of the young men wishing to enlist were found physically unfit, sought a solution that looked past the individual boy to the mother who bore him. Yet despite the relegation of girls to the singular identity as future mothers of boys, the focus on an evolutionarily fit motherhood made girls' education, girls' exercise, and girls' recapitulation culturally acceptable and, indeed, culturally necessary. Blackwell's argument that the family, rather than the individual, is the unit selected in evolution and her claim that the female's reproductive function does not deplete her energies for intellectual endeavors, Buckley's attention to the familial instincts that give rise to the social values and her insistence that motherhood is an evolving set of strategies that pushes the animal kingdom ever upward, and new initiatives promoting girls' health and outdoor activity chipped away at the Victorian ideal of the "angel of the house." However, there was a darker side to this newly empowered and physically robust image of motherhood. Girls were encouraged not only to improve their bodies and minds in order to care for children but also to make reproductive choices according to the new "science" of eugenics. This branch of the motherhood ethos sought to empower middle-class white girls at the cost of their non-white, working-class sisters and brothers.

Eugenics for girls

Francis Galton, Darwin's cousin, coined the term "eugenics" in 1883 as part of a project to save the English race from its own worst degenerative tendencies.[43] By constructing elaborate genealogies of eminent families and encouraging bachelors and bachelorettes to choose only spouses from family trees pure of instances of insanity, criminality, and degeneration, Galton hoped to improve future generations. By the end of the 1880s, eugenics seemed a promising domain for the assertion of a distinctly female agency, a science befitting the "New Woman." In *Love and Eugenics in the Late Nineteenth-Century Novel* (2003), Angelique Richardson argues, "social purists and eugenic feminists increasingly emphasized the importance of female choice of a reproductive partner, replacing male passion with female selection."[44] Women, she writes, could assume the responsibility for "introduc[ing] the idea of direction and progress into human development."[45] Maternal care for one's children was certainly powerful, but not nearly as powerful as being able to determine the character of those children in the first place. In the early decades of the twentieth century, with the rediscovery of Gregor Mendel's theory of genetics and its synthesis with evolutionary biology, eugenics gained scientific footing and popular appeal in England, where Galton had introduced it, and in the United States, where eugenic policies were codified as state law.[46] Eugenicists in both countries urged political measures and pedagogical programs aimed at educating youths in what became known as "civic eugenics." Because eugenics already appealed to late Victorian feminism, the target for this new program and the principles of sexual selection was not primarily boys, but girls.

In the last decade of the nineteenth century, selection became integral to the discourse surrounding motherhood. Like Blackwell's *Sexes Throughout Nature*, Eliza Burt Gamble's *The Evolution of Woman: An Inquiry into the Dogma of Her Inferiority to Man* (1893) maintains that "motherhood was the primary bond by which society was bound together," but this is a bond forged before the child is born or, indeed, conceived.[47] Gamble, a Michigan schoolteacher, draws from Darwin's *Descent of Man* the claim that physiological characteristics like birds' plumes and bucks' horns are the result of male competition for female interest and reproductive possibilities. To Gamble, this means that, in choosing her mate from among potential male suitors, "the female takes the place of the human breeder. In other words, she represents the intelligent factor . . . [S]he is the primary cause of the very characters through which man's superiority over woman has been gained."[48] In other words, the female fulfills the role not merely of the human breeder, but of personified (or deified) Natural Selection. And because the female designs her mate to suit herself, his superiority is only an illusion masking hers. Gamble writes, "as a stream may not rise higher than its source, or as the creature may not surpass its creator in excellence," the male of the species cannot best his female selector. She chooses which males reproduce and, therefore, which genetic mutations prevail and which are extinguished.

As with Blackwell, however, this near-deified authority does not unseat the female from her domestic duty. Continuing Blackwell's thoughts on energy consumption and conservation, Gamble maintains that, while the male wastes his energy in vain adaptations like plumes, horns, tusks, and other "appendages which lie outside the line of true development," "females have managed to do without."[49] These females are Blackwell's "overburdened mothers" with "little energy to spare," frugal Victorian housewives who "do without" for the good of their family. Gamble extends this self-sacrifice into the sexual realm, where she otherwise gives the female the unprecedented power of choice. This move is tellingly summed up in her description of sexual selection among birds: "the female made the male beautiful that she might endure his caressess" [*sic*].[50] Self-sacrificing even in the unwelcome act of copulation, Gamble's females demonstrate how this version of sexual selection was, according to Richardson, "assisted by the association of women with passionlessness which was fermenting in evangelical and biological discourse."[51] If women were free of the desire that ruled male sexual choices, they could be guided by reason and duty alone.

In her study of Gamble's contributions to evolutionary theory, Rosemary Jann writes, "Gamble's vision of true womanhood has more in common with the logic of domestic ideology that Nancy Armstrong traces through the Victorian novel, in which female virtue overcomes male aggression and competitiveness and subordinates it to nurturing love."[52] Gamble turns the females of all species into middle-class heroines exercising sexual modesty, prudent choice, and domestic economy.

Increasingly over the next two decades, this new account of the female's role in evolution was translated into a directive for young women and girls. In *The Awakening of Women; or, Woman's Part in Evolution* (1899), for instance, feminist reformer Frances Swiney pleads with female readers to "be scrupulously careful in choosing their partners in life, as to character rather than talent, to healthiness and purity of body and mind, rather than to affluence of position and station."[53] Swiney's advice to young women updates Galton's system, focusing on health rather than wealth and good qualities above good families. Such directives were underscored by medical professionals. Scottish physician Caleb Williams Saleeby extended his praise for "the vast importance of motherhood as a factor in the evolution of all the higher species of animals" into the nation's budding interest in eugenics.[54] In addition to Swiney's list of desirable genetic traits – character, health, and purity – Saleeby's sternly titled *Parenthood and Race Culture: A Outline of Eugenics* (1909) emphasizes that prospective mothers and fathers must select mates who want to be parents and who, thereby, exhibit their possession of a parenting "instinct": "when children are born only to those who love children, and who will tend to transmit their high measure of that parental instinct from which all love is derived, we shall bring to earth a heaven compared with which the theologians' is but a fool's paradise."[55] Not only will smart sexual selection stem the tide of degeneration, according to eugenicists like Saleeby and Swiney, but it will also propel the race to unimagined evolutionary heights.

Children's literature was receptive to the eugenic message. As early as the 1860s, Charles Kingsley's moralized evolution in *The Water-Babies: A Fairy Tale for a Land-Baby* (1863) hints at eugenic politics: his parable of the divergent family lineages resulting in the noble salmon and their debased trout cousins and his "History of the Doasyoulikes" show child readers the benefit of preserving only the evolutionarily "fit."[56] In the United States, and likewise in American children's literature, eugenics was more eagerly adopted and institutionalized as law. Across the Atlantic, according to Edwin Black's *War Against the Weak* (2003), Galton's "quaint theories of felicitous marriages among the better classes, yielding incrementally superior offspring, were discarded in favor of wholesale reproductive prohibition for the inferior classes."[57] In Jack London's *Before Adam* (1907), the hero belongs to the doomed tribe called "the Folk," but his progeny survives because he mates with a woman from the more evolutionarily viable "Fire People."[58] Discussing the novel, Lisa Hopkins argues that "the suggestive similarities between the Folk and Native Americans" overlay the United States' policies of genocide and eugenics onto London's primitive man fantasy.[59] Appealing specifically to girls, American author Jean Webster's *Dear Enemy* (1915) – a sequel to her girls' novel *Daddy Long-Legs* (1912) – introduces Sallie McBride, the director of an orphanage who is unequivocal about her mission to foster the best human specimens and, falling for a handsome eugenicist doctor, picks out the "unimpeachable heredity" of some of her charges and the "unspeakable heredity," "alcoholic heredity," and "morbid heredity" of others.[60] *Dear Enemy* resembles what literary critic Dana Seitler terms "regeneration narratives" in turn-of-the-century American literature, in which female protagonists right the wrongs of modern living by committing to eugenic maternity.[61]

The Girl Guides in the United Kingdom and the Girl Scouts and Camp Fire Girls in the United States did not teach their members sexual morality, eugenic or otherwise, but they nevertheless received approval from advocates of genetic engineering. In *Growing Girls*, Miller illuminates several links between these girl societies and the eugenic movement. For instance, the eugenic *Journal of Heredity* praised girls' clubs in a 1915 article that announced: "fitness for motherhood is a happy by-product of Camp Fire activities, which make for a splendid physique and intelligent control of one's own body and mind."[62] The Camp Fire Girls' founders Gulick and her husband Luther were more explicit than their counterparts in the Girl Guides and Girl Scouts; they advertised their program with the assertion that "Camp Fire education is helping to shape a new race."[63] Agnes Baden-Powell and Low employed eugenic language when their handbook, *How Girls Can Help Their Country*, said that "a weak, inform physique" was "nothing less than a crime."[64] Perhaps as a sign of the times, Miller notes that by the 1920 edition of *The Girl Scouts Handbook*, an almost word-for-word reprint of the earlier handbook, the criminalization of the weak body has been removed.[65] The United States' investment in eugenics started to recede after the First World War, but it had already left its mark (even if some of its visible traces were erased) on children's literature, female education, and girls' social clubs.

Though organizations like the Camp Fire Girls, the Girl Guides, and the Girl Scouts could seemingly support both recapitulation and eugenicist agendas, the idea that childhood development repeats the history of the species and the hope that informed sexual selection will provide future generations with only the best traits are not theoretically compatible. In fact, it was Mendel's work on genetics rediscovered in the early twentieth century that impelled a practicable theory of eugenics and that, not coincidentally, discredited recapitulation.[66] Recapitulation holds that organisms are determined by the position they achieve along an ascending ladder of forms, but genetics teaches that they are governed by genes alone: individual development cannot correct for inherited deficiencies. What the individual can control, according to eugenics, is which traits are perpetrated into the next generation. Narratively, recapitulation and eugenics also found contrasting genres: the first spawned violent adventures for boys and the second, idealistic romances for girls. Despite these irreconcilable differences, however, the fantasy of the girl rediscovering her primal nature by housekeeping and mothering in the (semi)wilds and the imperative for the same girl to choose the right set of genes from a selection of mates, improving herself and ensuring the success of her family group at the same time, came together in a significant piece of children's literature pivotally placed during mounting expectation of a world war.

Flower girls and mother hens

While *Sara Crewe; or, What Happened at Miss Minchin's Boarding School* (1888) is Burnett's more obvious school story, *The Secret Garden* inducts its characters Mary, Dickon Sowerby, and Colin Craven into a program of open air, outdoor education drawn along the lines of the Boy and Girl Scouts and the American summer camp.[67] Removing Mary from India and transporting her to England in its first chapters, Burnett's novel offers both a transgendering and a geographical inversion of the boy's recapitulation in Kipling's *Jungle Books* (1894 and 1894). For Kipling, as shown in the last chapter, the British had overshot the point of evolutionary perfection and were now in decline; rescuing the race meant reviving the boy's and the species' recapitulative past best represented by the colonial native intimate with the jungle beasts and the Indian landscape. For Burnett's girl, however, it is the English countryside – marked by the garden rather than the jungle – that enables her to reconnect with deep human history and enjoy the natural development that India was unable to provide. Burnett's replacement of India with England suggests that the girl's maternal development has opposite requirements to the boy's military ascent. From this reversal, however, *The Secret Garden*'s adoption of evolutionary theory into a narrative of female development drives Burnett's novel to confront questions about the content and character of girls' nature, the affective and eugenic components of motherhood, and the expansion of the customary focus on the individual to encompass the development of the family unit instead.

The literary trope of young men and boys leaving the urban centers of England and traveling to the colonies in order to regain their manhood is ubiquitous in Victorian and Edwardian fiction.[68] The late-nineteenth- and early-twentieth-century recapitulationists did not invent this wish-fulfilling and empire-affirming plot, but they obligingly gave it an evolutionary gloss. Hall best condensed the dominant sense that "our urbanized hothouse life ... tends to ripen everything before its time."[69] City life for Hall, like the overcivilized Western polities for Kipling, rushes its denizens through their natural stages of development, thrusting them into an old age well before their time. To reawaken the natural vigor of ontogenic and phylogenic youth, men must travel to the British colonies or the American West. But *The Secret Garden* reverses this route: it is India rather than England that causes premature ripening and decay. Transported from India after her parents' deaths to her uncle's Yorkshire estate, the ten-year-old Mary appears to the servants like an "old woman," without the natural vitality of childhood. [70] She explains to the gardener Ben Weatherstaff that "everything is hot, and wet, and green after the rains in India ... And I think things grow up in a night." Ben responds that in England, by contrast, the flowers "won't grow up in a night ... Tha'll have to wait for 'em" (39). While Burnett echoes turn-of-the-century evolutionists like Hall, as well as children's writers like Kipling, in imagining that different cultures represent varying degrees of evolutionary development and in advocating the slow development that allows ample time for childhood, she finds the right pace for female development only in England.

The evolutionary principle better exemplified in England than in India is motherhood. The obvious association of Mary with flowers – flowers that grow too fast in India, just right in England, the flowers of the secret garden that has been locked up and neglected for ten years, exactly Mary's age, etc. – has caused literary scholars to overlook Mary's association with animals. But the animals in Burnett's novel function as developmental markers and are evaluated, like those in Buckley's *Life and Her Children* and *Winners in Life's Race*, according to their parenting abilities. In India, Mary encounters insects and reptiles: for example, the snake that "slipped under the door" and left her all alone after her parents died from cholera

(6). The snake, a cold-blooded reptile that abandons its offspring as soon as they hatch, resembles Mary's own mother, neglectful of her daughter long before her fatal illness. Meanwhile, during the cholera outbreak, the Indians are "dying like flies" (5); here Burnett uses a common cliché but one that, in the animal imagery that runs throughout the novel, suggests that India offers only a base, insect-like form of life. Like the snake that does not care for its own family and the flies for which no one else cares, Mary is heartless and insignificant while in India. But when she moves to Yorkshire and befriends the English robins, she learns to sympathize with others. The English environment and its natural fauna work on Mary "until her blood had grown warm" (30). This "warm-bloodedness" operates in the same double manner as it did for Buckley: Mary is becoming more caring and unselfish, less like the reptiles and insects she knew in India and more like the advanced English birds.

As they were in Buckley's two-part natural history, birds are again the principal actors of *The Secret Garden*. Unlike the insects and reptiles for which there exists neither parenting nor childhood, the robin nestlings begin a slow maturation under their parents' watchful eyes. Once in Yorkshire, Mary meets Dickon, a peasant boy who lives with his family near her uncle's estate and who knows all the habits of the local wildlife.[71] Early in their friendship, he draws her attention to the careful way the robins build their nest: "Has tha' noticed how th' robin an' his mate has been workin' while we've been sittin' here? Look at him perched on that branch wonderin' where it'd be best to put that twig he's got in his beak . . . Tha' knew how to build tha' nest before tha' came out o' th' egg" (96). The robin is the perfect parent, building his nest without dearth, surfeit, or waste. Over the human characters whose homes are lacking (the desolate house of Mary's youth in India and the cold mansion of her English uncle), the birds have the advantage of instinct. As Dickon says, the robins know how to parent even before any actual hatchlings make demands on them. In contrast, Mary has no positive parental models of her own and has to learn from the birds how to be both a homemaker and a mother. Dickon instructs her about their work in the garden: "us is nest-buildin' too" (96). From the English birds, Mary learns what she never could from the insects and reptiles in India or from her own parents. Here, she is inducted into the natural lessons of motherhood.

Though largely left to explore her uncle's estate on her own rather than as part of a troop, Mary plays the part of a Girl Scout for much of *The Secret Garden*. In line with the ethos of girls' organizations, for example, being in nature gives Mary opportunities for friendships with animals. Though she has no friends when she first arrives in England, she quickly takes an interest in the robin perched on the wall of the concealed garden. Dickon tells her, "Aye, he's a friend o' yours," and Mary cannot contain her excitement: "'Do you think he is?' cried Mary eagerly. She did so want to know. 'Do you think he really likes me?'" (58). Her rehabilitation in the English air likewise signals *The Secret Garden*'s relevance to the recent extension of scouting, camping, and fresh-air exercise to girls. According to Miller's *Growing Girls*, girls' clubs promoted "plenty of good food, twenty-four-hour days in the open air, an intimate acquaintanceship with the fields and the woods, and a practical lesson in cleanliness and hygiene."[72] Mary's sour temperament and the forfeiture of her childhood in India are marked by her lack of fresh air – "fresh air" being a phrase that the novel repeats at least thirty times – and her poor appetite. Susan Sowerby, Dickon's mother and the novel's supreme maternal voice, advises the servants tending Mary to "let her play out in th' fresh air skippin' and it'll stretch her legs an' arms an' give her some strength in 'em" (43). The physical and moral effects of the "the fresh, strong, pure air" are immediate: "just as it had given her an appetite, and fighting with the wind had stirred her blood, so the same things had stirred her mind" (41). Burnett's girl readers – perhaps involved with the Scouts or the Guides – may have found commonalities with Mary's program of rejuvenation outside the walls of Misselthwaite Manor.

Burnett's insistence on the benefits of fresh air and her focus on the garden have led scholars to connect *The Secret Garden* and Friedrich Froebel's kindergarten.[73] Before Spencer penned his prescription for elementary education based on evolution, Froebel wrote in *The Education of Man* (1826), "out-door life, in open nature, is particularly desirable for young people; it develops, strengthens, elevates, and ennobles."[74] For Froebel, the garden is an apt metaphor for the ideal school because the space recalls an early moment in human history, not according to a biological narrative but a biblical one. He says, "in the mind of man, in the history of his mental development, in the growth of his consciousness, in the experience of every child from the time of his appearance on earth to the time when he consciously beholds himself in the garden of Eden, in beautiful nature spread out before him, there is repeated the history of the creation and development of all things."[75] Because the Garden of Eden was man's first home, the modern garden constitutes the young child's natural environment. The obvious metaphorical connection between Mary and flowers in *The Secret Garden* evokes a host of familiar literary, scientific, and pedagogical lineages that predate and extend Froebel's kindergarten. Phyllis Bixler, for instance, argues that Burnett revives Jean-Jacques

Rousseau, who "described the child itself as a young plant to be carefully tended."[76] James R. Kincaid identifies an entire genre of child-rearing manuals that play on "the child-botanical."[77] Maude Hines reveals a long history of children's literature that turns girls into flowers.[78] And tracing a "botanical vernacular" from Carl Linnaeus through the nineteenth century, Amy M. King isolates what she calls "the bloom narrative," in which marriage plots employ botanical metaphors to represent sexual courtship "without transgressing the boundaries of decorum."[79] As both Mary's classroom and the setting for her interactions with boys, Burnett's garden seems to tread familiar metaphorical territory.

But in the early twentieth century, botanical metaphors were taking on new significance in the increasingly public discourse about eugenics, to which Burnett's years of living in the United States had likely introduced her.[80] Flowers and other plants commonly featured in early genetic experimentation, from Dutch botanist Hugo de Vries's use of the primrose to demonstrate breeding and heredity to the centrality of the pea pod in Mendel's discovery of laws of genetic mutation. While individual plants practically functioned in genetic science, the garden as a collection of beautiful and beneficial flora, on the one hand, and unwanted weeds, on the other, became a metaphor in eugenic propaganda about whole biological systems and the dangers of unsupervised propagation. Joseph DeJarnett's poem, "Mendel's Law: A Plea for a Better Race of Men" (1921), for example, implores readers: "Look at the garden beds,/ The cabbage, the lettuce and turnips,/ Even the beets are thoroughbreds;/ Then look at the many children/ With hands like the monkey's paw,/ Bowlegged, flat headed, and foolish – / Bred true to Mendel's Law."[81] The characterization of some children as weeds appears just as often in works about childhood and literature for children. Jane Hume Clapperton's *Vision of the Future: Based on the Application of Ethical Principles* (1904), a manifesto for eugenic education, encourages young people to survey gardens and to observe "plants creep[ing] into unfavorable conditions" before the gardener asserts control, in order to illustrate the same need for reproductive laws in human society.[82] In Webster's *Dear Enemy*, Sallie converts the kindergarten metaphor into a eugenic flowerbed: she thinks, "there are so many possibilities in our child garden for every kind of flower. It has been planted rather promiscuously, to be sure, but though we undoubtedly shall gather a number of weeds, we are also hoping for some rare and beautiful blossoms."[83] Within the eugenic metaphor, Rousseau's and Froebel's gardens of self-developing children now required an exterminator.

Not to be overlooked, then, is the fact that Mary's rejuvenation in *The Secret Garden* occurs when she is busy weeding. Though she knows nothing about gardening, Mary's first act in the garden is rescuing the little green points suffocating among the weeds: "she searched about until she found a rather sharp piece of wood and knelt down and dug and weeded out the weeds and grass until she made nice little clear places around them" (48). A few pages later, Dickon explicitly describes the garden in terms of a Darwinian struggle for existence: "th' strongest ones has fair thrived on [being left alone]. The delicate ones has died out, but th' others has growed an' growed, an' spread an' spread" (61). Associating some children with flowers, *The Secret Garden* complementarily suggests that other children might be weeds. This extension of the analogy frames the plot of the novel when Mary is confronted with the choice between spending time outdoors with the poor but healthy Dickon and being ensconced inside the dark manor house with her rich but physically decrepit and emotionally disturbed cousin Colin. Her choice between these two playmates calls up the eugenic dilemma in quite clear terms: Dickon is "very clean" with "cheeks ... red as poppies" and "such round and such blue eyes" as Mary had never seen (57), while Colin has "a sharp, delicate face the color of ivory ... like a boy who had been ill" (73). Burnett's attentiveness to drawing up such criteria recalls Swiney's plea in *The Awakening of Women* to select "healthiness and purity of body" over "affluence of position and station." According to the eugenic script that was contemporaneously being geared to young girls (surely some members of Burnett's audience) the correct choice is obvious: Mary should pick the blooming Dickon over the weedy Colin.

The Secret Garden totters on the edge of this "regeneration narrative," to use Seitler's term, but ultimately resists it. Colin is not, after all, suffering from any inherited weakness; his humpback is a delusion cured by positive thoughts and "fresh air" exercises in the garden. At the novel's close, the three children are "a healthy likable lot," forming a fit "collection of sturdy little bodies and round red-cheeked faces, each one grinning in its own particular way" (168). But even before Colin's psychological rejuvenation, Mary refuses to make the eugenic choice seemingly put before her. Alternating between the garden and the manor, maintaining her friendships with both boys though separately, Mary "did not want to see Colin as much as she wanted to see Dickon," but, the narrator is sure to tell us, "she wanted to see [Colin] very much" (83). Mary may not understand this as sexual selection, but she does comprehend something of motherhood. In fact, Mary uses her education in the art of motherhood to avoid the eugenic choice: she invites Colin to join Dickon and her in the garden as their figurative son, whom they nurse and teach to walk just under the nest where the robins are teaching their chicks to fly. *The Secret Garden*, thus, casts aside eugenics to advocate instead for an expansive and empathetic foster family. Though the shift in the novel's attention from Mary to Colin and his recovery compromises feminist readings of the novel, Burnett's choice to expand her attention from the singular female protagonist to the family unit results from her rejection of the eugenic plot and her privileging instead an ideal of motherhood closer to Blackwell's and Buckley's: the good mother does not select among suitable mates, but sacrifices herself for the success of all her natural and adoptive (actual and figurative) progeny. The movement away from Mary testifies to her maturation as a prospective mother; the narrative form that female recapitulation takes demonstrates an evolution of the self outward, from a singular hero to a community constituted by multiple protagonists.

Given Burnett's adoption of the bird as nature's paradigmatic parent and the outward expansion of sympathy validated by the novel, it is no wonder that *The Secret Garden* also takes a "bird's eye view" similar to Buckley's fantasy of maternal omni-vision. Once Colin starts learning that his invalidism is only a delusion, the narrative shifts from the ground to the treetops and sees through the eyes of the father robin. Initially alarmed by Colin's clumsy ambulation, the observing robin remembers:

> [W]hen he himself had been made to learn to fly by his parents he had done much the same sort of thing. He had taken short flights of a few yards and then had been obliged to rest. So it occurred to him that this boy was learning to fly – or rather to walk. He mentioned this to his mate and when he told her that the Eggs would probably conduct themselves in the same way after they were fledged she was quite comforted and even became eagerly interested and derived great pleasure from watching the boy over the edge of her nest – though she always thought that the Eggs would be much cleverer and learn more quickly. (152–153)

The bird's identification with the boy enables the reader's identification with the bird; we are united because we were all once children in need of parental love and patience.[84] Burnett's use of the robins departs from Margaret Gatty's treatment of bird observers in "Inferior Animals" (1861), where a group of pontificating rooks assess man's evolution as inferior to their own.[85] Burnett's robins note the similarity of all children and the duty toward them shared by all the higher parents of the animal world. Though Burnett primarily uses the father robin's eyes, this point of view is aligned with the maternal gaze. A few pages later, Susan Sowerby, reiterates almost verbatim the robin's sentiments: "when [the children] told her about the robin and the first flights of the young ones she laughed a motherly little mellow laugh in her throat. 'I suppose learnin' 'em to fly is like learnin' children to walk" (161). The perfect mother, the father robin, the girl learning her lessons from both, and now the reader share the point of view that is the ethical directive of the novel: to see all nature's creatures as one's own children and to tend the whole world as if it were a nest filled with them.[86]

Burnett's use of the garden to reject eugenics forges an unlikely alliance between Burnett and Huxley. Perhaps because it was a popular eugenic metaphor, Huxley employed the garden in his anti-eugenic polemic *Evolution and Ethics* (1893–1894). Unlike eugenicists who argued that sexual selection must continue the work of natural selection, to weed out the weak, Huxley sought to establish a clear-cut division between natural processes and human ethics: what he dubs the "cosmic" and the "horticultural" processes. According to Huxley, human civilization began when man stopped adapting himself to his environment and started adapting his environment to himself; "in short," he says, civilization began when a previously wild patch of land "was made into a garden."[87] Huxley chooses the garden because the garden bears the signs of man's work fitting the landscape to his needs. "The horticultural process," he says, is composed "not of selection, but of that other function of the gardener, the creation of conditions more favorable than those of the state of nature."[88] If this is the work that the garden performs in Burnett's novel, then *The Secret Garden* might give us a coherent recapitulative narrative for the girl protagonist. Mary leaves India, where orphaned children rush toward maturity, and moves to England, where nature is rife with good mothers and a corresponding slow childhood. Here she matures from a flower to a bird to a gardener, bypassing the eugenic plot, and instead mimicking in her own development the stage of early human history when culture is born, selection (both natural and sexual) is deemphasized in favor of family survival, and individual evolution is replaced by communal civilization.

Imaginary gardens with real girls in them

Mary's evolution into figural motherhood may be a victory for human ethics (over selfish individualism and eugenic extermination), but most readers agree that it is a defeat for female agency. From the point that Colin regains the ability to walk, about two-thirds into the novel, the narrative takes him as its main focus, and pages elapse in which we barely hear Mary speak. Refusing to choose either Dickon or Colin as a mate, Mary escapes a eugenicist trap, but she relinquishes the power that writers like Gamble and Swiney thought women naturally possessed within an evolutionary paradigm. Fittingly, albeit disappointingly, while Mary is associated with birds, Colin is compared to a "new-born lamb," a more advanced mammal (115). The novel's reassurance that Colin, the English aristocratic white male, is not really crippled may have been a welcome salve on the eve of the First World War, but it does little to reassure the girl that her development has equal import to that of her more nationally significant brothers (or male cousins). Regardless of the novel's initial focus on Mary, Burnett figures the boy's rise to mastery as the inevitable continuation of the girl's move to motherhood. But the novel's characters are not determined by biology alone; indeed, evolution did not provide Burnett her only, or her primary, frame of reference. Though the novel promotes the physical and political superiority of boys over girls, *The Secret Garden* privileges creative agency over corporeal presence: the boy is the master of the "garden," but the girl controls its "secret."

The conclusion of *The Secret Garden* flaunts Colin's textual, biological, political, and economic dominance. When Colin finally recovers his legs, the children decide to race, and he "burst through [the garden gate] at full speed and, without seeing the outsider [his father], dashed almost into his arms" (171). Not only is Colin the "winner of the race," a title Buckley uses to designate evolutionary success, but he exhibits none other than the power of locomotion: that ineluctable sexual difference that, for Darwin, secured the male's biological superiority. Mary's physicality simply cannot compete with Colin's; the boy, stunted for a decade, easily surpasses the girl. Received by his father, Colin also asserts his place in the patrilineal descent that makes him the uncontested heir to the Craven estate. His preparation for this role is made clear when Mary and Dickon first carry him into the garden that they lovingly tended and he declares, "it is my garden now" (133). This is an odd assertion of authority within the novel. Earlier, Susan Sowerby expresses what sounds like a moral takeaway: "when I was at school," she says to the housekeeper at Misselthwaite Manor, "my jography told as th' world was shaped like a orange an' I found out before I was ten that th' whole orange doesn't belong to nobody . . . don't you – none o' you – think as you own th' whole orange or you'll find out you're mistaken, an' you won't find it out without hard knocks" (114). Less than twenty pages later, however, ten-year-old Colin affirms his ownership of the whole orange to no protest, and his claim, far from being challenged by the novel, is fully sanctioned by its conclusion. The last words of the novel again reinforce the diminishment of Mary and the narrative transcendence of not only the boy but also his title: "Master Colin!" (173).

The shift from Mary to Colin has understandably dissatisfied contemporary and modern readers, some of whom have tried to explain it away.[89] Bixler, for instance, casts the garden as the novel's protagonist: "if one regards the book's 'heroes' to be neither Mary nor Colin but rather its community of mothers centered in the secret garden," she says, then "the last part of *The Secret Garden* need not be considered disappointing."[90] But Colin's declaration that the garden is his property places this locus of the maternal community under male ownership, which hardly mollifies readers' frustration. The garden's transition from a communal space into a male-owned private property rather carries out the progression of civilization that Gamble describes in *The Evolution of Woman*. While Gamble asserts a continuum between female animals' power of selection and matriarchies in primitive human culture, she accounts for the current Victorian patriarchy by imagining an upheaval, wherein men seized "ownership of the soil" and secured patriarchal lines of inheritance and ultimately effected "the usurpation by man of the natural rights and privileges of woman."[91] According to Jann, Gamble's theory combined scant anthropological evidence about matriarchies and her recent reading of Fredric Engels.[92] Though *The Secret Garden* does not rise to a full Marxist condemnation of private property, Colin's usurpation alters the garden from the semi-wild and unclaimed space that the children shared.

Burnett does not deny Colin's claim to the land, but *The Secret Garden* relishes in the state of the garden before it comes under masculine control and ownership. For Mary (the girl) and Dickon (the peasant), the garden is most beautiful when it is not fully cultivated. Dickon says, "I wouldn't want to make it look like a gardener's garden, all clipped an' spick an' span ... It's nicer like this with things runnin' wild, an' swingin' an' catchin' hold of each other," and Mary agrees, pleading "don't let us make it tidy" (63). The children's resistance to Victorian rules of propriety differentiates *The Secret Garden* from earlier literature that moralized nature, like Maria Hack's *Harry Beaufoy* (1821) and Gatty's "Training and Restraining" (1855). Hack's Mrs. Beaufoy praises her son Harry's garden for its "order and design," and in Gatty's story, a girl sees her garden devastated by a storm and learns the dangers of giving in to passions and waywardness.[93] But Mary and Dickon enjoy the sensuality and physical healthiness of the half-wild garden. According to Nelson, Burnett "redefin[es] sexuality, and physicality in general, as selfless and good. The Angel is still present ... but she has become fertile."[94] More than this, however, Hack's and Gatty's obedient, tidy children have disappeared, and in their place are children creatively manipulating their environment for their own pleasure and in deference to their own ethical code. Mary's and Dickon's disdain for the tidy garden rejects the eugenic metaphor of the perfect garden with its flowers daintily ordered by types. This passage also expresses a nostalgia for the early stages of Huxley's "horticultural process," before human culture so segregated its dominions from the natural landscape and gardens became estates systemized and denaturalized by male-generated contracts and codicils.

Though *The Secret Garden* cedes the physical garden to Colin, the novel makes readers yearn for its status as the half-tended secret that Mary initiates and supervises. In addition to its training for motherhood, English nature conveys lessons in secrecy. Mary is the first to find the garden, but as soon as she learns that secrets are not only to be kept but also to be shared, secrets construct the three children as a family. Before Mary and Dickon physically transport Colin into the garden, she imaginatively transports her still bedridden cousin with the stories she tells him about the garden while it is still unclaimed and untidy:

> "I think it has been left alone so long – that it has grown all into a lovely tangle. I think the roses have climbed and climbed and climbed until they hang from the branches and walls and creep over the ground – almost like a strange gray mist ... Perhaps they are coming up through the grass – perhaps there are clusters of purple crocuses and gold ones – even now. Perhaps the leaves are beginning to break out and uncurl – and perhaps – the gray is changing and a green gauze veil is creeping – and creeping over – everything. And the birds are coming to look at it – because it is – so safe and still. And perhaps – perhaps – perhaps –" [Mary said] very softly and slowly indeed, "the robin has found a mate – and is building a nest." (106)

Mary speaks speculatively – "perhaps ... perhaps ... perhaps" – because she has not yet decided to tell Colin that she has found a way into the garden. Wary of making the garden seem too real and exposing that she has been inside, Mary tells Colin a version of the garden that mixes physical reality and imaginative dream. The "strange gray mist" that eerily changes into "a green gauze veil" that "is creeping – and creeping – over everything" is Mary's creation. Her provisional insertions ("perhaps"), participles ("coming," "beginning," "creeping," "building"), and repetitions ("climbed and climbed and climbed"), color the secret garden as her own invention distinct from the material garden that Colin will usurp by the novel's end. Even though the narrator irritatingly asserts that "Colin had more imagination than she had" (121) and predicts "the great scientific discoveries" he will make inside the real garden (138), the pulsating yet half-whispered secret that Mary breathes into Colin's ear is the garden that matters to the readers.

Secrecy opens up possibilities for communities and styles of communication that rest outside the discourses of male power. Discussing Mary's whispered description of the garden to Colin, Ruth Y. Jenkins writes that "translating the secret garden into symbolic language cannot be completed; the secret garden cannot exist without some aspect of the abject – unstable imagery and unconventional syntax."[95] Among *The Secret Garden*'s other irregular utterances, Jenkins includes Burnett's liberal use of Yorkshire dialect, Colin's midnight cries, and Dickon's drawing of a missel thrush in its nest to assure Mary that he will keep the garden a secret. While Jenkins provocatively links these multiple deviations from conventional forms of representation to the abject, which she associates with the novel's rhetoric of mothering and, specifically, female possibilities for creation, her focus on the abject overlooks the significance of the secret. It is during one of the novel's strange, interspecies speech fantasies that Mary discovers the key to unlock the abandoned garden: watching the robin, "she chirped, and talked, and coaxed and he hopped, and flitted his tail and twittered," and then when he starts to peck in the dirt looking for a worm, Mary catches sight of the buried key (40). This exchange is not altogether dissimilar from Mary's later intercourse with Colin, but here the inarticulateness of Mary and the robin's "speech" is clearly tied to the "secrecy" of the garden. Her attempt to approach nature has opened up the physical space of the garden and the imaginative space of the secret. Mary can share the secret with Dickon because, as he tells her, he has been "'keepin' secrets all th' time . . . secrets about foxes' cubs, an' birds' nests, an' wild things' holes, there'd be naught safe on th' moor. Aye, I can keep secrets" (59). In other words, being part of the secret entails having a custodial – elsewhere defined as both birdlike and maternal – relationship to nature. Thus, Dickon fittingly lets Mary know he can keep the garden a secret by drawing a mother missel thrush guarding its nest. Both the condition and the reward of mothering is secrecy.

The secret of *The Secret Garden* is Burnett's distinct literary response to evolutionary theory and recapitulation. Gatty's emphasis on literary design and Kingsley's insistence on fantasy serve to lead the child reader to a Divine God at work behind or beyond nature; Carroll's parodies and Kipling's playful pauses reveal the agency of the child either to model evolution or to defer development in favor of an even more potent intermediacy. But Burnett's secret refocuses our attention away from both God and the individual to the group and, in particular, to the ethos of friendship among the children and with nature. In contrast to Colin's "secret terrors" about his illusory disfiguring illness (104), the healthy, natural space of the garden is the secret that the children share. Burnett does not make this secret-sharing an a priori condition of childhood. Mary does not immediately tell Colin about the garden as she does Dickon; rather, "Mary had tried to be very cautious . . . [S]he wanted to discover whether he was the kind of boy you could tell a secret to" (89). We might describe both Mary's and Colin's character development as their becoming "the kind of [people] you could tell a secret to." Discovering the secret garden requires Mary's shedding of the premature age and self-centeredness that were the consequences of her early years in India, and sharing the secret necessitates her reorientation to being a part of a mutually nurturing community. The secret is the transition from Mary's vague inarticulate chirps at the robin who cannot really understand her to the verbal and imaginative play that constitutes storytelling with Colin and Dickon. With the secret, the individual evolves into a member of the group, and the knowledge of nature evolves into a story one tells about it.

The mental garden ultimately matters more than its material counterpart, and this will come as no surprise to readers familiar with Burnett's biography. Despite what I have been arguing about *The Secret Garden*'s creation of a recapitulative narrative for girls, evolutionary theory was not the most salient intellectual field for Burnett when she wrote the novel. Rather, *The Secret Garden* is Burnett's clearest expression of her faith in Christian Science. Christian Science, developed in the last quarter of the nineteenth century by American Mary Baker Eddy, rests on the belief that sicknesses of the body are wholly sicknesses of the soul and that all matter is ultimately illusory mental phenomena. In her foundational text *Science and Health, with Key to the Scriptures* (1875), Eddy argues that "all disease arises, like other mental conditions, from association"; brought on by bad thoughts, illness can be alleviated by positive thinking.[96] In *The Secret Garden*, Colin is cured by his mind as much as by the garden: the novel's final chapter affirms that "just mere thoughts" are "as good for one as sunlight" (163). Though the materialism of evolution does not accord with the spiritualism of Christian Science, Eddy took up the metaphor of the garden to combat eugenics, as would Huxley. In *Science and Health*, she writes,

> In the propagation of the human species is there not a greater responsibility, a more solemn charge, than in the culture of your garden, or raising stock to increase your flocks and herds? Nothing unworthy of perpetuity should be transmitted to children.

The formation and education of mortals must improve before the millennium can arrive. The most important education of the infant is to keep it mentally free from impurity. The Divine Mind best governs the human body, and develops it harmoniously. Mind, not matter, should govern man, from the cradle to the grave.[97]

The first paragraph, taken on its own, anticipates a eugenic claim: lurking in the garden – like those described by Clapperton and Webster – is some evil "unworthy of perpetuity," which should not be "transmitted to children." But the second paragraph clarifies that Eddy's "garden" is a mental space, and that its "impurities" are not bad genes but bad thoughts. This is not the Romantic garden where children are tended like plants, or the eugenic garden where degenerates are exterminated like weeds, or even Huxley's garden where the gardener fits the plurality of plants for survival. Rather, this garden manipulates these previous metaphors in order to transcend them: our own personal garden is entirely what our intellectual and imaginative abilities make of it.

Like this passage from Eddy, Burnett's novel initially nods toward eugenics to undermine it with an entirely nonbiological philosophy. But in its last chapter, *The Secret Garden* explicitly draws on Eddy's parallel between good thoughts as flowers and bad thoughts as weeds: the narrator asserts that "surprising things can happen to any one who, when a disagreeable or discouraged thought comes into his mind, just has the sense to remember in time and push it out by putting in an agreeable determinedly courageous one. Two things cannot be in one place. 'Where you tend a rose, my lad/ A thistle cannot grow'" (163–164). The thistle here is not illness, as it would be in eugenic discourse, but rather the thought of illness. Therefore, while Mary weeds the physical garden but rejects the eugenic extension to Victorian tidiness or the sexual selection that would weed out Colin's genetic line in favor of the more robust Dickon's, the novel rewards its characters for gardening their mental plots. Mary finds a place for sickly Colin besides hearty Dickon, but she must only allow the best thoughts to grow in the garden of her imagination and uproot the bad. The narrator says, "when her mind gradually filled itself with robins, and moorland cottages crowded with children . . . with springtime and with secret gardens coming alive day by day, and also with a moor boy and his 'creatures,'" there was "no room left for the disagreeable thoughts" (163). Ironically, one of the most disagreeable thoughts to be eugenically eradicated in *The Secret Garden* is eugenics itself. But even more critical to the narrative of human development advocated by the novel is this passage's insistence on the "secret gardens coming alive day by day" and the importance of imagination far more than property in the successful preservation of life.

In her final piece of nonfiction, *In the Garden* (1925), published one year after her death, Burnett poeticizes the labors of the gardener and calls the assertion of human artifice over the natural space "a revelation of one's power to imagine and one's determination to create."[98] She does not reference Huxley, but this fantasy of the garden is an extrapolation of his metaphor in *Evolution and Ethics*. For Huxley, the garden was the site where human morality tussled with natural instinct and won, while for Burnett, the garden is a blank canvas on which to create. Physical nature is no match for the human imagination. *The Secret Garden* makes no such unequivocal or coherent philosophical statement. The garden is a place where Mary is flower and gardener, girl and bird, Colin's mother and his inferior, author and interloper: a dizzying array of associations that leave readers both extolling Burnett's feminist impulses and lamenting her paternalistic results. But, as I have argued, *The Secret Garden* sincerely considers the nineteenth-century efforts to reclaim evolution for girls. A prematurely aged hothouse plant, Mary moves to England where she begins her maturation anew, in the right environment and at the right pace. In this superior habitat, she becomes a figurative bird and symbolic mother: the joint pinnacle of phylogenic and ontogenic female progress. Then her biological development stops, perhaps because Burnett could not see past the same limitations that had halted the Victorian feminists who preceded her. She had no need to, however, because the novel itself demonstrates the weakening of Burnett's commitment to materiality and her attraction to an alternate theory of immaterial mind. Outside the strictures of biology, the little girl is more than a flower or bird, more than a gardener or mother. She is an author, creator, and secret keeper.

The nineteenth-century narrative of evolutionary recapitulation was not fertile ground for girls. Women writers like Blackwell, Gamble, Swiney, Buckley, Webster, and Burnett attempted to cull out a developmental course that favored female agency: toward becoming an altruistic mother, a discriminating sexual selector, a eugenic handmaiden, a nesting bird, a moral lens onto the organic world, or an author of imaginary gardens. In *The Secret Garden*, Burnett stretched the girl's developmental story outside the strictly biological (or even metaphorically biological) to establish a fantastical relationship between women and nature, where the girl could take control. Complex and dynamic portraits of wild girls reliving the animal and primitive stages of the human past would come later in the twentieth century: Scott O'Dell's *The Island of the Blue Dolphins* (1960), for example, transforms the true story of a Nicoleño Indian girl abandoned on an island into a feminized blend of *Robinson Crusoe* and *The Jungle Books*, and Jean Craighead George's *Julie of the Wolves* (1972) similarly translates aspects of Kipling's tale to the Alaskan wilderness and makes an Eskimo girl companion to a pack of arctic wolves.[99] Both twentieth-century children's novels allow their female protagonists to embrace the bestial development that was foreclosed, or allowed in only the most limited way, to Victorian and Edwardian mommies-to-be. Reversing Mowgli's trajectory, transplanting Mary from India to England, and placing her in a garden rather than a jungle, *The Secret Garden* is the Edwardian era's female counterpart to *The Jungle Books*. Girl heroines would have to wait another half century to enter that male centered story, yet perhaps as O'Dell's and George's works attest, they still could not be both white and wild.

Mary's closer literary kin might be Nancy Drew and Trixie Belden: girl detectives who, with one or two faithful sidekicks, solve mysteries with titles like *The Secret of the Old Clock* (1930) and *The Secret of the Old Mansion* (1948).[100] For Burnett, the secret is both an invitation into the world of storytelling, where Mary's power lies, and a chance for Burnett's readers, like Kipling's, to follow a narrative lacuna that is also a fictional pause. The girl's recapitulation, by virtue of being stunted not by her reproductive function but by the mechanisms of male authority, recalls this nascent moment of human history: the moment when nature comes under the control of human artifice and imagination. In its advocacy of outdoor exercise and healthy bodies for girls as well as boys, *The Secret Garden* mimics the developments in girls' education and girls' social organizations that also came into existence at the beginning of the twentieth century. Recapitulation had contributed, against its own masculinist drives, to the girls' access to the natural and the primitive. And even more like the boys' literature – whose audience always included girl readers anyway – *The Secret Garden* lets the girl pause in girlhood, in the glory of pretend motherhood before sexual choice, marriage, and child-bearing. This invitation to pretend, to weave stories about the garden's continual coming into being, may never achieve the power of possession that only boys enjoyed even in the first decades of the twentieth century. But much like the books already discussed in the study, *The Secret Garden* extols the power of storytelling and secret sharing to preserve, to augment, and to improve on biological evolution.

Conclusion
Recapitulation reconsidered

In 1872, anthropologist and folklorist Edward Clodd wrote a child's version of Charles Darwin's *The Descent of Man, and Selection in Relation to Sex*, published the previous year. Fittingly titled *The Childhood of the World: A Simple Account of Man in Early Times*, Clodd's text promises to reveal "the history of the most wonderful living thing that this world has ever seen."[1] "You will perhaps think that I am about to describe to you some curly-haired, big-tusked, fierce-looking monster," he says, teasing his readers, but it is "the *Story of Man*" that he tells, which "is really the story of *yourself*."[2] As my book has shown, Victorian and Edwardian children were encouraged to see the story of the species as the story of themselves even more literally, as they were cast into the recurring roles of animal and primitive. Concerns about universal education and the cultural dominance of the sciences led literary authors to adopt and to adapt the recapitulative plot. This book has argued that evolutionary discourse – and literary writers' alternating enthusiasm for and resistance to it – shaped children's literature into the genre we know today. The era from 1860 to 1920 has been called the genre's Golden Age, though the name is misleading. Victorian and Edwardian children's literature did not seek to escape social, political, and scientific issues but engaged with the challenges posed to both the child and the text. Evolutionary recapitulation was both an intriguing metaphor and a disciplinary threat, and it became the impetus for some of the best-loved books of English literature. In the twentieth century, recapitulation faded as a serious scientific theory, and it lost its place in popular culture, but it nevertheless retained a place in theories of childhood in the next century and beyond.

At the close of the nineteenth century, the fissures between divergent versions of evolutionary theory were deepening. Neo-Lamarckism was threatening to displace an increasingly unpopular Darwinism. According to Peter J. Bowler in *Evolution: The History of an Idea* (1983), the progressive, purposeful direction of Lamarckian evolution remained more appealing than the haphazardness of random variation and natural selection proposed by Darwin.[3] In 1889, the most strident of the Darwinian holdouts, German evolutionary biologist August Weismann demonstrated the fallacy of Lamarck's inheritance of acquired characters by amputating the tails off mice and showing that no offspring were born with missing or shortened tails as a consequence.[4] Neither Weismann's dogmatism nor his "orgy of mutilation," in Bowler's words, won over many adherents, but he significantly suggested the concept of a "germ plasm," a material substance on which information about morphological structure is encoded and passed on from parent to child independent of alterations to the parent during its lifetime.[5] Though Weismann found few immediate advocates, his germ plasm fitted nicely with Francis Galton's introduction of eugenics and biometrics, also in the 1880s, sparked other biologists and botanists like Hugo de Vries to seek better theories of mutation, and laid the groundwork for the later synthesis between Darwinism and Mendelian genetics. At each stage, this growing attention to hard-wired heredity is at odds with both Lamarckism and recapitulation: organisms do not repeat the evolution of their species to reach and then to surpass the level of their parents if the destination of their development is always already inherited wholesale in their genes.[6]

While these challenges to the inheritance of acquired characteristics were slowly gaining ground, the status that morphology enjoyed in the second half of the nineteenth century was coincidentally shrinking. Evolutionary biologists were raising questions that morphologists could not answer: among them were whether a common ancestor or convergent evolution is responsible for certain structural similarities (among crustaceans, insects, and arachnids, for instance); whether adaptive anomalies (such as flightless birds) are the result of primitive transitions between species or later-occurring degenerations; and what was the origin of vertebrates.[7] Morphology had risen in esteem in the latter half of the century because it accorded with Thomas H. Huxley's vision of professionalized science, taking practitioners out of the field where they often had no more claim to authority than amateur naturalists on Sunday strolls and putting them into exclusive academic institutions and medical laboratories where access was restricted. However, just as lab work marked a professional advance over fieldwork, experiment proved another step above observation, and soon scientists like Weismann who were manipulating organisms and then genes achieved higher esteem than morphologists who dissected animals merely to observe anatomical structures. Michael Ruse, in *Monad to Man: The Concept of Progress in Evolutionary*

Biology (1996), also charts a late-century move away from the idealism of Ernst Haeckel, who had codified the so-called biogenetic law of recapitulation.[8] For these reasons, among others, William Bateson's publishing of Gregor Mendel's work in 1902 kicked off, according to historian Garland E. Allen, a "revolt against morphology" that would finally disprove Lamarckism and end any scientific adherence to the theory of recapitulation.[9]

The synthesis between Darwinian natural selection and Mendelian genetics was not immediate. Initially geneticists' assumptions about sudden mutations seemed as antagonistic to the gradual adaptation of Darwinism as did its hard-wiring conflict with Lamarck's inheritance of acquired characters. But, after Thomas Hunt Morgan's conclusion that mutations in fruit flies increase their genetic variations, which can then be naturally selected, Darwinism merged with genetics to become the basis of twentieth- and twenty-first-century biology.[10] As a result, recapitulation was shelved as another nineteenth-century misunderstanding about evolution. According to Stephen Jay Gould, "as long as the mechanism of heredity lay shrouded in mystery, recapitulationists could always postulate a convenient and purely hypothetical set of laws to yield their preferred results."[11] Once the new science of genetics lifted this shroud, however, recapitulation was consigned to the grave not only by scientists but by the next generation of pedagogues as well. In *The Psychology of Elementary Education* (1925), for example, A. S. Edwards discourages teachers and school officials from taking the analogy between ontogeny and phylogeny too literally:

> The worst criticism of the theory seems to be that the parallelism of race and individual cannot be made out. It may have been useful, and probably has been. With no better theory for the organization of some elementary education, it undoubtedly served a purpose in helping to give suggestion for various activities of young children. We shall follow a wiser course in doing our best to determine what are the best things children can be led to do at each age, quite irrespective of what we think the race did or did not do.[12]

Edwards admits that, in drawing attention to the stages of child development, recapitulation offered a useful early blueprint for organizing the child's education. But the blueprint needed embellishment that was sound in both theory and practice, and the analogy between individual and species could only be carried so far. The narrative of the individual's rehearsal and mastery of his ancestors' evolutionary stages seemed now wholly the stuff of fantasy, unusable in actual laboratories, nurseries, or classrooms, where it had held sway for the previous half century.

In psychology and literature, however, recapitulation did not altogether disappear. Rather, it mutated into a much more powerful cultural formulation: Freudian psychoanalysis. In *Darwin's Influence on Freud: A Tale of Two Sciences* (1990), Lucille Ritvo argues that Darwin's "struggle for existence" underlies Sigmund Freud's description of psychic drives, competing with each other under a veneer of psychological coherence.[13] Freud likely learned about evolutionary theory through Darwin's German followers, like Haeckel. It is not surprising, then, to find the recapitulation hypothesis recurrent in his writings. *The Interpretation of Dreams* (1900) maintains that dream life recalls not only the dreamer's childhood experiences but also the collective prehistory: "behind this childhood of the individual," there is "a picture of a phylogenic childhood – a picture of the development of the human race, of which the individual's development is in fact an abbreviated recapitulation influenced by the chance circumstances of life."[14] According his preface to the third edition of *Three Essays on Sexuality* (1914), in sexual development, "ontogenesis may be regarded as a recapitulation of phylogenesis."[15] One's mental disposition, Freud writes, "is ultimately the precipitate of earlier experience of the species to which the more recent experience of the individual ... is super-added." What separates the healthy individual from the neurotic is the extent to which he has moved through the animal, primitive stages toward a modern, adult negotiation of desires and impulses. The Oedipal conflict, in particular, rehearses a phase of early human evolution that every (male) individual must pass through; in *Totem and Taboo* (1913), Freud explains that the boy's hatred of his father repeats the prehistoric moment when the young members of "Darwin's primal horde" banded together to kill the overbearing patriarch.[16] And in *Moses and Monotheism* (1939), he insists that religion is rooted in shared primal experience and that all men "bring the experiences of their species with them into their own new existence" as individuals.[17]

Though psychoanalysis seems rooted in recapitulation, its development reveals Freud's departure from this biological model, not because of its scientific implausibility but because it did not quite suit his psychological theories. For Freud, distinct sexual phases (polymorphous perversity, narcissism, etc.) replace recapitulation's focus on graduated levels of animal species or primitive civilizations.[18] Development, for Freud, also shifts from a predetermined evolutionary sequence to the achievement of a cohered and integrated consciousness. *Three Essays* describes sexual organization in succession, but a decade and a half later, *Civilization and Its Discontents* (1929) stresses the mental simultaneity of psychic drives:

"nothing that has once come into existence will have passed away and all the earlier phases of development continue to exist alongside the latest one."[19] Searching for a metaphor for the collection of unconscious material, Freud initially attempts to use the animal kingdom, but he finds it too marred by extinction. The psychic material in our unconscious, in contrast, never goes extinct. Freud then turns to embryology but finds it similarly compromised because "the earlier phases of development are in no sense still preserved."[20] Finally, he settles on archeology for a very different model of the mind: here inorganic material survives collected and intact. In Freud's later descriptions, then, the human mind does not move through successive stages, developing or decaying like an individual body or the animal kingdom at large; rather it accrues without loss like a timeless repository of archeological artifacts.

Though Freud shifted away from the metaphor of recapitulation, the analogy between ontogeny and phylogeny has proven resilient in popular culture, showing up in parenting self-help manuals. In *The Common Sense Book of Baby and Child Care* (1946), the first best seller of its kind, Dr. Benjamin Spock told new parents: "babies start off in the womb as a single tiny cell, just the way the first living thing appeared in the ocean . . . Toward the end of the first year of life, when they learn to clamber to their feet, they're celebrating that period millions of years ago when our ancestors got up off all fours."[21] Though this idea has little bearing on Spock's practical advice, his assertion that ontogeny recapitulates phylogeny has appeared in at least fifty million copies of the book sold worldwide.[22] In a more recent best seller, *The Happiest Toddler on the Block* (2004), Dr. Harvey Karp claims that "the starting place" to raising well-behaved children "is your child's level of *evolution*."[23] To the toddler's progressive stages, Karp gives names like "charming chimp-child" and "knee-high Neanderthal," domesticating Darwinism for an American audience frustratingly squeamish about evolution. As Kenneth B. Kidd shows in *Making American Boys: Boyology and the Feral Tale* (2004), advice to parents of boys over the last twenty-five years frequently asserts their essential wildness: Robert Bly's *Iron John: A Book About Men* (1990) says, "the boy is mythologically living through the past history of man," and Michael Gurian's *The Wonder of Boys: What Parents, Mentors and Educators Can Do to Shape Boys into Exceptional Men* (1996) holds that "things have not changed much since the first humans started walking about the African savannah."[24] Back-to-nature movements give children of both sexes an inherent connection to a primitive past. Richard Louv's *Last Child in the Woods: Saving Our Children from Nature-Deficient Disorder* (2006) argues that children need to have ample opportunities to play outside because "genetically, we are essentially the same creatures as we were at the beginning" of human history.[25] Even the seemingly tireless discourse about mothering has taken up recapitulation's call of the wild: actress and neuroscientist Mayim Bialik's *Beyond the Sling: A Real-Life Guide to Raising Confident, Loving Children the Attachment Parenting Way* (2012) tells moms-to-be that they have "a primal, ancient, and elegant instinct" that, though "smothered in recent years," must be revived for the sake of their atavistic infants.[26]

Recapitulation has not made a comparable comeback in elementary education, but the disciplinary struggle between the sciences and the humanities certainly has. In the United States, national and state governments have established initiatives in the STEM (science, technology, engineering, and mathematics) fields at the expense of attention to the arts and humanities, and the United Kingdom, too, has established a National STEM Centre. Though much debate has intervened between the Victorian period and our own – C. P. Snow and F. R. Leavis's "Two Cultures" debate and the "culture wars" of the 1980s and 1990s – reasons given for funding STEM are notably familiar. After the 1851 Great Exhibition sparked Britain's interest in the role of science and technology in empire building, Queen Victoria announced: "the advancement of the fine arts and of practical science will be readily recognised by you as worthy of the attention of a great and enlightened nation."[27] According to the U. S. Department of Education's (DOE's) Web site in 2015, "the United States has become a global leader, in large part, through the genius and hard work of its scientists, engineers and innovators. Yet today, that position is threatened as comparatively few American students pursue expertise in the fields of science, technology, engineering and mathematics."[28] President Barack Obama put the nation's need to get students into STEM fields in terms of a global competition; the DOE reports his saying that we must "move from the middle to the top of the pack in science and math," and he has established an initiative called "Race to the Top."[29] Obama stresses the importance of the sciences but, unlike Queen Victoria, is silent on the subject of the arts. Meanwhile, Grace Richards's "Oh the Humanities! Why STEM Shouldn't Take Precedence Over the Humanities" (2014) claims that, according to the U. S. National Center for Education Statistics, "nearly 1.5 million elementary students are without music, nearly 4 million are without the visual arts, and . . . more than 23 million, are educated without dance and theatre."[30]

Proponents for the arts and humanities are making arguments for their relevance. As if echoing Matthew Arnold, the 2013 Commission of the

Humanities and Social Sciences, sponsored by the American Academy of Arts and Sciences, reported that these disciplines offer "a source of national memory and civic vigor, cultural understanding and communication, individual fulfillment and the ideals we hold in common."[31] In "The Wedge Driving Academe's Two Families Apart: Can STEM and the Human Sciences Get Along?" (2013), David Hollinger uses the opposite tactic, arguing not that the humanities and social sciences preserve traditional ways of thinking but that they are the best means of challenging and revising them: "the humanities deserve support," he writes, "not because they always get things right – often they do not – but because they are the great risk takers in the tradition of the Enlightenment."[32] Public campaigns critical of STEM-myopia include attempts to include an "A" for "Art," converting STEM to STEAM, or turning the acronym into word and making the "stem" merely a utilitarian trunk supporting the "flower" of the arts and humanities.[33] Actor and celebrity children's book author John Lithgow, speaking at a National Medal of Arts and National Humanities Medal ceremony, said that the "stem" can only reproduce with the "bloom" that the study of history, philosophy, and literature provides.[34] Coincidentally, Herbert Spencer used the same metaphor to devalue art and literature when he wrote, in *Education: Intellectual, Moral, and Physical* (1860), that the sciences are "the root and leaves [which] are intrinsically of greater importance because on them the evolution of the flower depends."[35] The UK's *Guardian* weighed in with Paul Smith's "Move Over, STEM: Why the World Needs Humanities Graduates" (2014), contending that globalization requires humanities-trained citizens attuned to cultural contexts. Challenging a pseudo-religio-historical narrative that also sounds Spencerian, Smith writes, "God did not create chemistry on the first day, social anthropology on the second, and area studies on the third. The world was and is created of light, form, time, materiality, biological life and human experience."[36]

Children's literature might not seem the most likely place for addressing these concerns, especially if we accept Jacqueline Rose's claim in *The Case of Peter Pan, or in The Impossibility of Children's Fiction* (1984), that children's literature insists upon a simplistic relationship among the child, the text, and the state.[37] Rose's argument focuses on J. M. Barrie's *Peter Pan* in part because Barrie rewrote the story at least four times: from a collection of photographs of the Llewelyn-Davies boys called *The Boy Castaways of Black Lake Island* (1899), to his novel *Little White Bird* (1902), to the play *Peter Pan; or, The Boy Who Wouldn't Grow Up* (1904), to his novelization of the play, *Peter and Wendy* (1911).[38] For Rose, the most indicative revision is the loss of the origin myth of the story itself: in *Little White Bird*, the narrator tells the story of Peter Pan to a boy named David, while claiming that the story is created collaboratively between adult and child. When this narrative situation is eclipsed in the play *Peter Pan* and the novel *Peter and Wendy*, Rose argues, the revised texts repress "the idea that there could be a problem at just that level of communication, a troubling intention and address."[39] But Barrie's changes from *Little White Bird* to *Peter and Wendy* also reveal a shift from a recapitulative model of childhood psychology to a psychoanalytic one.[40] As the title of Barrie's earlier novel hints, Peter's escape from the nursery to live with the birds in Kensington Gardens is an apt relocation; according to the mythology Barrie invents for his eternal boy, all children are birds before they are born, and "they are naturally a little wild during the first few weeks, and very itchy at the shoulders, where their wings used to be."[41] But this animal prehistory is missing in *Peter and Wendy*; instead Barrie offers a portrait of the child's mind that jumbles together psychic material resonant with Freud's archeological metaphor. "Have you ever seen a map of a person's mind?," Barrie's narrator asks, and then he describes the mind as a simultaneous collection of "coral reef and rakish-looking crafts . . . and savages and lonely lairs, and gnomes . . . also first day at school, religion, fathers, the round pond, needlework, murders, hangings"; the list goes on, "and it is all rather confusing, especially as nothing will stand still."[42]

If *Peter and Wendy*'s fantasy of disordered but dynamic youth (with no remaining trace of the animal) is the paradigmatic example of children's literature, then the result is a mixture of Romantic nostalgia and Freudian ego-construction that has little to say about the relative merits of the disciplines in the course of humanization. But here I have argued that, contrary to children's literature scholarship that bookends the turns of the nineteenth and twentieth centuries as first Romanticism and then Freudianism, there was a third formulation distinct to the Victorian age, born of a late-nineteenth-century confluence of Victorian science, schooling, and literature. Recapitulating his way from bestiality to humanity, the post-Darwinian child was neither the static innocent of the Romantics nor the dynamic nexus of drives that Freud proposed. The animal and primitive child of Victorian biology, pedagogy, and children's literature, is a missing link in our scholarly histories of childhood. Similar to the Romantic ingénue, the animal child has a deep affinity with nature, but he was not – as Rose claims about pre-Freudian constructs of the child – a linguistic and political blank. The recapitulating child brought with him a preinscribed set of pedagogical expectations that intervened into a crisis about universal public education. In accord with the Freudian psyche, this child is only partially aware of the mental inheritance that must be worked through in order to achieve a healthy adulthood, but unlike the discourse of psychoanalysis, recapitulation posited a teleological pedagogy that children's writers preserved, parodied, and perverted. I have argued that children's literature was uniquely poised to take on the challenge of the bestial child and his pedagogical prospects because, far from denying textuality, the genre was long troubled with the cleavage between nature and text, doing and reading, science and literature.

This book has focused on the ways in which Victorian and Edwardian children's authors, primarily in Britain though glancing at America, adopted recapitulation as a particularly literary challenge. The pedagogy of recapitulation proposed by Spencer placed such importance on spontaneous play – which Spencer understood as the universal means by which animals learn – and scientific method – which he argued was merely a more sophisticated form of play that drove human evolution – that it left no place for literature. Reading was not an activity open to our early ancestors, he claimed, and thus had no part in our ascent. As the effects of civilization rather than its causes, according to Spencer, literature and art best be left to our leisure moments after the real work of self-preservation and environmental manipulation was done. In response to the rise of the sciences in cultural esteem, thanks in no small parts to Spencer and the search for a "universal" pedagogical program capable of serving newly compulsory education, children's authors like Margaret Gatty, Charles Kingsley, Lewis Carroll, Rudyard Kipling, and Frances Hodgson Burnett argued back – through their children's texts – that art and literature, indeed, are essential to both individual development and its intergenerational corollary of human evolution. Though these authors each employed the analogy between individual development and human evolution, they rarely shared the same vision for the goal toward which these parallel courses tend. What links their texts together, however, is the central role each ceded to literature in the child's ultimate achievement and maintenance of humanity.

The authors examined here validated the power of literature by enhancing and emphasizing the literariness of their genre. In so doing, they twisted children's literature into productive and enduring new shapes. The twentieth century and the beginning of the twenty-first century have demonstrated how persistently popular the literary modes and techniques of the Victorian and Edwardian age still remain. The Christianizing fantasy of Kingsley's *Water-Babies* (1863) makes a return in C. S. Lewis's

The Chronicles of Narnia (1950–1956) and even in Philip Pullman's skeptical trilogy, *His Dark Materials* (1995–2000).[43] The parodic turn of Carroll's *Alice's Adventures in Wonderland* (1865) reappears in the upturned fairy tales of Roald Dahl's *Revolting Rhymes* (1982) and Jon Scieszka's *The Stinky Cheese Man, and Other Fairly Stupid Tales* (1992).[44] Kipling's valuation of the bestial pause in *The Jungle Books* (1894 and 1895) notably informs Maurice Sendak's award-winning classic *Where the Wild Things Are* (1963) as well as Piers Torday's recent *The Last Wild* trilogy (2013–2015).[45] And Burnett's investment in the secret-sharing multiple protagonists of *The Secret Garden* (1911) is renewed in texts like E. L. Konigsburg's *From the Mixed-Up Files of Mrs. Basil E. Frankweiler* (1967) and the doubly secret and anonymously authored Pseudonymous Bosch's *The Secret Series* (2007–2011).[46] The Victorian and Edwardian responses to recapitulation have now been dispersed across children's texts with diverse themes and developmental goals, but the literary traditions established by the authors featured in this study must be understood alongside the more material changes to children's culture that the theory of recapitulation also produced: outdoor youth organizations like the Boy Scouts and the Camp Fire Girls, the American invention of the summer camp, and the shift in pedagogical practice to student-based learning.

The idea that the child repeats the animal and primitive stages of the species' past and rehearses human progress in an exacting, evolutionarily prescribed order no longer contributes to any serious pedagogical or psychological theory of childhood. But the theory of evolution is far from irrelevant to child development. Twenty-first-century evolutionary psychologists and behavioralists now refer to a stage called "middle childhood," after parental dependency has passed but before the onset of puberty, during which time the child is primarily acculturated. In *The Evolution of Childhood: Relationships, Emotion, Mind* (2010), neuroscientist and biologist Melvin Konner describes this "pause" in cognitive development and argues that this "partial breaking process . . . has in turn made possible what most distinguishes us from apes: imbuing a child with a culture."[47] In other words, culture is not the flower on Spencer's scientific root: a late addition to self-preservation that occurred at the end of humanity's ascent and one that should be complementarily recovered only at the end of childhood. Rather, acculturation occurs during a prolonged middle stage of development, after the pressures of survival dissipate and before the burdens of reproduction begin, and it is the expansion of this middle space for cultural acquisition that made us human and that continues to humanize us. Human evolution does not dictate a twelve-step program through graduated levels of animality or savagery, but it does require a pause, not unlike the pause celebrated in *The Jungle Books* and *The Secret Garden*. Modern evolutionary theory, thus, suggests a bridge between Spencer's insistence that we attend to our inherited biology and Arnold's contention that "a power of reading, well trained and well guided, is perhaps the best among the gifts which it is the business of our elementary schools to bestow."[48] When Konner talks about culture, he does not mean only literary culture. But for the modern child, literature introduces its readers to cultural values and cultural complexities, and it teaches strategies for entering into culture, for negotiating selfhood within it, and for instituting change. Children's literature might, then, be just what our evolution ordered.

Postscript: prescript

Few twenty-first-century children's books explicitly invoke the nineteenth-century theory of recapitulation. The unwieldiness of Haeckel's multi-syllabic law – "ontogeny recapitulates phylogeny" – matched with the absurd literalness of the theory, its scientific inaccuracy, and its long-standing use in racist hierarchies and imperialist justifications make it seem sometimes better left alone, or transformed into Freudian psychoanalysis or Spock's and Karp's avuncular advice. But children's writer Mordicai Gerstein has recently revived the analogy between the modern child and the primitive. The first layout of Gerstein's *The First Drawing* (2013) asks the reader to "imagine. . . you were born before the invention of drawing, more than thirty thousand years ago."[49] On the first page, the illustration shows a modern child in jeans and a t-shirt, his beagle resting at his feet, and his hand holding a pencil and poised to start writing on the blank canvas in front of him [Figure 11]. On the second page, the white wall of the modern world has disappeared, ceding its place to an airy vista, and before it stands the same child figure, but now in a leather tunic and sandals, his hand on the head of a great wolf where the docile beagle once snoozed. Gerstein's book presents a clan of cave dwellers before the dawn of drawing or writing and a lonely prehistoric boy who loves to watch animals and sometimes fancies that the clouds in the sky and the shadows in the cave mimic their aspects. Eventually, the boy takes a burnt stick and traces a mammoth's form on the cave wall, creating the first ever drawing. All the time Gerstein calls this character "you" because the first drawing any child makes replicates this primitive moment in which art was invented.

Imagine...

you were born before the invention of drawing, more than thirty thousand years ago.

Figure 11 From *The First Drawing* by Mordicai Gerstein, n.p. Text and illustrations copyright © 2013 by Mordicai Gerstein.

In the Author's Note at the end of *The First Drawing*, Gerstein credits the 1994 discovery of the cave paintings in Chauvet-Pont-d'Arc, in southern France, for inspiring his book. Next to the approximately thirty-thousand-year-old paintings of horses, rhinoceroses, reindeers, mammoths, and lions was also found an ancient child's footprint.[50] It is this last finding that moved Gerstein; he writes, "for someone who has drawn all his life, it has always seemed obvious that whoever invented drawing must have been a child ... When I read of the child's footprint in the cave, I said to myself, 'Aha! I was right!'"[51] He does not mention that dating techniques have revealed the footprint to be three to five thousand years newer than the cave paintings, and thus not the trace remnant of any of the artists.[52] But, of course, this does not really matter, in part because the recapitulative analogy between child and animal, or child and primitive, still lingers in conversations about child development, and in part because of another association between childhood and cave painting forged in the Victorian age. The first cave paintings seen by modern Europeans were at Altamira in Cantabria, Spain. According to the oft-told story of their discovery, in 1879, explorer Don Marcelina Sanz de Sautuola brought his eight-year-old daughter, Maria, on an expedition in search of prehistoric bone carvings; as the seasoned explorer scanned the cave floor for his spoils, Maria looked up and became the first modern person to glimpse the sixteen-thousand-year-old paintings on the walls.[53] The link between the child and the first painters is thus overdetermined but enticing. As the originators, the discoverers, the heirs, and the modern versions of the early cave painters, children carry with them the species' first impulses to artistic creation.

Given young Maria's discovery at Altamira in 1879, it might be surprising that Victorian and Edwardian histories of human evolution overlook artistic achievements like cave paintings. Speculative accounts of human history like Clodd's *Childhood of the World*, Frederick Starr's *Some First Steps in Human Progress* (1901), and Minnie J. Reynold's *How Man Conquered Nature* (1914) feature early man's manufacture of tools, discovery of how to make fire, and agricultural and industrial advancements, but the creation of art does not enter the story.[54] The Altamira cave paintings mark a deep failing of Victorian culture to understand the early peoples that they were so obsessed with charting and defining. By the time that de Sautuola published an account of his (or his daughter's) findings in 1880, the paintings were thought to be frauds, done perhaps by de Sautuola himself. In *The Mind in the Cave: Consciousness and the Origins of Art* (2002), his study of the paintings at Altamira, Lascaux, and Chauvet, David Lewis-Williams says that "the elaborately executed art on the ceiling in the Altamira cave did not fit current notions of Paleolithic 'savagery'; it was too 'advanced' for the period."[55] According to Lewis-Williams, the "implacable and virulent skepticism" exhibited by de Sautuola's contemporaries "is today considered one of the great scandals of the study of Upper Paleolithic art." By the discovery of the Chauvet cave in 1994, the mind of the public was a little more open, but the three explorers to find the paintings – Jean-Marie Chauvet, Eliette Brunel Deschamps, and Christian Hillaire – still feel the need to underscore how the caves disprove our misconceptions about "primitive" peoples. From the caves, they say, we learn that "art did not have a linear evolution from clumsy and crude beginnings," and therefore, "our view of the beginnings of artistic creation and even of the psyche of these first modern humans has been changed."[56] Early humans were not children; we do not get imagine ourselves as them grown up.

The analogy between species and individual generated fallacies about the development of both, and we can from our retrospective vantage point find in recapitulation only a quaint corner of nineteenth-century pseudo-science. Or we can, along with Gerstein, recognize that within the association between the child and the primitive, as between the child and the animal, there is an inexorable and even enlightened quest to discover "the story of ourselves" – the common core of our humanity or, beyond anthropocentrism, the qualities that we share with all living beings. Gerstein's *First Drawing* idealistically tries to show us that what binds modern humans with each other and with our primitive ancestors is the desire to create art and to translate the images that we both see and invent into physical marks with which we can communicate. What the Victorian and Edwardian writers studied here – Gatty, Kingsley, Carroll, Kipling, and Burnett – proposed was that any story of our origins, our development, and our future as individuals and as a species is incomplete without an attention to art and literature. The recuperation of our presumed evolutionary past in *Parables from Nature, The Water-Babies, Alice's Adventures in Wonderland, The Jungle Books*, and *The Secret Garden* is an attempt to reunite the modern, urbanized child with a lost nature more attuned to his evolving body and consciousness. They are also explorations into the power of literature to humanize us. Such works will not solve the twenty-first-century institutional crisis in the arts and humanities, but they might remind us that art and literature are not going anywhere. Or to reframe it from the perspective of the children's genre we have been investigating here, human beings cannot go anywhere, and have indeed never gotten anywhere, without the imagination fostered by literature and the arts.

Notes

Introduction

1. Charles Kingsley, *The Water-Babies: A Fairy Tale for a Land-Baby*, 1863, 4th ed., illus Linley Sambourne (London: Macmillan and Company, 1890), 105–106. *The Water-Babies* first ran as a serial in *Macmillan's Magazine* from August 1862 to March 1863.
2. Ibid., 67.
3. Ibid., 106.
4. See William Hone, *The Year Book of Daily Recreation and Information*, 1832 (London: Ward, Lock, Bowden and Company, 1892), 351.
5. Charles Darwin, *The Descent of Man, and Selection in Relation to Sex*, 1871 (Princeton, NJ: Princeton University Press, 1981), 29.
6. The same edition with Robinson's illustrations was published in London by Constable and Company, 1915.
7. George Boas, *The Cult of Childhood* (Dallas, TX: Spring Publications, Inc., 1966), 14.
8. George K. Behlmer, *Child Abuse and Moral Reform in England, 1870–1908* (Stanford, CA: Stanford University Press, 1982), 53. See also Harriet Ritvo, *The Animal Estate: The English and Other Creatures in the Victorian Age* (Cambridge, MA: Harvard University Press, 1987), 133; and Kathryn Bond Stockton, *The Queer Child; or Growing Sideways in the Twentieth Century* (Durham, NC: Duke University Press, 2009), 65.
9. Louis Robinson, M.D., "Darwinism in the Nursery," *Eclectic Magazine of Foreign Literature, Science, and Art*, 54:6 (December 1891), 846–854 (851). Robinson's essay was also published in *Nineteenth Century*, 30 (1891), 831–842.
10. S. S. Buckman, "Babies and Monkeys," *The Popular Science Monthly*, 46 (January 1895), 371–388 (374). Buckman's essay was previously published in *Nineteenth Century*, 36 (1894), 727–743. Sally Shuttleworth offers an excellent reading of Robinson's and Buckman's essays in *The Mind of the Child: Child Development in Literature, Science, and Medicine, 1840–1900* (Oxford: Oxford University Press, 2010), 245–263.
11. Milicent Washburn Shinn, *The Biography of a Baby* (Boston, MA: Houghton, Mifflin and Company, 1900), 6 and 26.

12. James Sully, *Studies of Childhood* (New York: D. Appleton, 1896), 5. An earlier version of Sully's work appeared in the January 1895 issue of *The Popular Science Monthly*, two essays ahead of Buckman's piece.

13. Charles Darwin, Notebook B, in Paul H. Barrett, Peter J. Gautrey, Sandra Herbert, David Kohn, and Sydney Smith (eds.), *Charles Darwin's Notebooks, 1836–1844: Geology, Transmutation of Species, Metaphysical Enquiries* (Ithaca, NY: Cornell University Press, 1987), 167–236 (190, Note 78).

14. Focusing on the theory of modification expressed in *Origin of Species*, Stephen Jay Gould claims that "Darwin had accepted the observations of von Baer – a flat denial of recapitulation and its obvious evolutionary meaning." Robert Richards, in contrast, analyzes the reliance on recapitulation in Darwin's earlier notebooks and essays and argues for "its critical role in the formation of the theory." See Gould, *Ontogeny and Phylogeny* (Cambridge, MA: The Belknap Press of Harvard University Press, 1977), 71–72, and Richards, *The Meaning of Evolution: The Morphological Construction and Ideological Reconstruction of Darwin's Theory* (Chicago, IL: University of Chicago Press, 1992), 92. Dov Ospovat gives a more measured argument and a subtle teasing out of Darwin's uses of recapitulation and his distinctions from von Baer, arguing that Darwin only "abandoned recapitulation when it began to lose favor among the younger biologists whose opinions he respected." See Ospovat, *The Development of Darwin's Theory: Natural History, Natural Theology, and Natural Selection, 1838–1859* (Cambridge: Cambridge University Press, 1981), 152.

15. Herbert Spencer, "The Development Hypothesis," 1852, in Herbert Spencer, *Illustrations of Universal Progress; A Series of Discussions*, 1864 (New York: D. Appleton and Company, 1865), 377–383.

16. Robert Chambers, *Vestiges of the Natural History of Creation*, 1844 (New York: Leicester University Press, 1969), 272–273.

17. Gould, *Ontogeny and Phylogeny*, 13.

18. Gillian Beer, *Darwin's Plots: Evolutionary Narrative in Darwin, George Eliot and Nineteenth-Century Fiction*, 1983 (Cambridge: Cambridge University Press, 2000), 12.

19. Ospovat, esp. "Natural History after Cuvier" and "Darwin and the Branching Conception" in *The Development of Darwin's Theory*, 115–169; Peter J. Bowler, *Evolution: The History of an Idea*, 1983, 25th Anniversary ed. (Berkeley, CA: University of California Press, 2009), esp. "The Reception of Darwin's Theory" and "The Eclipse of Darwinism," 177–273; Adrian Desmond, *Archetypes and Ancestors: Palaeontology in Victorian London, 1850–1875* (Chicago, IL: University of Chicago Press, 1982), esp. "Creative Continuity," 56–83; Adrian Desmond, *The Politics of Evolution: Morphology, Medicine, and Reform in Radical London* (Chicago, IL: University of Chicago Press, 1989),

esp. "Importing the New Morphology," 25–100; and Richards, *The Meaning of Evolution.*

20. Shinn, *Biography of a Baby,* 7–8.

21. Louis Robinson, "Darwinism in the Nursery," 848.

22. William Byron Forbush, *The Boy Problem: A Study in Social Pedagogy* (Boston, MA: The Pilgrim Press, 1901), 9. Forbush says that he borrowed the phrase "candidate for humanity" from the American psychologist G. Stanley Hall.

23. For histories of education in Great Britain and especially the 1870 Elementary Education Act, see Charles Birchenough, *History of Education in England and Wales from 1800 to the Present Day,* 1914 (London: University Tutorial Press, 1938); P. H. J. H. Gosden (ed.), *How They Were Taught: An Anthology of Contemporary Accounts of Learning and Teaching in England, 1800–1950* (Oxford: Basil Blackwell, 1969); J. S. Hurt, *Elementary Schooling and the Working Classes, 1860–1918* (London: Routledge & Keegan Paul, 1979); Donald K. Jones, *The Making of the Education System, 1851–81* (London: Routledge & Keegan Paul, 1977); David Layton, *Science for the People: The Origins of the School Science Curriculum in England* (New York: George Allen & Unwin Lts., 1973); and J. Stuart Maclure (ed.), *Educational Documents: England & Wales 1816–1968,* 1969 (London: Methuen and Company, Ltd., 1972).

24. A similar act making elementary school compulsory was passed in Scotland in 1872.

25. See above and additionally Neil J. Smelser, *Social Change and Social Paralysis: British Working-Class Education in the Nineteenth Century* (Berkeley, CA: University of California Press, 1991), 64–97.

26. See Layton, *Science for the People,* for extended discussions of the contributions of each.

27. Herbert Spencer, *Education: Intellectual, Moral, and Physical,* 1860 (New York: D. Appleton and Company, 1896), 21. For a discussion of Spencer's influence on educational policy, see Birchenough, *History of Education,* 285–313.

28. Spencer, *Education,* 73 and 74.

29. See, for example, Humphrey Carpenter, *Secret Gardens: The Golden Age of Children's Literature from Alice's Adventures in Wonderland to Winnie-the-Pooh* (Boston, MA: Houghton Mifflin Company, 1985); and Gillian Avery, "Fairy Tales with a Purpose" and "Fairy Tales for Pleasure" in Donald J. Gray (ed.), *Alice in Wonderland,* 1971, 2nd ed. (New York: W. W. Norton and Company, 1992), 321–330.

30. Peter J. Bowler, *Biology and Social Thought: 1850–1914* (Berkeley, CA: Office for History of Science and Technology, University of California at Berkeley, 1993), 29.

31. Richard Owen, "Report on British Fossil Reptiles," Part 2, in *Report BAAS* (1841), 60–204 (202). Quoted in Desmond, *Politics of Evolution*, 13.

32. For a discussion of Geoffroy Saint-Hilaire, see Gould, *Ontogeny and Phylogeny*, 47–48; and for a discussion of Cuvier, see Martin J. S. Rudwick, *Georges Cuvier, Fossil Bones, and Geological Catastrophes: New Translations & Interpretations of the Primary Texts* (Chicago, IL: University of Chicago Press, 2008), 253–268.

33. Serres's articles, collectively titled "Recherches d'anatomie transcendente," were published in the *Annales des Sciences Naturelles*. For a fuller discussion of Serres's contributions to the theory of recapitulation, see Gould, *Ontogeny and Phylogeny*, 47–52.

34. Étienne Serres, "Principes d'embryogénie, de zoogénie et teratogénie," in *Mémoires de l'Academie des Sciences de l'Institut Impérial de France* (Paris: De l'Imprimerie de Firmin Didot Frères, 1860), xx: 1–943 (834). Quoted in Gould, *Ontogeny and Phylogeny*, 38.

35. John Fletcher, *Rudiments of Physiology*, 3 vols. (Edinburgh: Carfrae, 1835–1837), I: 78. Quoted in Desmond, *Politics of Evolution*, 71.

36. Karl Ernst von Baer, *Entwicklungsgeschichte der Thiere: Beobachtung und Reflexion* (Königsberg: Bornträger, 1828), 207. Quoted in Gould, *Ontogeny and Phylogeny*, 55.

37. Chambers, *Vestiges*, 212. Carpenter's discussion of von Baer appears in William B. Carpenter, *Principles of General and Comparative Physiology*, 1839, 3rd ed. (Philadelphia, PA: Blanchard & Lea, 1851), esp. 580–582.

38. Charles Darwin, "Autobiography" in Frances Darwin (ed.), *The Autobiography of Charles Darwin and Selected Letters*, 1892 (New York: Dover Publications, Inc., 1958), 5–58 (46).

39. Ibid.

40. Ernst Haeckel, *The Evolution of Man: A Popular Exposition of the Principal Points of Human Ontogeny and Phylogeny*, 1874 (New York: D. Appleton and Company, 1897), 6–7.

41. Edward J. Larson, *Evolution: The Remarkable History of a Scientific Theory* (New York: Modern Library, 2006), 114.

42. Desmond suggestively speculates that the lack of maritime exploration among the preunification German states necessarily turned German evolutionists away from hopes of collecting new fossils and toward proving descent via embryology. See Desmond, *Archetypes and Ancestors*, 148–149.

43. Herbert Spencer, *An Autobiography*, 2 vols. (London: Williams and Norgate, 1904), I: 384.

44. Herbert Spencer, "Progress: Its Law and Cause" in Herbert Spencer, *Illustrations of Universal Progress*, 1–60 (2–3). This essay was originally published in *The Westminster Review*, 67 (April 1857), 445–447, 451, 454–456, 464–465.

45. Spencer, *Education*, 64.
46. Ibid., 110.
47. Ibid., 123.
48. Levi Seeley, *Elementary Pedagogy* (New York: Hinds, Noble & Eldredge, 1906), 75–76.
49. Arthur Penryn Stanley, *The Life and Correspondence of Thomas Arnold, D.D.*, 2 vols. (London: B. Fellowes, 1844), 1: 74.
50. Thomas Hughes, *Tom Brown's Schooldays*, 1857 (Oxford: Oxford University Press, 1989), 195 and 204.
51. See Layton, *Science for the People*, 13–34.
52. See Smelser, *Social Change and Social Paralysis*, 64–97.
53. *The Quarterly Educational Magazine and Record of the Home and Colonial School Society* (1848), 1: 51. Quoted in Layton, *Science for the People*, 25–26.
54. Spencer, *Education*, 124–125.
55. Layton, *Science for the People*, 32
56. Birchenough, *History of Education*, 292.
57. "Speech by Mr. W. E. Forster, Vice President of the Council, "Introducing the Elementary Education Bill, in the House of Commons – February 17th, 1870" in Maclure (ed.), *Educational Documents*, 98–105 (104).
58. See Hurt, *Elementary Schooling and the Working Classes*, 52–74.
59. Matthew Arnold, "General Report for the Year 1876" and "General Report for 1878" in *Reports on Elementary Schools, 1852–1882* (London and New York: Macmillan and Company, 1889), 186–224.
60. Matthew Arnold, "General Report for the Year 1852" in *Reports on Elementary Schools*, 1–20 (20).
61. Matthew Arnold, "General Report for the Year 1876" in *Reports on Elementary Schools*, 186–200 (200).
62. Ibid.
63. For a more involved, though speculative, discussion on the connection between Arnold and Spencer, see Anthony Kearney, "Matthew Arnold and Herbert Spencer: A Neglected Connection in the Victorian Debate About Scientific and Literary Education," *Nineteenth-Century Prose*, March 22, 2001; reprinted and available via *The Free Library* at www.thefreelibrary.com/ Matthew+Arnold+and+Herbert+Spencer%3a+a+neglected+connection+in+the . . . -a0188997974.
64. See R. H. Super, "The Humanist at Bay: The Arnold-Huxley Debate" in U. C. Knoepflmacher and G. B. Tennyson (eds.), *Nature and the Victorian Imagination* (Berkeley, CA: University of California Press, 1977), 231–245; and Carol T Christ, "The Victorian University and Our Own," *Journal of Victorian Culture*, 12:3 (2008), 287–294.

65. John Locke, *Some Thoughts Concerning Education*, 1693 (Oxford: Clarendon Press, 1989), 208.
66. Jean-Jacques Rousseau, *Émile: or, On Education*, 1762 (London: Everyman, 1995), 95.
67. Richard Edgeworth, "Address to Mothers" in Maria Edgeworth, *Early Lessons*, 4 vols., 1814, 6th ed. (London: R. Hunter, 1829), III: xxiii–xxiv. Quoted in Alan Richardson, *Literature, Education, and Romanticism: Reading as Social Practice, 1780–1832* (Cambridge: Cambridge University Press, 1994), 132.
68. Sarah Trimmer, *An Easy Introduction to the Knowledge of Nature, and Reading the Holy Scriptures. Adapted to the Capacities of Children*, 1780, 10th ed. (London: T. Longman and O. Rees, G.G. and J. Robinson, 1799), 13.
69. Richardson, *Literature, Education, and Romanticism*, 133.
70. Boas, *Cult of Childhood*, 11; Carpenter, *Secret Gardens*, 6; and James Holt McGavran (ed.), *Romanticism and Children's Literature in Nineteenth-Century England* (Athens, GA: University of Georgia Press, 1991), 9.
71. Jacqueline Rose, *The Case of Peter Pan; or, The Impossibility of Children's Fiction*, 1984 (Philadelphia, PA: University of Pennsylvania Press, 1993), 1.
72. Marah Gubar, *Artful Dodgers: Reconceiving the Golden Age of Children's Literature* (Oxford: Oxford University Press, 2009), 6.
73. Ibid., 5.
74. William Wordsworth, "Ode," 1807, in Stephen Gill (ed.), *William Wordsworth: The Major Works* (Oxford: Oxford University Press, 1984), 297–302 (299).
75. U. C. Knoepflmacher, "The Balancing of Child and Adult: An Approach to Victorian Fantasies for Children," *Nineteenth-Century Fiction*, 37:4 (March 1983), 497–530 (497).
76. Alan Rauch, *Useful Knowledge: The Victorians, Morality, and the March of Intellect* (Durham, NC: Duke University Press, 2001); Tess Cosslett's *Talking Animals in British Children's Fiction, 1786–1914* (Aldershot: Ashgate, 2006); and Caroline Sumpter, *The Victorian Press and the Fairy Tale* (Basingstoke: Palgrave, 2008).
77. The influence of recapitulation on arts education goes well beyond literature. For instance, music historian Bennett Zon recently demonstrated the influence of the theory of recapitulation on nineteenth-century children's musical education. See Zon, "The 'Non-Darwinian' Revolution and the Great Chain of Musical Being" in Bernard Lightman and Bennet Zon (eds.), *Evolution and Victorian Culture* (Cambridge: Cambridge University Press, 2014), 196–226.
78. Joseph Jacobs, *The Fables of Æsop, Selected, Told Anew and Their History Traced*, illus. Richard Heighway, 1889 (London: Macmillan and Company, 1894), XXI.

79. Sumpter, *The Victorian Press*, 42.

80. Andrew Lang (ed.), *The Violet Fairy Book*, 1901 (New York: Dover Publications, 1966), VIII.

81. W. T. Harris, "Introduction to the Home Reading Book Series by the Editor" in Charles Dickens and Ella Boyce Kirk, *The Story of Oliver Twist, by Charles Dickens, Condensed for Home and School Reading* (New York: D. Appleton and Company, 1897), V–X (VIII).

82. Ibid., XIII.

83. See Rauch, *Useful Knowledge*, 22–59, for an excellent discussion on these kinds of explicitly pedagogical texts.

84. Matthew Arnold, *Culture and Anarchy: An Essay in Political and Social Criticism* (London: Smith, Elder and Company, 1869), VIII.

85. James A. Secord, *Victorian Sensation: The Extraordinary Publication, Reception, and Secret Authorship of Vestiges of the Natural History of Creation* (Chicago, IL: University of Chicago Press, 2000); Geoffrey Cantor, Gowan Dawson, Graeme Gooday, Richard Noakes, Sally Shuttleworth, and Jonathan R. Topham (eds.), *Science in the Nineteenth-Century Periodical: Reading the Magazine of Nature* (Cambridge: Cambridge University Press, 2004); and Aileen Fyfe and Bernard Lightman (eds.), *Science in the Marketplace: Nineteenth-Century Sites and Experiences* (Chicago, IL: University of Chicago Press, 2007).

86. Kenneth B. Kidd, *Making American Boys: Boyology and the Feral Tale* (Minneapolis, MN: University of Minnesota Press, 2004); and Dana Seitler, *Atavistic Tendencies: The Culture of Science in American Modernity* (Minneapolis, MN: University of Minnesota Press, 2008).

87. See, in particular, George Levine, *Darwin and the Novelists: Patterns of Science in Victorian Fiction* (Cambridge, MA: Harvard University Press, 1988).

88. Bernard Lightman and Bennett Zon, "Introduction," in Lightman and Zon (eds.), *Evolution and Victorian Culture*, 1–16 (7).

89. Gowan Dawson, *Darwin, Literature, and Victorian Respectability* (Cambridge: Cambridge University Press, 2007), 7.

90. Anne DeWitt, *Moral Authority, Men of Science, and the Victorian Novel* (Cambridge: Cambridge University Press, 2013), 6.

91. Ibid.

chapter 1   The child's view of nature

1. William Wordsworth, *The Prelude; or, The Growth of a Poet's Mind*, 1805 (New York: D. Appleton and Company, 1850), Book v: 122.

2. Margaret Gatty, *Parables from Nature, First and Second Series, with a Memoir by Her Daughter, Juliana Horatia Ewing*, illus. P. H. Calderon,

W. Holman Hunt, E. Burne Jones, Otto Speckter, G. H. Thomas, John Tenniel, M. E. Edwards, Lorenz Fröhlich, Harrison Weir, J. Wolf, et al., 2 vols. (London: George Bell and Sons, 1885 and 1886), II: 71. This two-volume set includes all thirty-six of Gatty's *Parables from Nature* that were originally published by Bell and Daldy in five series: 1855, 1857, 1861, 1864, and 1871. All further references to Gatty's *Parables from Nature* are to the George Bell and Sons edition and will be cited parenthetically in text.

3. For the histories of science education and working-class instruction in the Victorian elementary school, see George C. T. Bartley, *The Schools for the People, Containing the History, Development, and Present Working of Each Description of English Schools for the Industrial and Poorer Classes* (London: Bell and Daldy, 1871); George A. Foote, "The Place of Science in the British Reform Movement, 1830–1850," *Isis*, 42 (1951), 92–208; P. H. J. H. Gosden, *How They Were Taught: An Anthology of Contemporary Accounts of Learning and Teaching in England, 1800–1950* (Oxford: Basil Blackwell, 1969); the History of Education Society (ed.), *Studies in the Government and Control of Education since 1860* (London: Methuen, 1970); David Layton, *Science for the People: The Origins of the School Science Curriculum in England* (New York: George, Allen & Unwin, 1973); J. S. Hurt, *Elementary Schooling and the Working Classes, 1860–1918* (London: Routledge & Kegan Paul, 1979); and Neil J. Smelser, *Social Paralysis and Social Change: British Working-Class Education in the Nineteenth Century* (Berkeley, CA: University of California Press, 1991).

4. Quoted in Bartley, *Schools for the People*, 124.

5. Norman Morris, "State Paternalism and *Laissez-Faire* in the 1860s" in the History of Education Society (ed.), *Studies in the Government and Control of Education*, 13–25 (23).

6. Henry Barnard, *Object Teaching and Oral Lessons on Social Science and Common Things* (New York: F. C. Brownell, 1860), 34. According to Bartley, science courses were on the rise. He reports that, from 1861 to 1870, the number of science classes subject to state set examinations grew from 82 to 2,204, and the number of pupils taking the examinations rose from 438 in 1859 to over 34,000 in 1870; see Bartley, *The Schools for the People*, 137–138. But science textbooks were not readily available until the 1890s; see James A. Secord's section on "Science" in Leslie Howsam et al., "What Victorians Learned: Perspectives on Nineteenth-Century Schoolbooks," *Journal of Victorian Culture*, 12:2 (Autumn 2007), 262–285 (272–276).

7. John Hedley Brooke, *Science and Religion: Some Historical Perspectives* (Cambridge: Cambridge University Press, 1991), 200.

8. Richard Owen, "Report on British Fossil Reptiles," Part II, in *Report BAAS* (1841), 60–204 (202). Quoted in Adrian Desmond, *The Politics of Evolution:*

Morphology, Medicine, and Reform in Radical London (Chicago, IL: University of Chicago Press, 1989), 13.

9. Andrew Carnegie, *The Gospel of Wealth, and Other Timely Essays* (New York: The Century Company, 1901).

10. John Brooke and Geoffrey Cantor, *Reconstructing Nature: The Engagement of Science and Religion* (Oxford: Oxford University Press, 1998), 176–184.

11. Isaac Watts, *A Discourse on the Education of Children and Youth*, 1760, in Isaac Watts, *The Improvement of the Mind*, 1837 (New York: Cosimo, Inc., 2007), 285–269 (291).

12. For my discussion of Lewis Carroll's parodying of Watts, see Chapter 3 of this book.

13. J. Aiken, MD, and Mrs. (Anna) Barbauld, "Nineteenth Evening: Eyes, and no Eyes; or, The Art of Seeing" in *Evenings at Home; or, The Juvenile Budget Opened: Consisting of a Variety of Miscellaneous Pieces for the Instruction and Amusement of Young Persons*, 6 vols., 1793, 11th ed. (London: Baldwin, Cradock, and Joy, 1816), IV: 95–112. Versions of this story appear throughout nineteenth-century fictional works for children, including Charles Kingsley's Madame How and Lady Why; or, First Lessons in Earth Lore for Children, 1869, 3rd ed. (London: Strathan and Company, 1873), VIII–XII.

14. Dinah Maria Craik, *Our Year: A Child's Book in Prose and Verse*, illus. Clarence Dobell (Cambridge: Macmillan, 1860), 34.

15. W. Percival Westell, *Every Boy's Book of British Natural History*, with contributions from Sidney Newman Sedgwick and Sir John Lubbock (London: Royal Tract Society, 1906), 4 and 11.

16. Greg Myers, "Science for Women and Children: The Dialogue of Popular Science in the Nineteenth Century" in John Christie and Sally Shuttleworth (eds.), *Nature Transfigured: Literature and Science, 1700–1900* (Manchester: Manchester University Press, 1989), 171–200 (179).

17. Sarah Trimmer, *An Easy Introduction to the Knowledge of Nature, and Reading the Holy Scriptures. Adapted to the Capacities of Children*, 1780, 10th ed. (London: T. Longman and O. Rees, G. G. and J. Robinson, 1799), 142.

18. Charlotte Smith, *Conversations, Introducing Poetry: Chiefly on Subjects of Natural History for the Use of Children and Young Persons*, 1804 (London: T. Nelson & Sons, 1863), 7, http://babel.hathitrust.org/cgi/pt?id=nyp .33433009360391;view=1up;seq=13.

19. Westell, *Every Boy's Book*, 1.

20. William Paley, *Natural Theology; or, Evidence of the Existence and Attributes of the Deity, Collected from the Appearances of Nature*, 1802 (Oxford: Oxford University Press, 2006), 8.

21. Priscilla Wakefield, *Mental Improvement; or, The Beauties and Wonders of Nature and Art, Conveyed in a Series of Instructive Conversations*, 1794–1797 (East Lansing, MI: Colleagues Press, 1995), 3.

22. Ibid., 17.

23. Maria Hack, *Harry Beaufoy; or, The Pupil of Nature*, 1821 (Philadelphia, PA: Thomas Kite, 1828), 111, http://babel.hathitrust.org/cgi/pt?id=njp .32101063604183;view=1up;seq=3.

24. Ibid., 7.

25. Ibid., 10–11. Only in historical retrospect does Mrs. Beaufoy's insistence that Harry see animals, including humans, as machines seem oddly in line with Thomas H. Huxley's later argument to the same effect in "On the Hypothesis that Animals are Automata, and Its History," 1874, in Thomas H. Huxley, *Collected Essays*, 9 vols. (New York: Greenwood Press, 1968), 1: 199–250.

26. Paley, *Natural Theology*, 163–164.

27. Hack, *Harry Beaufoy*, 25.

28. Smith, *Conversations, Introducing Poetry*, 50–51.

29. Wakefield, *Mental Improvement*, 5.

30. Ibid., 20.

31. Ibid., 31.

32. There are, roughly, one hundred uses of "see," seventy of "look,' and ninety of "notice," and sixty of "observe" in the first edition of *Origin of Species*. See Charles Darwin, "On the Origin of Species, by Means of Natural Selection; or, the Preservation of Favoured Races in the Struggle for Existence" in Charles Darwin, *On the Origin of Species: A Facsimile of the First Edition* (1859), 1964 (Cambridge, MA: Harvard University Press, 2000).

33. Worthington Hooker, MD, *The Child's Book of Nature, For the Use of Families and Schools, in Three Parts*, 1874, Rev. ed. (New York: Harper & Brothers, 1886), II: 163–164.

34. Mrs. C. C. Campbell, *Natural History for Young Folks* (London: T. Nelson and Sons, 1884), 13.

35. J. G. Wood, *The Boy's Own Book of Natural History*, 1861 (London: George Routledge and Sons, 1897), 1.

36. Hooker, *The Child's Book*, 127.

37. Ibid., 161.

38. James Johonnot, *Friends in Feathers and Fur, and Other Neighbors, for Young Folks*, 1884 (New York: D. Appleton and Company, 1888), 5.

39. Gillian Beer, *Darwin's Plots: Evolutionary Narrative in Darwin, George Eliot and Nineteenth-Century Fiction*, 1983 (Cambridge: Cambridge University Press, 2000), 114.

40. Bernard Lightman, "'The Voices of Nature': Popularizing Victorian Science" in Bernard Lightman (ed.), *Victorian Science in Context* (Chicago, IL:

University of Chicago Press, 1997), 187–211 (194); and Alan Rauch, "Parables and Parodies: Margaret Gatty's Audiences in the *Parables from Nature*," *Children's Literature*, 25 (1997), 137–152 (140 and 142).

41. For biographies of Gatty, see Christabel Ward Maxwell, *Mrs. Gatty and Mrs. Ewing* (London: Constable, 1949); Wendy Katz, in *The Emblems of Margaret Gatty* (New York: AMS Press, 1993); and Suzanne Le-May Sheffield, *Revealing New Worlds: Three Victorian Women Naturalists* (London: Routledge, 2001).

42. Sheffield, *Revealing New Worlds*, 32 and 36.

43. Rauch, "Parables and Parodies," 145 and 144.

44. Tess Cosslett, *Talking Animals in British Children's Fiction, 1786–1914* (Aldershot: Ashgate, 2006), 98–99.

45. U. C. Knoepflmacher, "The Balancing of Child and Adult: An Approach to Victorian Fantasies for Children," *Nineteenth-Century Fiction*, 37:4 (1983), 497–530 (497).

46. Margaret Gatty to William Henry Harvey, May 4, 1861. Quoted in both Rauch, "Parables and Parodies," 145, and Sheffield, *Revealing New Worlds*, 30.

47. Karl Ernst von Baer, *Entwicklungsgeschichte der Thiere: Beobachtung und Reflexion* (Königsberg: Bornträger, 1828), 203–204. Quoted in Stephen Jay Gould, *Ontogeny and Phylogeny* (Cambridge, MA: Harvard University Press, 1977), 54.

48. In *Talking Animals*, Cosslett reads "Whereunto?" as an example of Gatty's propensities to "carnival," in which "comedy and irony threaten to destabilize the order and hierarchy Gatty is ostensibly committed to" (103). Cosslett asks intriguing questions but too quickly explains away the narrative and moral complications of the text by assuming that the story is, again, "not primarily written for children" (104).

49. Tess Cosslett, "Child's Place in Nature: Talking Animals in Victorian Children's Fiction," *Nineteenth-Century Contexts*, 23:4 (2002), 475–495 (482).

50. Myers, "Science for Women and Children," 180.

51. Margaret Gatty, *Parables from Nature, with Notes on the Natural History*, illus. P. H. Calderon, W. Holman Hunt, Otto Speckter, Lorenz Frolich, E. Burne Jones, Harrison Weir, J. Tenniel, J. Wolf, et al. (London: George Bell and Sons, 1888), 474.

52. Ibid., 485.

53. Ibid., 469.

54. Katz discusses the similarities between Gatty and Newman's religious thought and rhetorical strategies, particularly their uses of analogy, in *Emblems of Margaret Gatty*, 235–239; Maxwell focuses on Gatty's criticisms of the Tractarian Movement, of which Newman was a principal part, in *Mrs. Gatty and Mrs. Ewing*.

55. Gatty, *Parables from Nature, with Notes on the Natural History*, 477.
56. Thomas H. Huxley, "Prolegomena," 1894, in *Evolution and Ethics, and Other Essays* (New York: D. Appleton and Company, 1899), 1–45 (13).
57. Peter Kropotkin, *Mutual Aid: A Factor in Evolution*, 1902 (New York: McClure Phillips and Company, 1903), IX. The idea of "mutual aid" as a driving principle of evolution will be further discussed in Chapter 5.
58. Knoepflmacher, "Balancing of Child and Adult," 508–509.
59. Ibid., 503.
60. Ibid., 508 and 497.
61. Gatty, *Parables from Nature, with Notes on the Natural History*, 470.
62. Cannon Schmitt, "Evolution and Victorian Fiction" in Bernard Lightman and Bennett Zon (eds.), *Evolution and Victorian Culture* (Cambridge: Cambridge University Press, 2014), 17–38 (26).
63. Rudyard Kipling, "Something of Myself," 1937, in Rudyard Kipling, *Something of Myself, and Other Autobiographical Writings*, ed. Thomas Pinney (Cambridge: Cambridge University Press, 1990), 1–134 (22).
64. See Lightman, "'The Voices of Nature,'" 192.
65. Mrs. Henry Mackarness (ed.), *The Young Lady's Book: A Manual of Amusements, Exercises, Studies, and Pursuits* (London: George Routledge and Sons, 1876), 41.

chapter 2   Amphibious tendencies

1. Charles Kingsley, *The Water-Babies: A Fairy Tale for a Land-Baby*, 1863, 4th ed., illus. Linley Sambourne (London: Macmillan, 1890). *The Water-Babies* was originally serialized in *Macmillan's Magazine* from August 1862 to March 1863. Further references, except those noted below, are to the 1890 edition and will be cited parenthetically in text. An earlier version of my argument about Kingsley's *Water-Babies* and Spencer's pedagogical theories appeared in Jessica Straley, "Of Beasts and Boys: Kingsley, Spencer, and the Theory of Recapitulation," *Victorian Studies*, 49:4 (Summer 2007), 583–609.
2. See J. Stuart Maclure, (ed.), *Educational Documents: England & Wales 1816–1968*, 1969 (London: Methuen and Company. Ltd. 1975), 79–80.
3. See Matthew Arnold, *Reports on Elementary Schools, 1852–1882* (London and New York: Macmillan and Company, 1889); and Charles Dickens, *Hard Times*, 1854 (London: Penguin Books, 2003).
4. See Kingsley's collected lectures in Charles Kingsley, *The Works of Charles Kingsley*, 28 vols. (London: Macmillan and Company, 1880). Many of these lectures will be discussed individually.
5. Charles Kingsley, "Workmen of England," Placard, 1848. Reprinted in Frances Eliza Grenfell Kingsley (ed.), *Charles Kingsley, His Letters, and*

Memories of His Life, 2 vols., 1877 (New York: Charles Scribner's Sons, 1889), 1: 95–96 (96).

6. Ibid.

7. Benita Cullingford, *British Chimney Sweeps: Five Centuries of Sweeping* (Chicago, IL: New Amsterdam, 2000), 111.

8. For more detail on the history of the nineteenth-century school, see David Layton, *Science for the People: The Origins of the School Science Curriculum in England* (New York: George Allen & Unwin Ltd., 1973); R. C. Olby, G. N. Cantor, J. R. R. Christie, and M. J. S Hodge, *Companion to the History of Modern Science* (London: Routledge, 1990), 946–959, excerpted in William H. Brock, *Science for All: Studies in the History of Victorian Science and Education* (Aldershot: Ashgate Publishing Company, 1996), x; and Charles Birchenough, *History of Elementary Education in England and Wales from 1800 to the Present Day*, 1914 (London: University Tutorial Press, 1938).

9. See James A. Secord, "Science" in Leslie Howsam, Christopher Stray, Alice Jenkins, James A. Secord, Anna Vaniskaya, "What Victorians Learned: Perspectives on Victorian Schoolbooks," *Journal of Victorian Culture*, 12:2 (Autumn 2007), 262–285 (272–276). Much of the education in natural history received by children appeared in scientific dialogues for the middle-class home; these books are discussed in greater detail in Chapter 1.

10. Johann Gaspar Spurzheim, *Education: Its Elementary Principles, Founded on the Nature of Man*, 12th American ed. (New York: Fowlers and Wells, 1847), 14.

11. Ibid., 15.

12. Charles Darwin, "A Biographical Sketch of an Infant," *Mind: A Quarterly Review of Psychology and Philosophy*, 2 (1877), 285–294.

13. Johann Heinrich Pestalozzi, "How Gertrude Teaches Her Children," 1801. Quoted at length in Edward Biber, *Henry Pestalozzi, and His Plan of Education: Being an Account of His Life and Writings* (London: John Souter, 1831), 159–183(174).

14. Biber, *Henry Pestalozzi, and His Plan of Education*, 178.

15. Pestalozzi, "How Gertrude Teaches Her Children," in Ibid.,174

16. Henry Edwards, *Elementary Education: The Importance of Its Extension in Our Own Country* (London: Longman and Company, 1844), 10, https://books .google.com/books?id=tjYiAQAAMAAJ&printsec=frontcover&dq=elementary +education+edwards&hl=en&sa=X&ved=0ahUKEwiahvPd_73JAhVJ6GMK HRlRAFoQ6AEIMTAC#v=onepage&q=elementary%20education% 20edwards&f=false.

17. See Ann Taylor Allen, "Children Between Public and Private Worlds: The Kindergarten and Public Policy in Germany, 1840-Present" in

Roberta Wollons (ed.), *Kindergartens and Cultures: The Global Diffusion of an Idea* (New Haven, CT: Yale University Press, 2000), 16–41 (19).

18. Herbert Spencer, *Education: Intellectual, Moral, and Physical,* 1860 (New York: D. Appleton and Company, 1896), 103.

19. Ibid., 32.

20. Ibid., 64.

21. Herbert Spencer, *"Progress: Its Law and Cause,"* 1857, in Herbert Spencer, *Illustrations of Universal Progress: A Series of Discussions,* 1864 (New York: D. Appleton and Company, 1865), 1–60. This essay was originally published in *The Westminster Review,* 67 (April 1857), 445–447, 451, 454–456, 464–465.

22. Spencer, *Education,* 123.

23. Ibid., 124–125.

24. Birchenough, *History of Elementary Education,* 292; for a discussion of Spencer's influence on educational policy, see 285–313.

25. See Olby et al., *Companion to the History of Modern Science,* 958.

26. Spencer, *Education,* 78–79.

27. Augustus De Morgan, *Remarks on Elementary Education in Science: An Introductory Lecture* (London: John Taylor, 1830), 3.

28. Thomas H. Huxley, *On the Educational Value of the Natural History Sciences,* Lecture delivered July 22, 1854 (London: John van Voorst, 1854), 12.

29. Spencer, *Education,* 22.

30. Ibid., 61.

31. See John Locke, *Some Thoughts Concerning Education,* 1693 (Oxford: Clarendon Press, 1989), 177–178.

32. Spencer, *Education,* 92.

33. Ibid., 191.

34. Charles Kingsley, *Alton Locke: Tailor and Poet,* 1850 (London: Cassell and Company, Ltd., 1967); *Westward Ho!* (Chicago and New York: Rand, McNally and Company, 1855); and *The Heroes; or, Greek Fairy Tales for My Children,* 1855 (London and New York: Macmillan and Company, 1885).

35. Charles Kingsley, "The Science of Health" in *Health and Education,* 1874 (New York: D. Appleton and Company, 1893), 1–25 (1).

36. Ibid., 4–5.

37. Ibid., 7.

38. Ibid.

39. Ibid., 9–10.

40. Charles Kingsley, "How to Study Natural History," Lecture delivered at Reading, 1846, in *Works of Charles Kingsley,* XIX: 289–310 (291).

41. Charles Kingsley, "Science," Lecture delivered at the Royal Institution, 1866, in *Works of Charles Kingsley,* XIX: 229–257 (248). Neither *Works of Charles Kingsley* nor *Health and Education* gives a date for this lecture, but the year

1866 is indicated by Frances Kingsley (ed.), *Charles Kingsley, His Letters, and Memories of His Life*, 368.

42. For a history of "muscular Christianity" and Kingsley's role in the development of the idea, see Bruce Haley, *The Healthy Body and Victorian Culture* (Cambridge, MA: Harvard University Press, 1977).

43. Charles Kingsley, *Glaucus; or, The Wonders of the Shore*, 3rd ed. (Cambridge: Macmillan and Company, 1855), 39.

44. Charles Kingsley, *Town Geology*, 1872, in *Works of Charles Kingsley*, XIX: 3–151 (13–14).

45. Gillian Beer, *Darwin's Plots: Evolutionary Narrative in Darwin, George Eliot and Nineteenth-Century Fiction*, 1983 (Cambridge: Cambridge University Press, 2000), 120.

46. Alan Rauch, *Useful Knowledge: The Victorians, Morality, and the March of Intellect* (Durham, NC: Duke University Press, 2001), 183.

47. For contemporary writings on the fear of degeneration among the working classes, see John Cantlie, *Degeneration Amongst Londoners*, Lecture delivered at the Parkes Museum of Hygiene, January 27, 1885 (London: Field and Tuer, 1885).

48. See, for example, Q. D. Leavis, "The Water-Babies," *Children's Literature in Education*, 23 (1976), 155–163 (157); and John Goldthwaite, *The Natural History of Make-Believe: A Guide to the Principal Works of Britain, Europe, and America* (Oxford: Oxford University Press, 1996), 73.

49. Beer, *Darwin's Plots*, 126.

50. In *Adolescence: Its Psychology and Its Relations to Physiology, Anthropology, Sociology, Sex, Crime, Religion and Education*, 2 vols., 1904 (New York: D. Appleton and Company, 1920), American psychologist G. Stanley Hall uses the child's likeness to an amphibian to argue for a recapitulative pedagogy that can counter the tendency for degeneration. He compares the current education system's premature lessons in modern civility to "the old error of amputating the tadpole's tail rather than letting it be absorbed to develop the legs that make a higher life on land possible" (II: 231). Hall's recapitulative theories are discussed at greater length in Chapter 4.

51. Naomi Wood, "A (Sea) Green Victorian: Charles Kingsley and *The Water-Babies*," *The Lion and the Unicorn*, 19:2 (December 1995), 233–252 (244).

52. William Paley, *Natural Theology; or, Evidence of the Existence of Attributes of the Deity, Collected from the Appearances of Nature*, 1802 (Oxford: Oxford University Press, 2006), 7–15.

53. Kingsley's illustrations of degeneration also borrow from Scottish geologist Hugh Miller's *The Foot-Prints of the Creator* (1849), his momentarily popular rebuttal to Robert Chambers's *Vestiges of the Natural History of*

Creation (1844). Unlike contemporary natural theologians, Miller did not maintain that all organic forms had been static since Creation, but rather that they had retrogressed. He finds his most conspicuous example of this physical decline – evidence of an analogous moral decline – among fish. The flounder, for instance, exhibits everywhere "misarrangement and misorder," especially in its "squint eyes," its "strangely asymmetrical" jaws and its "wry mouth – twisted in the opposite direction, as if to keep up such a balance of deformity as that which the breast-hump of a hunchback forms to the hump behind." See Hugh Miller, *The Foot-Prints of the Creator; or, The Asterolepis of Stromness*, 1849, 15th ed. (Boston, MA: Guild and Lincoln, 1873), 160 and 163.

54. Sloth, or indeed the mammal called a sloth, figures more dominantly in Alton's Locke's dream vision of his own recapitulation through prehistoric mammalian forms in Kingsley's novel of the same title. In "The Sins of Sloths," Alan Rauch reads Kingsley's use of the sloth, and his antediluvian ancestor the Megatherium, as "the impossibility of advancement" that contrasts with the "potential in the direst adversity" represented by *The Water-Babies'* eft. See Alan Rauch, "The Sins of Sloths: The Moral Status of Fossil Megatheria in Victorian Culture" in Deborah Denenholz Morse and Martin A. Danahay (eds.), *Victorian Animals Dreams: Representations of Animals in Victorian Literature and Culture* (Surrey: Ashgate Publishing Limited, 2007), 215–228 (223).

55. Charles Kingsley, "The Natural Theology of the Future," Lecture delivered at Scion College, 1871, in *Works of Charles Kingsley*, XIX: 313–336 (332). Reworking Paley's insistence in *Natural Theology* that evidence of design necessitates belief in a Designer, Kingsley argues that "if there be evolution, there must be an evolver" (330).

56. Jean-Baptiste Lamarck, *Zoological Philosophy: An Exposition with Regard to the Natural History of Animals*, 1809, trans. Hugh Elliot (London: Macmillan and Company, Ltd., 1914), 119–124.

57. Kingsley, "The Natural Theology of the Future," 314.

58. Caroline Sumpter, *The Victorian Press and the Fairy Tale* (Basingstoke: Palgrave, 2008), 74.

59. Jonathan Padley, "Marginal(ized) Demarcator: (Mis)Reading *The Water-Babies*," *Children's Literature Association Quarterly*, 34:1 (Spring 2009), 51–64 (58 and 57).

60. Humphrey Carpenter, *Secret Gardens: The Golden Age of Children's Literature from Alice's Adventures in Wonderland to Winnie-the-Pooh* (Boston, MA: Houghton Mifflin Company, 1985), 24.

61. Goldthwaite, *Natural History of Make-Believe*, 73.

62. Padley, "Marginal(ized) Demarcator," 54.

63. William Wordsworth, "Ode," 1807, in Stephen Gill (ed.), *William Wordsworth: The Major Works* (Oxford: Oxford University Press, 1984), 297–302 (299).

64. Ibid.

65. Charles Kingsley, *The Water-Babies: A Fairy Tale for a Land-Baby* (London: Macmillan, 1863), 155. The paragraph containing this sentiment, as well as the next paragraph about Locke (discussed below), disappeared by the 1890 edition of the book.

66. Charles Kingsley, "The Tree of Knowledge," 1879, in *Health and Education*, 52–68(56).

67. The relationship between recapitulation theory and female development is discussed in Chapter 5.

68. Kingsley, "How to Study Natural History," 299.

69. John Locke, *An Essay Concerning Human Understanding*, 1689 (Oxford: Clarendon Press, 1975), 156.

70. Ibid., 157.

71. Kingsley, *The Water-Babies* (1863), 155.

72. Richard Owen, "On the Characters, Principles of Division, and Primary Groups of the Class Mammalia," *Journal of the Proceedings of the Linnean Society of London*, 2.5 (June 1857), 1–37. The thesis was repeated in "The Gorilla and the Negro," *Athenaeum*, No. 1743 (March 23, 1861), 395–397; and in "On the Zoological Significance of the Brain and Limb Characteristics of the Gorilla, as Contrasted with Those of Man," *Medical Times and Gazette* (October 1862), 373–374.

73. Thomas H. Huxley, *Man's Place in Nature, and Other Anthropological Essays*, 1863 (New York: D. Appleton and Company, 1919), 98. Huxley responded first to Owen in "Man and the Apes," *Athenaeum*, No. 1744 (March 30, 1861), 43, again in "The Brain of Man and Apes," *Medical Times and Gazette* (October 1862), and a third time in *Man's Place in Nature*. The debate was popularly satirized; the October 18, 1862 edition of *Punch*, for instance, included a poem entitled "The Gorilla's Dilemma" that contemplates, "Must I humbly take rank as quadruman,/ As OWEN maintains that I ought:/ Or rise into brotherhood human,/ As HUXLEY has flatt'ringly taught?" (164). The first stanza of the poem from *Punch* is reprinted in Jerold Savory and Patricia Marks (eds.), *The Smiling Muse: Victoriana in the Comic Press* (Cranbury, NJ: Associated University Press, 1985), 60.

74. The narrator repeats this assertion almost word for word as the final sentence of the book (330).

75. Kingsley, "How to Study Natural History," 301.

76. Letter 3426 – Charles Kingsley to Charles Darwin (January 31, 1862). Darwin Correspondence Project. www.darwinproject.ac.uk/entry-3426. Darwin's response is also available on the DCP site.

77. Cannon Schmitt, *Darwin and the Memory of the Human: Evolution, Savages, and South America* (Cambridge: Cambridge University Press, 2009), 117. Schmitt discusses Kingsley's letter and Darwin's response to it, 49 and 116–118.

78. Ibid., 118.

79. Board of Education, *Suggestions for the Consideration of Teachers and Others Concerned in the Work of Public Elementary Schools* (London: His Majesty's Stationery Office, 1905), 35. *The Water-Babies* is recommended in a revised edition, reprinted with revision of the parts relating to English, Arithmetic, Geography, History and Singing (London: His Majesty's Stationery Office, 1912), 36.

80. Charles Kingsley, *The Water-Babies: A Fairy-Tale for a Land-Baby, Adapted for Use in Schools*, Bell's Literature Readers, illus. Eva Roos (London: George Bell & Sons, 1908), 79.

81. Charles Kingsley and Coral Woodward, *Kingsley's Water-Babies, Arranged for Youngest Readers* (Boston, MA: Educational Publishing Company, 1898).

82. Miles Gloriosus, Review of "Charles Kingsley: *The Water-Babies*," *School and Home Education*, 36:3 (November 1916), 78. The edition under discussion is J. H. Strickney (ed.), *The Water Babies*, illus. Florence Liley Young (Boston, MA: Ginn and Company, 1916).

83. Charles Kingsley and Winifred Howard, *The Water-Babies, Adapted and Re-Told with Copious Natural History Notes and a Scheme of Correlated Lessons and Handwork*, illus. Margaret Ashworth (London: Sir Isaac Pitman, Ltd., 1913).

84. Ibid., 153.

85. See, on Dreiser, Bert Bender, *Evolution and "the Sex Problem": American Narratives during the Eclipse of Darwinism* (Kent, OH: The Kent State University Press, 2004), 116; and on Heinlein, William H. Patterson, *Robert Heinlein: In Dialogue with His Century*, 2 vols. (New York: Tor Books, 2010), II: 24.

86. Philip Henry Gosse, *Romance of Natural History*, 2 vols., 1860–1861, 4th. ed (London: James Nisbet and Company, 1861), I: v.

chapter 3   Generic variability

1. Lewis Carroll, *Alice's Adventures in Wonderland*, illus. John Tenniel, 1865, in *Alice's Adventures in Wonderland* and *Through the Looking-Glass*, ed. Hugh Haughton (London: Penguin Books, 1998), 11. The first edition of *Alice's Adventures in Wonderland* was published by Macmillan and Company in 1865, and the first edition of *Through the Looking-Glass and What Alice Found There*, also illustrated by Tenniel, was published by Macmillan and Company in 1872. Further references to both Carroll's *Alice's Adventures in*

Wonderland and *Through the Looking-Glass* are to the Penguin edition and will be cited parenthetically in text.

2. William Empson, "*Alice in Wonderland*: The Child as Swain" in *Some Versions of Pastoral* (New York: New Directions, 1935), 253–294 (255).

3. Nancy Lacey Schwartz, "The Dodo and the Caucus Race," *Jabberwocky*, 6:1 (Winter 1977), 3–15 (3).

4. Donald Rackin, "Blessed Rage: The *Alices* and the Modern Quest for Order" in *Alice's Adventures in Wonderland and Through the Looking-Glass: Nonsense, Sense, and Meaning* (New York: Twayne Publishers, 1991), 77.

5. U. C. Knoepflmacher, *Ventures into Childland: Victorians, Fairy Tales, and Femininity* (Chicago, IL: University of Chicago Press, 1998), 176.

6. Robert Polhemus, *Comic Faith: The Great Tradition from Austen to Joyce* (Chicago, IL: University of Chicago Press, 1980), 261. Rose Lovell-Smith provocatively suggests in "The Walrus and the Carpenter" that Carroll's portrayal of these predatory beachcombers is a parody of Margaret Gatty's "Whereunto?" (1861). See Rose Lovell-Smith, "'The Walrus and the Carpenter': Lewis Carroll. Margaret Gatty, and Natural History for Children," *Australasian Victorian Studies Journal*, 10 (2004), 43–69.

7. Rose Lovell-Smith, "The Animals of Wonderland: Tenniel as Carroll's Reader," *Criticism*, 45:4 (2003), 383–415 (385). In another article about Wonderland's animals, "Eggs and Serpents: Natural History Reference in Lewis Carroll's Scene of Alice and the Pigeon," *Children's Literature*, 35 (2007), 27–53, Lovell-Smith argues that the Pigeon episode specifically borrows from a common "egg thief" motif of Victorian natural history books.

8. For a discussion of the overlaps between *Wonderland* and *The Water-Babies*, see John Goldthwaite, *The Natural History of Make-Believe: A Guide to the Principal Works of Britain, Europe, and America* (New York: Oxford University Press, 1996), 123–125 and 131–133.

9. Isaac Watts, "Against Idleness and Mischief" in Isaac Watts, *Divine and Moral Songs for the Use of Children*, 1715 (London: John Van Vorst, 1848), 49–50 (50).

10. A. Dwight Culler, "The Darwinian Revolution and Literary Form" in George Levine and William Madden (eds.), *The Art of Victorian Prose* (Oxford: Oxford University Press, 1968), 224–246 (240). For further consideration of Carroll's attitude toward evolutionary theory, see Morton N. Cohen, *Lewis Carroll: A Biography* (New York: Alfred A. Knopf, 1995), 350–352.

11. William Paley, *Natural Theology; or, Evidence of the Existence of Attributes of the Deity, Collected from the Appearances of Nature*, 1802 (Oxford: Oxford University Press, 2006), 15.

12. Sarah Trimmer, *An Easy Introduction to the Knowledge of Nature, and Reading the Holy Scriptures. Adapted to the Capacities of Children*, 1780, 10th ed. (London: T. Longman and O. Rees, G.G. and J. Robinson, 1799), 82.

13. Ibid., 38.

14. Tom Hood, *From Nowhere to the North Pole: A Noah's Ark-Æological Narrative* (London: Chatto and Windus, 1875), 9.

15. Ibid., 102.

16. Ibid., 101.

17. Ibid., 95.

18. Charles Kingsley, *The Water-Babies: A Fairy Tale for a Land-Baby*, 1863, 4th ed., illus. Linley Sambourne (London: Macmillan and Company, 1890), 105–106.

19. Hood, *From Nowhere to the North Pole*, 55–56.

20. Kingsley, *The Water-Babies*, 108.

21. Albert and George Gresswell, *The Wonderland of Evolution* (London: Field & Tuer, 1884), 55. I want to thank Bernard Lightman for drawing my attention to this delightfully strange book during the North American Victorian Studies Association conference in Montreal (November 2010).

22. Kingsley, *The Water-Babies*, 69–70.

23. Edward Lear, *Nonsense Botany*, 1888 (Hyattsville, MD: Rebecca Press, 1983), 2–3 and 30–31.

24. Lovell-Smith's "The Animals of Wonderland" discusses Tenniel's use of natural history images in this illustration, 388–391.

25. Susan Stewart, *nonsense: Aspects of Intertextuality in Folklore and Literature* (Baltimore, MD: The Johns Hopkins University Press, 1979), 34–36.

26. Wim Tigges, "An Anatomy of Nonsense" in Wim Tiggs (ed.), *Explorations in the Field of Nonsense* (Amsterdam: Rodopi, 1987), 23–46(27).

27. Charles L. Dodgson (Lewis Carroll), *Curiosa Mathematica: Part I, A New Theory of Parallels*, 1888 (London: Macmillan and Company, 1890), xv.

28. Gideon Algernon Mantell, *The Wonders of Geology*, 2 vols. (London: Relfe and Fletcher, 1838); and Samuel Griswold Goodrich, *The Wonders of Geology, by the Author of Peter Parley's Tales* (Philadelphia, PA: Thomas, Cowperthwaite and Company, 1846).

29. See Thomas H. Huxley, "Science and Culture," 1880, in *Science and Education*, 1898 (New York: P. F. Collier & Son, 1905); and Matthew Arnold, "Literature and Science," 1882, in *Essays in Criticism, Second Series: Contributions to 'The Pall Mall Gazette' and Discourses in America* (London: Macmillan and Company, Ltd., 1903), 317–348.

30. Arnold, "Literature and Science," 333.

31. Matthew Arnold, "General Report for the Year 1861" in *Reports on Elementary Schools, 1852–1882* (London and New York: Macmillan and Company, 1889), 90–95 (93).

32. Ibid., 91–92.

33. Ibid., 95.

34. Stewart, *nonsense*, 57–84; and Linda Hutcheon, *A Theory of Parody: The Teaching of Twentieth-Century Art Forms* (New York: Methuen, 1985), 6.

35. Samuel Johnson and John Walker (ed.), *A Dictionary of the English Language*, 1755 (London: John Williamson and Company, 1839), 678.

36. Joseph A. Dane considers the possibility that parody is a degradation (and an essentially parasitic form) in *Parody: Critical Concepts Versus Literary Practices, Aristophanes to Stern* (Norman, OK: University of Oklahoma Press, 1988), 6.

37. Hutcheon, *Theory of Parody*, 35–36 and 97.

38. Margaret Gatty, "A Lesson of Faith," 1855, in *Parables from Nature, First and Second Series, With a Memoir by Her Daughter, Juliana Horatia Ewing*, illus. P. H. Calderon, W. Holman Hunt, E. Burne Jones, Otto Speckter, G. H. Thomas, John Tenniel, M. E. Edwards, Lorenz Fröhlich, Harrison Weir, J. Wolf, etc., 2 vols. (London: George Bell and Sons, 1885 and 1886), I: 1–5. Gatty's fiction is discussed in Chapter 1.

39. Charles Darwin, Notebook D in Paul H. Barrett, Peter J. Gautrey, Sandra Herbert, David Kohn, and Sydney Smith (eds.), *Charles Darwin's Notebooks, 1836–1844: Geology, Transmutation of Species, Metaphysical Enquiries* (Ithaca, NY: Cornell University Press, 1987), D40, D41, D62e, and D63e.

40. Robert Southey, "The Old Man's Comforts, and How He Gained Them," 1799. Quoted in Carroll, *Alice's Adventures in Wonderland*, 307–308 (308).

41. This ordering of the chapters, however, omits "A Wasp in a Wig," a chapter Carroll wrote to appear between "It's My Own Invention" and "Queen Alice" but was not published as part of *Looking-Glass*.

42. Matthew Arnold, "General Report for the Year 1872" in *Reports on Elementary Schools*, 162–170 (163).

43. Lewis Carroll, "Doublets: A Word Puzzle," 1879, in Lewis Carroll, *Diversions & Digressions of Lewis Carroll*, ed. Stuart Dodgson Collingwood (New York: Dover Publications, Inc., 1961), 275–286 (278).

44. Ibid., 282 and 283.

45. Fanny Umphelby, *The Child's Guide to Knowledge, Being a Collection of Useful and Familiar Questions and Answers on Every-Day Subjects, Adapted for Young Persons, and Arranged in the Most Simple and Easy Language. By a Lady*, 1825, 55th ed. (London: Simpkin Marshall, 1884), 1.

46. Greg Myers, "Science for Women and Children: The Dialogue of Popular Science in the Nineteenth Century" in John Christie and Sally Shuttleworth (eds.), *Nature Transfigured: Literature and Science, 1700–1900* (Manchester: Manchester University Press, 1989), 171–200 (179).

47. Ibid., 195.

48. Paley, *Natural Theology*, 7.

49. Ibid., 158.

50. Charles Lyell, *Principles of Geology: Being an Attempt to Explain the Former Changes of the Earth's Surface, By Reference to Causes Now in Operation*, 3 vols., 1830–1833 (London: Penguin, 1997), I.7: 67.

51. See William Buckland, *Geology and Mineralogy Considered with Reference to Natural Theology*, 2 vols., 1836 (Philadelphia, PA: Carey, Lea, and Blanchard, 1837). Discussed in Peter J. Bowler, *Evolution: The History of an Idea*, 1983, 25th Anniversary ed. (Berkeley, CA: University of California Press, 2009), 116–120.

52. Terry Caesar, "I Quite Forget What – Say a Daffodily: Victorian Parody," *ELH*, 51:4 (1984), 795–818 (796–797).

53. George Levine, *Darwin and the Novelists: Patterns of Science in Victorian Fiction* (Cambridge, MA: Harvard University Press, 1988), 37.

54. Stewart, *nonsense*, 143.

55. *Alice's Adventures under Ground: A Facsimile of the Original Lewis Carroll Manuscript*, 1864 (Ann Arbor, MI: University Microfilms, Inc., 1964), 66. According to Haughton's introduction Carroll's *Alice's Adventures in Wonderland*, xxxv, Carroll's diaries report that he finished the manuscript of *under Ground* in 1863, but he did not present it to Alice Liddell until 1864.

56. Ibid., 72. This exchange is repeated in Carroll, *Wonderland*, 71.

57. See Haughton's notes in Carroll, *Alice's Adventures in Wonderland*, 344 and 339.

58. G. E. Farrow, *The Wallypug of Why*, 1895. Excerpted in Carolyn Sigler (ed.), *Alternative Alices: Visions and Revisions of Lewis Carroll's Alice Books* (Lexington, KY: University of Kentucky Press, 1997), 243–267 (250).

59. Juliana Horatia Ewing, "Amelia and the Dwarfs" in Mrs. Alfred (Margaret) Gatty (ed.), *Aunt Judy's Christmas Volume for Young People*, 8 (London: Bell and Daldy, 1870), 259–275(263), http://babel.hathitrust.org/cgi/pt?id=nyp .33433082288402;view=1up;seq=271.

60. Christina Rossetti, *Speaking Likenesses* (London: Macmillan and Company, 1874), 26.

61. See, for example, Sandra Beckett, "Parodic Play with Paintings in Picture Books," *Children's Literature*, 29 (2001), 175–195.

62. Arnold, "Literature and Science," 347.

63. Ibid., 331–332.

chapter 4   The cure of the wild

1. See J. Stuart Maclure (ed.), *Educational Documents: England & Wales 1816–1968*, 1969 (London: Methuen and Company, Ltd., 1972); J. S. Hurt, *Elementary Schooling and the Working Classes, 1860–1918* (London: Routledge & Kegan Paul, 1979), 75–100; the History of Education Society (ed.), *Studies in the Government and Control of Education since 1860* (London: Methuen,

1970); and Jacqueline Rose also discusses the consolidation of the school board in *The Case of Peter Pan; or, The Impossibility of Children's Fiction, 1984* (Philadelphia, PA: University of Pennsylvania Press, 1993).

2. See Board of Education, *Suggestions for the Consideration of Teachers and Others Concerned in the Work of Public Elementary Schools* (London: His Majesty's Stationery Office, 1905).

3. Rudyard Kipling, "Slaves of the Lamp (Part II)," 1899, in Isabel Quigley (ed.), *The Complete Stalky & Co.* (Oxford: Oxford University Press, 1987), 279–297 (281).

4. Victorian discussions of degeneration include E. Ray Lankester, *Degeneration: A Chapter in Darwinism* (London: Macmillan and Company, 1880); John Cantlie, *Degeneration Amongst Londoners*, Lecture delivered at the Parkes Museum of Hygiene, January 27, 1885 (London: Field and Tuer, 1885); and Max Nordau, *Degeneration*, 1892 (Lincoln, NE: University of Nebraska Press, 1968). Modern critical works discussing Victorian fears of degeneration include Edward J. Chamberlain and Sander L. Gilman (eds.), *Degeneration: The Dark Side of Progress* (New York: Columbia University Press, 1985); and Daniel Pick, *Faces of Degeneration: A European Disorder, 1848–1918* (Cambridge: Cambridge University Press, 1989).

5. Lankester, *Degeneration*, 32.

6. Rudyard Kipling, "One View of the Question" in *Many Inventions*, 1893 (New York: Doubleday, Page, and Company, 1914), 79–105 (89, 98, 92).

7. Rudyard Kipling, "In the Rukh" in *Many Inventions*, 222–264 (236).

8. Ibid., 254.

9. Rudyard Kipling, *The Jungle Books*, ed. Daniel Karlin (London: Penguin Books, 1987), 40 and 256. The individual stories that make up *The Jungle Book* and *The Second Jungle Book* appeared in magazines, such as *St. Nicholas* and *McClure's Magazine*, between 1894 and 1895; see E. W. Martindell, *A Bibliography of the Works of Rudyard Kipling* (London: The Bookman's Journal, 1922). The text of the Penguin edition is based on the first edition of *The Jungle Book*, illus. J. Lockwood Kipling, W. H. Drake, and P. Frenzeny (London: Macmillan and Company, 1894) and the first edition of *The Second Jungle Book*, illus. J. Lockwood Kipling (London: Macmillan and Company, 1895). Further references are to the Penguin edition and will be cited parenthetically in text.

10. Zohreh T. Sullivan, *Narratives of Empire: The Fictions of Rudyard Kipling* (Cambridge: Cambridge University Press, 1993), 28.

11. Jane Hotchkiss, "The Jungle Eden: Kipling, Wolf Boys, and the Colonial Imagination," *Victorian Literature and Culture*, 29:2 (2001), 435–449 (448).

12. Don Randall, *Kipling's Imperial Boy: Adolescence and Cultural Hybridity* (New York; Palgrave, 2000), 16.

13. Hotchkiss notably disagrees with the assertion of "In the Rukh" as the end to Mowgli's story, though she maintains the dichotomy inherent in the postcolonial reading.
14. Randall, *Kipling's Imperial Boy*, 67.
15. Ibid., 72.
16. In his autobiography, *Something of Myself* (1937), Kipling says that he wrote "In the Rukh" before any of the stories from *The Jungle Books*; see Rudyard Kipling, *Something of Myself*, 1937, in Rudyard Kipling, *Something of Myself, and Other Autobiographical Writings*, ed. Thomas Pinney (Cambridge: Cambridge University Press, 1990), 1–134 (67). But according to Charles Carrington's *Rudyard Kipling: His Life and His Work* (London: Macmillan, 1955), his wife, Caroline Balestier Kipling, claimed in her diaries that "Mowgli's Brothers" was written before "In the Rukh." In *Kipling and the Children* (London: Elek Books Ltd., 1965), Roger Lancelyn Green says that Caroline's diary only speaks of revisions, and thus her journals should not trump Kipling's recollections (110–112).
17. According to Karlin's "Note on the Text" of *The Jungle Books*, the "Outward Bound" edition of *The Jungle Books* (1897) and a later Sussex edition follow this pattern (28–29). Kipling extracted the Mowgli saga from the two children's collections and rewrote it as *The Jungle Play* around 1900. Unlike *The Jungle Books*, *The Jungle Play* does include a marriage plot. In his introduction to the only published version of the play, Thomas Pinney writes that "*The Jungle Play* is that 'story for grown-ups'" that "Tiger-Tiger!" promises. See Rudyard Kipling, *The Jungle Play*, c. 1900, ed. Thomas Pinney (London: The Penguin Press, 2000).
18. G. Stanley Hall, *Adolescence: Its Psychology and Its Relations to Physiology, Anthropology, Sociology, Sex, Crime, Religion and Education*, 2 vols., 1904 (New York: D. Appleton and Company, 1920), II: 45–46.
19. Ibid., I: XI and II: 231.
20. Ibid., II: 60 and 66.
21. Here is also Kipling's refashioning of Margaret Gatty's *Parables from Nature* (1855–1871), which he read and imitated as a young writer. See Kipling, *Something of Myself*, 22. Instead of critiquing human vision, as Gatty's creatures do, each of Kipling's animals showcases its Darwinian adaptations.
22. Hall, *Adolescence*, II: 65.
23. Ibid., II: 65.
24. Allen MacDuffie, "*The Jungle Books*: Rudyard Kipling's Lamarckian Fantasy," *PMLA*, 129:1 (2014), 18–34; and Seth Lerer, *Children's Literature: A Reader's History from Aesop to Harry Potter* (Chicago, IL: University of Chicago Press, 2009). Lerer's work, in turn, cites my dissertation on which this book is based: "How the Child Lost Its Tail: Evolutionary Theory, Victorian Pedagogy, and

the Development of Children's Literature, 1860–1920" (Ph.D., dissertation, Stanford University, 2005).

25. MacDuffie, "Kipling's Lamarckian Fantasy," 22.
26. Rudyard Kipling, *Just So Stories*, 1902 (New York: Everyman's Library, 1992).
27. Herbert Spencer, "Progress: Its Law and Cause," 1857, in Herbert Spencer, *Illustrations of Universal Progress; A Series of Discussions*, 1864 (New York: D. Appleton and Company, 1865), 1–60 (10). This essay was originally published in *The Westminster Review*, 67 (April 1857), 445–447, 451, 454–456, 464–465.
28. Karl Ernst von Baer, *Entwicklungsgeschichte der Thiere: Beobachtung und Reflexion* (Königsberg: Bornträger, 1828), 203–204. For more information about von Baer and his objections to recapitulation, and Spencer's adoption of his theories, see Stephen Jay Gould, *Ontogeny and Phylogeny* (Cambridge, MA: Harvard University Press, 1977), 55, and my discussion in the Introduction of this book.
29. Edward Drinker Cope, *The Primary Factors of Organic Evolution* (Chicago, IL: The Open Court Publishing Company, 1896), 173.
30. Ibid., v–vii. Cope says that he is specifically responding to George Romanes's *Post-Darwinian Questions* (1895)
31. Rudyard Kipling, *Kim*, 1901 (New York: Everyman's Library, 1995).
32. Randall, *Kipling's Imperial Boy*, 158.
33. Satya P. Mohanty, "Drawing the Color Line: Kipling and the Culture of Colonial Rule" in Dominick LaCapra (ed.), *The Bounds of Race: Perspectives on Hegemony and Resistance* (Ithaca, NY: Cornell University Press, 1991), 311–343 (316).
34. Hall, *Adolescence*, 1: x.
35. Tess Cosslett, *Talking Animals in British Children's Fiction, 1786–1914* (Aldershot: Ashgate, 2006), 130.
36. Ibid., 130 and 131.
37. Ibid., 136.
38. Sue Walsh, *Kipling's Children's Literature: Language, Identity, and Constructions of Childhood* (Aldershot: Ashgate, 2010), 58.
39. See Stephen Benson, "Kipling's Singing Voice: Setting the *Jungle Books*," *Critical Survey*, 13:3 (2001), 40–60.
40. T. S. Eliot (ed.), *A Choice of Kipling's Verse*, 1941 (London: Faber & Faber, 1963), 5. In *Kipling, the Poet* (London: Secker and Warburg, 1994), Peter Keating discusses this claim, recognizing that eighteenth and early- to mid-nineteenth-century novels contained poetry often as epigraphs to prose chapters. By the end of the Victorian period, the practice was rare, and Kipling's extensive use of poetry within the prose form, which gave (as I am suggesting) equal weight to the two forms, justifies Eliot's argument that Kipling's "mixed form" was something new.

41. Benson, "Kipling's Singing Voice," 49.
42. Ibid., 52.
43. Monique Morgan, *Narrative Means, Lyric Ends: Temporality in the Nineteenth-Century British Long Poem* (Columbus, OH: The Ohio State University Press, 2009), 3–4.
44. Kathryn Bond Stockton, *The Queer Child; or Growing Sideways in the Twentieth Century* (Durham, NC: Duke University Press, 2009), 7 and 92.
45. Neil Cocks, "Hunting the Animal Boy," *The Yearbook of English Studies*, 32 (2002), 177–185.
46. Marah Gubar, *Artful Dodgers: Reconceiving the Golden Age of Children's Literature* (Oxford: Oxford University Press, 2009), 38.
47. Herbert Spencer, *Education: Intellectual, Moral, and Physical*, 1860 (New York: D. Appleton and Company, 1896), 106.
48. See Karl Groos, *The Play of Animals*, trans. Elizabeth Baldwin (New York: D. Appleton and Company, 1898) and *The Play of Man* 1901, trans. Elizabeth Baldwin (New York: D. Appleton and Company, 1912).
49. Hall, *Adolescence*, 1: 202.
50. See Robert Baden-Powell, *Scouting for Boys*, 1908 (Oxford: Oxford University Press, 2004) and Lord (Robert) Baden-Powell, *The Wolf Cub's Handbook*, 1916, 9th ed. (London: C. Arthur Pearson, 1938). For more on the Scouts and Baden-Powell's ideas about boyhood, see Robert H. MacDonald, *Sons of the Empire: The Frontier and the Boy Scout Movement, 1890–1918* (Toronto: University of Toronto Press, 1993); and in reference to Baden-Powell's debt to Kipling, see Hugh Brognan, *Mowgli's Sons: Kipling and Baden-Powell's Scouts* (London: Jonathan Cape, 1987).
51. MacDonald, *Sons of the Empire*, 132.
52. Baden-Powell, *The Wolf Cub's Handbook*, Dedication.
53. Ibid., 25.
54. Ibid., 61.
55. Ibid., 62.
56. Ibid., 40–41.
57. Hall, *Adolescence*, 1: x.
58. "Visit to Canada," Newspaper clipping (September 25, 1910). Quoted in MacDonald, *Sons of the Empire*, 146.
59. Baden-Powell, *The Wolf-Cub's Handbook*, 225.
60. Ibid., 60–61.
61. Edgar Rice Burroughs, *Tarzan of the Apes*, 1914 (London: Penguin Books, 1990), 174 and 189.
62. Dana Seitler, *Atavistic Tendencies: The Culture of Science in American Modernity* (Minneapolis, MN: University of Minnesota Press, 2008), 133.

63. Gail Bederman, *Manliness & Civilization: A Cultural History of Gender and Race in the United States, 1880–1917* (Chicago, IL: University of Chicago Press, 1995), 171 and 175.

64. Burroughs, *Tarzan of the Apes*, 53.

65. See Jean-Jacques Rousseau, *Émile: or, On Education*, 1762 (London: Everyman, 1993), 176–177; and Karl Marx, *Capital: A Critique of Political Economy*, 3 vols., 1867, ed. Frederick Engels, trans. Samuel Moore and Edward Aveling (Chicago, IL: Charles H. Kerr and Company, 1915), 1: 88–91, excerpted in Daniel Defoe, *Robinson Crusoe*, 1719, Norton Critical Edition, 2nd ed., ed. Michael Shinagel (New York: W. W. Norton and Company, 1994), 274–277.

66. Burroughs, *Tarzan of the Apes*, 115.

67. Ibid., 167.

68. See Murray N. Rothbard, *Education: Free and Compulsory* (Auburn, AL: The Ludwig von Mises Institute, 1999); and Nancy E. Walker, Catherine M. Brooks, and Lawrence S. Wrightsman, *Children's Rights in the United States: In Search of a National Policy* (Thousand Oaks, CA: Sage Publications, Inc., 1999).

69. G. Stanley Hall, "The Ideal School as Based on Child Study," *National Education Association Journal of Addresses and Proceedings*, Washington D.C. (1901), 475–482 and 488.

70. See Barbara Beatty, "'The Letter Killeth': Americanization and Multicultural Education in Kindergartens in the United States, 1856–1920" in Roberta Wollons (ed.), *Kindergartens and Cultures: The Global Diffusion of an Idea* (New Haven, CT: Yale University Press, 2000), 42–58 (49–51).

71. John Dewey, *The School and Society: Being Three Lectures*, 1899, 2nd ed. (Chicago, IL: University of Chicago Press and New York: McClure, Phillips and Company, 1900), 62.

72. Ibid., 34–36.

73. Lora Romero, *Home Fronts: Domesticity and Its Critics in the Antebellum United States* (Durham, NC: Duke University Press, 1997), 41.

74. Kenneth B. Kidd, *Making American Boys: Boyology and the Feral Tale* (Minneapolis, MN: University of Minnesota Press, 2004), 15.

75. See Daniel Francis, *The Imaginary Indian: The Image of the Indian in Canadian Culture* (Vancouver: Arsenal Pulp Press, 1992), 144–168.

76. Ernest Thompson Seton, *The Gospel of the Redman: An Indian Bible*, 1936 (San Diego, CA: Book Tree, 2006).

77. Ernest Thompson Seton, *Wild Animals I Have Known* (New York: Grosset & Dunlap, 1898), 12.

78. Francis, *The Imaginary Indian*, 146.

79. Ernest Thompson Seton, *Two Little Savages: Being the Adventures of Two Boys Who Lived as Indians and What They Learned*, 1903 (New York: Grosset & Dunlap, 1911).

80. Francis, *The Imaginary Indian*, 146.

81. Charles Alexander Eastman, *Indian Boyhood*, 1902 (Garden City, NJ: Doubleday, Page and Company, 1915), Dedication.

82. Seton, *Two Little Savages*, 46–47.

83. Ibid., 326.

84. Ibid., 56.

85. Lee Frew argues that Seton's representation of white boys "playing Indian," staking out an intimate relationship with the physical environment in the early twentieth-century in the absence of any actual Native Americans, engages in a particularly Canadian fantasy of "settler nationalism," which seeks to usurp rather than recall the native peoples' prior claim to North American lands. See Lee Frew, "Settler Nationalism and the Foreign," *University of Toronto Quarterly*, 82:2 (January 2013), 278–297.

86. For a discussion about the relationship between the Boy Scouts and the Woodcraft Indians, see Francis, *The Imaginary Indian*, 153–158.

87. "The Camp Conference, Secretary's Report, 1905–6," 35–36. Quoted in Leslie Paris, *Children's Nature: The Rise of the American Summer Camp* (New York: New York University Press, 2008), 30.

88. Paris, *Children's Nature*, 23.

89. Ibid., 9.

90. Rudyard Kipling, "A Counting-Out Song" in *Land and Sea Tales for Scouts and Scout Masters* (Garden City, NJ: Doubleday, Page and Company, 1923), 318–322 (319–320).

91. Edward Burnett Tylor, *Primitive Culture: Researches into the Development of Mythology, Philosophy, Religion, Art and Custom*, 2 vols. (London: John Murray, 1871), 1: 70 and 65.

92. Henry Carrington Bolton, *The Counting-Out Rhymes of Children: Their Antiquity, Origin, and Wide Distribution* (New York: D. Appleton and Company, 1888), 41; and Alexander Francis Chamberlain, *The Child: A Study in the Evolution of Man*, 1900 (New York: Charles Scribner's Sons, 1903), 277.

chapter 5   Home grown

1. G. Stanley Hall, *Adolescence: Its Psychology and Its Relations to Physiology, Anthropology, Sociology, Sex, Crime, Religion and Education*, 2 vols., 1904 (New York: D. Appleton and Company, 1920), 11: 208. Chapter 4 deals more extensively with Hall and his concept of male adolescence.

2. Ruth Hubbard, "Have Only Men Evolved?", 1979, in *The Politics of Women's Biology*, 1990 (New Brunswick, NJ: Rutgers University Press, 1997), 87–106 (95).

3. Charles Darwin, *The Descent of Man, and Selection in Relation to Sex*, 1871 (Princeton, NJ: Princeton University Press, 1981), 253.

4. Elaine Morgan, *The Descent of Woman* (New York: Bantam, 1973), 3–4. Quoted in Hubbard, "Have Only Men Evolved," 95.

5. Angelique Richardson, *Love and Eugenics in the Late Nineteenth Century* (Oxford: Oxford University Press, 2003), 35.

6. See Charlotte Perkins Stetson (Gilman), *Women and Economics: A Study of the Economic Relation Between Men and Women as a Factor in Social Evolution* (Boston, MA: Small, Maynard and Company, 1898), 160 and 141.

7. Otis Tufton Mason, *Woman's Share in Primitive Culture*, 1895 (New York: D. Appleton and Company, 1897), 2–3.

8. Herbert Spencer, "Psychology of the Sexes," *Popular Science Monthly*, 4 (1873), 30–38 (30).

9. Ibid., 32.

10. Thomas H. Huxley, Letter to Charles Lyell (March 17, 1860). Quoted in Bernard Lightman, *Victorian Popularizers of Science: Designing Nature for New Audiences* (Chicago, IL: University of Chicago Press, 2007), 99.

11. Antoinette Brown Blackwell, *The Sexes Throughout Nature* (New York: G. P. Putnam's Sons, 1875), 18–19.

12. Ibid., 7.

13. Ibid., 113.

14. Ibid., 96.

15. Ibid., 84.

16. Ibid., 116.

17. Herbert Spencer, "Progress: Its Law and Cause," 1857, in Herbert Spencer, *Illustrations of Universal Progress; A Series of Discussions*, 1864 (New York: D. Appleton and Company, 1865), 1–60 (2). This essay was originally published in *The Westminster Review*, 67 (April 1857), 445–447, 451, 454–456, 464–465.

18. Blackwell, *The Sexes Throughout Nature*, 25.

19. Ibid., 61 and 200.

20. Ibid., 38.

21. Arabella Buckley, *Life and Her Children: Glimpses of Animal Life from the Amœba to the Insects*, 1880 (New York: D. Appleton and Company, 1882); and Arabella Buckley, *The Winners in Life's Race; or, The Great Backboned Family* (New York: D. Appleton and Company, 1883).

22. Buckley, *Winners in Life's Race*, 351.

23. Barbara T. Gates, "Revisioning Darwin with Sympathy" in Barbara T. Gates and Ann Shteir (eds.), *Natural Eloquence: Women Reinscribe Science* (Madison, WI: University of Wisconsin Press, 1997), 164–178 (169). For a longer discussion of this female tradition of sympathy in nature writing, see Barbara T. Gates, *Kindred Nature: Victorian and Edwardian Women Embrace the Living World* (Chicago, IL: University of Chicago Press, 1998).

24. See Peter Kropotkin, *Mutual Aid: A Factor in Evolution*, 1902 (New York: McClure Phillips and Company, 1903). Kropotkin cites Karl Kessler's "On the Law of Mutual Aid" (Lecture delivered at the Russian Congress of Naturalists in 1880) as the origin of his own ideas; see Kropotkin, *Mutual Aid*, 6–8.

25. Buckley, *Winners in Life's Race*, 299, 184, and 185. Just Buckley's Lamarckian ladder is worth noting; earlier natural histories customarily repeated an ordering of animals that had no evolutionary logic, but was so entrenched in the genre that Jane Loudon, the author of the enormously popular *The Entertaining Naturalist* (1849), admitted that "I could not persuade myself either to displace the Lion from the situation he has held so long at the commencement of the book, or to remove the Whales and other Cetacea from the place they have held near the fishes." See Mrs. (Jane) Loudon, *The Entertaining Naturalist; Being Popular Descriptions, Tales, and Anecdotes of More than Five Hundred Animals, Comprehending All the Quadrupeds, Birds, Fishes, Reptiles, Insects, &c. of Which a Knowledge is Indispensible to Polite Education*, 1849 (London: Henry G. Bohn, 1850), V–VI.

26. Buckley, *Winners in Life's Race*, 278, 287, and 289.

27. Ibid., 350.

28. Ibid., 173.

29. Ibid., 184.

30. Ibid., 151.

31. Ibid., 138 and 139.

32. Buckley, *Life and Her Children*, 13.

33. Buckley, *Winners in Life's Race*, 334.

34. Ibid., 352 and 350.

35. Sally Mitchell relates that the number of girls in secondary schools rose from 20,000 to 185,000 between 1897 and 1920; see Sally Mitchell, *The New Girl: Girls' Culture in England, 1880–1915* (New York: Columbia University Press, 1995), 80. For more on school lessons for Victorian girls, including needlework, also see Jane Martin, *Women and the Politics of Schooling in Victorian and Edwardian England* (London: Leicester University Press, 1999), 71–91.

36. Claudia Nelson, *Boys Will Be Girls: The Feminine Ethic and British Children's Fiction, 1857–1917* (New Brunswick, NJ: Rutgers University Press, 1991), 25.

37. Mitchell, *The New Girl*, 106.

38. Ibid., 122–123. Chapter 4 discusses the Boy Scouts and links between it and the theory of recapitulation.

39. Juliette Low, *How Girls Can Help Their Country, Adapted from Agnes Baden-Powell and Sir Robert Baden-Powell's Handbook* (Savannah, GA: M. S. & D. A. Byck, 1917), 98.

40. Hartley Davis, in collaboration with Mrs. Luther Halsey (Charlotte) Gulick, "The Camp-Fire Girls," *Outlook* (May 25, 1912), 181–189. Quoted in Susan Miller, *Growing Girls: The Natural Origins of Girls' Organizations in America* (New Brunswick, NJ: Rutgers University Press, 2007), 167.

41. Miller, *Growing Girls*, 158–191.

42. Low, *How Girls Can Help Their Country*, 29–47 and 8.

43. Francis Galton, *Inquiries into the Human Faculty and Its Development* (London: Macmillan and Company, 1883).

44. Richardson, *Love and Eugenics*, 49.

45. Ibid., 50. Sally Shuttleworth's *The Mind of the Child: Child Development in Literature, Science, and Medicine, 1840–1900* (Oxford: Oxford University Press, 2010) contains a fascinating discussion of eugenics in relation to the baby show, 233–237.

46. See Edwin Black, *War Against the Weak: Eugenics and America's Campaign to Create a Master Race* (New York: Four Walls Eight Windows, 2003).

47. Eliza Burt Gamble, *The Evolution of Woman: An Inquiry into the Dogma of Her Inferiority to Man*, 1893 (New York: G. P. Putnam's Sons, 1894), 60.

48. Ibid., 29.

49. Ibid., 27 and 26.

50. Ibid., 31.

51. Richardson, *Love and Eugenics*, 57.

52. Rosemary Jann, "Revising the Descent of Woman: Eliza Burt Gamble" in Gates and Shteir (eds.), *Natural Eloquence*, 147–163 (159). Jann is referring to Nancy Armstrong's *Desire and Domestic Fiction: A Political History of the Novel* (Oxford: Oxford University Press, 1987).

53. Frances Swiney, *The Awakening of Women; or, Woman's Part in Evolution* (London: George Redway, 1899), 101.

54. Caleb Williams Saleeby, *Parenthood and Race Culture: An Outline of Eugenics*, 1909 (New York: Moffat, Yard and Company, 1911), 166.

55. Ibid., 176.

56. Charles Kingsley, *The Water-Babies: A Fairy Tale for a Land-Baby*, 1863, illus. Linely Sambourne (London: Macmillan and Company, 1890), 229–237. Kingsley's *The Water-Babies* is discussed at length in Chapter 2.

57. Black, *War Against the Weak*, 208.

58. Jack London, *Before Adam*, 1907 (Lincoln, NE: University of Nebraska Press, 2000).

59. Lisa Hopkins, "Jack London's Evolutionary Hierarchies: Dogs, Wolves, and Men" in Lois A. Cuddy and Claire M. Roche (eds.), *Evolution and Eugenics in American Literature and Culture, 1880–1940: Essays on Ideological Conflict and Complicity* (Lewisburg, PA: Bucknell University Press, 2003), 89–101 (98).

60. Jean Webster, *Dear Enemy* (New York: Grosset & Dunlap, 1915), 228, 311, 305, and 260.

61. See Dana Seitler's chapter "Unnatural Selection: Mothers, Eugenic Feminism, and Regeneration Narratives" in *Atavistic Tendencies: The Culture of Science in American Modernity* (Minneapolis, MN: University of Minnesota Press, 2008), 175–198.

62. A. E. Hamilton, "Putting Over Eugenics," *Journal of Heredity*, 6 (June 1915), 281–288. Quoted in Miller, *Growing Girls*, 195.

63. Charlotte Vetter Gulick, Radio Talk (March 1926), Box 508, Special Collections, University of Maine at Orono. Quoted in Miller, *Growing Girls*, 197.

64. Low, *How Girls Can Help Their Country*, 98.

65. Miller, *Growing Girls*, 195.

66. See Peter J. Bowler, *Evolution: The History of an Idea*, 1983, 25th Anniversary ed. (Berkeley, CA: University of California Press, 2009), 260–264; and Michael Ruse, *Monad to Man: The Concept of Progress in Evolutionary Biology* (Cambridge, MA: Harvard University Press, 1996), 285–320. The synthesis of Mendel's and Darwin's theories is discussed further in the Conclusion.

67. Frances Hodgson Burnett, *Sara Crewe; or, What Happened at Miss Minchin's* (New York: Charles Scribner's Sons, 1888). Summer Camp is discussed further in Chapter 4.

68. Just to name a few of the most obvious examples: Wilkie Collins, *The Woman in White* (1860); Charles Dickens, *Great Expectations* (1861); H. Rider Haggard, *She* (1887); and Thomas Hardy, *Tess of the D'Urbervilles* (1892).

69. Hall, *Adolescence*, I: XI.

70. Frances Hodgson Burnett, *The Secret Garden*, 1911, ed. Gretchen Holbrook Gerzina (New York: W. W. Norton and Company, 2006), 11 and 26. *The Secret Garden* began serialization in *The American Magazine* in October 1910. The first edition of the book was published by Frederick A. Stokes in New York and Heinemann in London in 1911. Further references are to the Norton edition, and will be cited parenthetically in text.

71. Dickon perhaps draws his surname, Sowerby, from British naturalist James Sowerby (1757–1822).

72. Miller, *Growing Girls*, 192.

73. See, for example, Jerry Phillips, "The Mem, Sahib, the Worthy, the Rajah, and His Minions: Some Reflections on the Class Politics of *The Secret Garden*," *The Lion and the Unicorn*, 17 (1993), 168–194; Máire Messenger Davies, "'A Bit of Earth': Sexuality and the Representation of Childhood in Text and Screen Versions of *The Secret Garden*," *The Velvet Light Trap*, 48 (2001), 48–58; Jane Darcy, "The Edwardian Child in the Garden: Childhood in the Fiction of Frances Hodgson Burnett" in Adrienne E. Gavin and Andrew Humphries (eds.), *Childhood and Edwardian Fiction: Worlds Enough and Time* (New York: Palgrave, 2009), 75–88; and Ruth Y. Jenkins, "Frances Hodgson Burnett's *The Secret Garden*: Engendering Abjection's Sublime," *Children's Literature Association Quarterly*, 36:4 (Winter 2011), 426–444.

74. Friedrich Froebel, *The Education of Man*, 1826, trans. W. N. Hailmann, 1887 (New York: D. Appleton and Company, 1895), 309, http://babel.hathitrust.org/cgi/pt?id=uc1.$b249450;view=1up;seq=3. Jenkins quotes the same passage and links it to Burnett's novel; see "Engendering Abjection's Sublime," 428.

75. Froebel, *The Education of Man*, 40.

76. Phyllis Bixler, "Gardens, Houses, and Nurturant Power in *The Secret Garden*" in James Holt McGavran (ed.), *Romanticism and Children's Literature in Nineteenth-Century England* (Athens, GA: University of Georgia Press, 1991), 208–224 (209).

77. James R. Kincaid, *Child-Loving: The Erotic Child and Victorian Culture* (New York: Routledge, 1992), 90.

78. Maude Hines, "'He Made *Us* Very Much Like the Flowers': Human/Nature in Nineteenth-Century Anglo-American Children's Literature" in Sidney I. Dobrin and Kenneth B. Kidd (eds.), *Wild Things: Children's Culture and Ecocriticism* (Detroit, MI: Wayne State University Press, 2004), 16–30 (27).

79. Amy M. King, *Bloom: The Botanical Vernacular in the English Novel* (Oxford: Oxford University Press, 2007), 7.

80. For biographies of Frances Hodgson Burnett, see Gretchen Gerzina, *Frances Hodgson Burnett: The Unexpected Life of the Author of The Secret Garden* (New Brunswick, NJ: Rutgers University Press, 2004); and Ann Thwaite, *Waiting for the Party: The Life of Frances Hodgson Burnett, 1849–1924* (London: Faber, 1994).

81. Joseph DeJarnette, MD, "Mendel's Law: A Plea for a Better Race of Men" (New York: Cold Spring Harbor, 1921). Available at University of Virginia's Claude Moore Health Services Library's online collection of eugenic texts, Exhibit 4.3. See www.hsl.virginia.edu/historical/eugenics/exhibit4-3.cfm.

82. Jane Hume Clapperton, *A Vision of the Future: Based on the Application of Ethical Principles* (London: Swan Sonnenscien and Company, Ltd, 1904), 252, https://babel.hathitrust.org/cgi/pt?id=nyp.33433081957072;view=1up; seq=7.

83. Webster, *Dear Enemy*, 97.

84. The year after *The Secret Garden* was published, Burnett wrote a memoir about the real bird – a daily visitor in her garden in Kent – on which, she claims, the fictional robin was based. In *My Robin* (New York: Frederick A. Stokes, 1912), Burnett presents the relationship between human and bird as a romantic and suggestively sexual one. She writes, "he loved me. The low song trilled in his little pulsating scarlet throat was mine" (49) and "he loved my robin sounds, he loved my whispers, his dewy dark eyes looked into mine as if he knew we two understood strange tender things others did not" (52). Their romance survives an imposter robin that tries to woo her and the robin's flirtation with a female of his own species, but it ends when Burnett moves back to the United States.

85. Margaret Gatty, "Inferior Animals," 1861, in *Parables from Nature, First and Second Series, with a Memoir by Her Daughter, Juliana Horatia Ewing*, illus. P. H. Calderon, W. Holman Hunt, E. Burne Jones, Otto Speckter, G. H. Thomas, John Tenniel, M. E. Edwards, Lorenz Fröhlich, Harrison Weir, J. Wolf, etc., 2 vols. (London: George Bell and Sons, 1885 and 1886), II: 24–36. Chapter 1 discusses Gatty's *Parables from Nature* in more detail.

86. This technique is also not entirely new to Burnett; one chapter of *A Little Princess*, Burnett's expanded version of *Sara Crewe*, presents the actions of human characters through the consciousness of a rat, Melchisedec, who befriends Sara. See *A Little Princess*, 1905 (New York: Penguin Books, 2002), 80–89.

87. Thomas H. Huxley, "Prolegomena," 1894, in *Evolution and Ethics, and Other Essays* (New York: D. Appleton and Company, 1899), 1–45 (9).

88. Ibid., 43.

89. In "Gardens, Houses, and Nurturant Power," Bixler defends the feminism in Burnett's central metaphor of the maternal garden, while in *Boys Will Be Girls*, Nelson finds female agency in the garden's sexuality. In contrast, Danielle E. Price is more critical about the nineteenth-century language of "enclosure, imprisonment, instruction, and beautification" equally prescribed for plants and girls that she sees running throughout Burnett's novel; see Danielle E. Price, "Cultivating Mary: The Victorian Secret Garden," *Children's Literature Association Quarterly*, 26:1 (2001), 4–14 (4).

90. Bixler, "Gardens, Houses, and Nurturant Power," 213.

91. Gamble, *The Evolution of Woman*, 172.

92. Jann, "Revising the Descent of Woman," 155–156.

93. Maria Hack, *Harry Beaufoy; or, the Pupil of Nature*, 1821 (Philadelphia, PA: Thomas Kite, 1828), 7, http://babel.hathitrust.org/cgi/pt?id=njp .32101063604183;view=1up;seq=3; and Margaret Gatty, "Training and Restraining," 1855, in *Parables from Nature*, 1: 23–26.

94. Nelson, *Boys Will Be Girls*, 28.

95. Jenkins, "Engendering Abjection's Sublime," 434.

96. Mary Baker Eddy, *Science and Health, with Key to the Scriptures*, 1875, 40th ed. (Boston, MA: Mary Baker Eddy, 1889), 333.

97. Ibid., 61–62.

98. Frances Hodgson Burnett, *In the Garden* (Boston, MA: The Medici Society of America, 1925), 13. Here Burnett admits that she is less gracious than Mary about the weeds that grow alongside the more desirable plants. She writes, "I love to kneel down on the grass at the edge of a flower bed and pull out the weeds fiercely and throw them into a heap by my side. I love to fight with those who can spring up again almost in a night and taunt me . . . I am afraid that I absolutely know what hate is when I come upon a dozen flaunting ragweeds which while my back was turned have sprung up in a bed of lovely, tender, colored snapdragons, trying to pretend that they are only part of their foliage" (20–21).

99. Scott O'Dell, *The Island of the Blue Dolphins*, 1960 (Boston, MA: Houghton Mifflin Harcourt, 2010); and Jean Craighead George, *Julie of the Wolves*, 1972 (New York: Harper Collins, 2003).

100. *The Secret of the Old Clock* (New York: Grosset & Dunlap, 1930) was the first Nancy Drew mystery, written by the Edward Stratemeyer Syndicate under the pseudonym Carolyn Keene. The first Trixie Belden mystery was Julia Campbell Tatham, *The Secret of the Old Mansion* (Racine, WI: Western Publishing Company, 1948). In *The Secret of the Old Mansion*, Trixie ends up investigating a mystery while spending the summer at home, while her brothers are at a summer camp.

Conclusion

1. Edward Clodd, *The Childhood of the World: A Simple Account of Man in Early Times*, 1872 (London: Macmillan and Company, 1873), 3.

2. Ibid., 3–4.

3. Peter J. Bowler, *Evolution: The History of an Idea*, 1983, 25th Anniversary ed. (Berkeley, CA: University of California Press, 2009), 224–273.

4. See August Weismann, *Essays upon Heredity and Kindred Biological Problems*, 2 vols., 1889 (Oxford: Clarendon Press, 1892), 1: 444–445.

5. Bowler, *Evolution*, 253–256 (255).

6. For more on the eclipse of scientific theories of recapitulation, see Stephen Jay Gould, *Ontogeny and Phylogeny* (Cambridge, MA: The Belknap Press of Harvard University Press, 1977), 167–206.

7. For the tension between morphology and professionalization, see Bowler, *Evolution*, 230–34.

8. Michael Ruse, *Monad to Man: The Concept of Progress in Evolutionary Biology* (Cambridge, MA: Harvard University Press, 1996), 289.

9. Garland E. Allen, *Life Science in the Twentieth Century* (New York: Wiley, 1975). Allen is quoted in Bowler, *Evolution*, 230. Bateson's book was *Mendel's Principles of Heredity* (Cambridge: Cambridge University Press, 1902).

10. The experiments that Morgan performed, along with A. H. Sturtevant, H. J. Muller, and C. B. Bridges, are discussed in Bowler, 269–273 and in Edward J. Larson, *Evolution: The Remarkable History of a Scientific Theory* (New York: Modern Library, 2006), 166–174.

11. Gould, *Ontogeny and Phylogeny*, 202.

12. A. S. Edwards, *The Psychology of Elementary Education* (Boston, MA: Houghton Mifflin Company, 1925), 17.

13. Lucille Ritvo, *Darwin's Influence on Freud: A Tale of Two Sciences* (New Haven, CT: Yale University Press, 1990), 60–63. For other discussions of Freud's use of recapitulation, see Frank Sulloway, *Freud: Biologist of the Mind* (New York: Basic Books, 1983); and Dana Seitler, *Atavistic Tendencies: The Culture of Science in American Modernity* (Minneapolis, MN: University of Minnesota Press, 2008).

14. Sigmund Freud, *The Interpretation of Dreams*, 1900, trans. James Strachey (New York: Avon Books, 1965), 587–588.

15. Sigmund Freud, "Preface to the Third Edition," 1914, in *Three Essays on the Theory of Sexuality*, 1905, trans. James Strachey (Mansfield Centre, CT: Martino Publishing, 2011), 9–10 (10).

16. Sigmund Freud, *Totem and Taboo*, 1913, in Sigmund Freud, *The Origins of Religion: The Pelican Freud Library*, Vol. XIII, ed. James Strachey and Albert Dickenson, trans. James Strachey (London: Penguin Books, 1990), 43–224 (202).

17. Sigmund Freud, *Moses and Monotheism: Three Essays*, 1939, in Freud, *The Origins of Religion*, 237–386 (346).

18. See Seitler, *Atavistic Tendencies*, 31–54 and 94–128, for a fuller discussion of Freud's link between animality and sexuality.

19. Sigmund Freud, *Civilization and Its Discontents*, 1929, trans. and ed. James Strachey (New York: W. W. Norton and Company, 1961), 18.

20. Ibid., 19.

21. Benjamin Spock and Michael B. Rothenberg, *Dr. Spock's Baby and Childcare*, 1946 (New York: Pocket Books, 1985), 291.

22. See Thomas Maier, *Dr. Spock: An American Life* (New York: Basic Books, 2003), 462.

23. Harvey Karp, MD, *The Happiest Toddler on the Block: The New Way to Stop the Daily Battle of Wills and Raise a Secure and Well-Behaved One- to Four-Year -Old* (New York: Bantam Dell, 2004), 8.

24. Robert Bly, *Iron John: A Book About Men* (Boston, MA: Addison Wesley, 1990), quoted in Kenneth B. Kidd *Making American Boys: Boyology and the Feral Tale* (Minneapolis, MN: University of Minnesota Press, 2004), 172; and Michael Gurian, *The Wonder of Boys: What Parents, Mentors and Educators Can Do to Shape Boys into Exceptional Men* (New York: Penguin Books, 1996), 7.

25. Richard Louv, *Last Child in the Woods: Saving Our Children from Nature-Deficit Disorder* (Chapel Hill, NC: Algonquin Books of Chapel Hill, 2006), 43.

26. Mayim Bialik, *Beyond the Sling: A Real-Life Guide to Raising Confident, Loving Children the Attachment Parenting Way* (New York: Touchstone, 2012), 12.

27. Quoted in George C. T. Bartley, *The Schools for the People Containing the History, Development, and Present Working of Each Description of English Schools for the Industrial and Poorer Classes* (London: Bell and Daldy, 1871), 124.

28. See U. S. Department of Education Web site: www.ed.gov/stem.

29. Ibid.

30. Grace Richards, "Oh, the Humanities! Why STEM Shouldn't Take Precedence Over the Humanities," 2014, Arizona State University Project Humanities Web site: http://humanities.asu.edu/oh-humanities-why-stem-shouldnt-take-precedence-over-arts.

31. Commission on the Humanities and Social Sciences, *The Heart of the Matter* (Cambridge, MA: The American Academy of Arts and Sciences, 2013), 9: www.humanitiescommission.org/_pdf/hss_report.pdf. Quoted in David A. Hollinger, "The Wedge Driving Academe's Two Families Apart: Can STEM and the Human Sciences Get Along?", *The Chronicle of Higher Education* (October 14, 2013): http://chronicle.com/article/Why-Cant-the-Sciencesthe/142239/.

32. Hollinger, "The Wedge Driving Academe's Two Families Apart."

33. Richards, "Oh, the Humanities!"

34. Quoted in Cathy N. Davidson, Paula Barker Duffy, and Martha Wagner Weinberg, "Why STEM is Not Enough (and We Still Need the Humanities)." The writers are members of the National Council on the Humanities; their article was posted on Valerie Strauss's blog *The Answer Sheet* on *The Washington Post* (March 5, 2012): www.washingtonpost.com/blogs/answer-sheet/post/why-stem-is-not-enough-and-we-still-need-the-humanities/2012/03/04/gIQAniScrR_blog.html.

35. Herbert Spencer, *Education: Intellectual, Moral, and Physical*, 1860 (New York: D. Appleton and Company, 1896), 73.

36. Paul Smith, "Move Over, Stem: Why the World Needs Humanities Graduates," *The Guardian* (March 19, 2014): www.theguardian.com/higher-education-network/blog/2014/mar/19/humanities-universities-global-stem.

37. Jacqueline Rose, *The Case of Peter Pan; or, The Impossibility of Children's Fiction*, 1984 (Philadelphia, PA: University of Pennsylvania Press, 1993).

38. *The Boy Castaways of Black Lake Island* is an unpublished book that existed in only two copies; while one was lost, the other is available in the General Collection, Beinecke Rare Book Room and Manuscript Library at Yale University. The photos are also republished in Andrew Birkin, *J. M. Barrie & The Lost Boys: The Love Story that Gave Birth to Peter Pan* (New York: Clarkson N. Potter, Inc. 1979).

39. Rose, *The Case of Peter Pan*, 21.

40. In "Peter Pan as Darwinian Creation Myth" (1994), R. D. S. Jack reads the play in terms of an evolutionary struggle, arguing that Peter is "frozen in the tableau form," while Wendy "is the fluid, adaptable, real figure at one with the demands of evolutionary development." R. D. S. Jack, *"Peter Pan* as Darwinian Creation Myth," *Literature and Theology*, 8:2 (June 1994), 157–173 (166).

41. J.M. Barrie, *The Little White Bird* (London: Hodder and Stroughton, 1902), 159. Rose argues that Barrie's myth of the child's bird prehistory functions as a "disavowal of origins, or conception"; see Rose, *The Case of Peter Pan*, 25.

42. J. M. Barrie, *Peter and Wendy*, 1911, in *Peter Pan: Peter and Wendy* and *Peter Pan in Kensington Gardens* (London: Penguin Books, 2004), 1–149 (9).

43. C. S. Lewis, *The Chronicles of Narnia*, 1950–1956 (New York: Harper Collins, 2004); and Philip Pullman, *His Dark Materials Trilogy: The Golden Compass, The Subtle Knife,* and *The Amber Spyglass*, 1995–2000 (New York: Laurel Leaf, 2003).

44. Roald Dahl, *Revolting Rhymes* (London: Puffin Classics, 1982); and Jon Scieszka, *The Stinky Cheese Man, and Other Fairly Stupid Tales* (New York: Viking Juvenile, 1992).

45. Maurice Sendak, *Where the Wild Things Are* (New York: Harper Collins, 1963); and Piers Torday, *The Last Wild* (New York: Viking Juvenile, 2013), *The Dark Wild* (New York: Viking Juvenile, 2014), and *The Wild Beyond* (New York: Viking Juvenile, 2015).

46. E. L Konigsburg, *From the Mixed-Up Files of Mrs. Basil E. Frankweiler* (New York: Simon & Schuster, 1967); and Pseudoymous Bosch, *The Secret Series: Complete Collection*, 2007–2011 (New York: Little, Brown Books for Young Readers, 2012).

47. Melvin Konner, *The Evolution of Childhood: Relationships, Emotion, Mind* (Cambridge, MA: The Belknap Press of Harvard University Press, 2010), 280 and 282.

48. Matthew Arnold, "General Report for the Year 1878" in *Reports on Elementary Schools, 1852–1882* (London and New York: Macmillan and Company, 1889), 201–224 (214).

49. Mordicai Gerstein, *The First Drawing* (New York: Little, Brown and Company, 2013), n.p.

50. A photographic image of the footprint, along with beautiful photographs of the panels themselves, is printed in Jean-Marie Chauvet, Eliette Brunel Deschamps, Christian Hillaire, *Dawn of Art: The Chauvet Cave, the Oldest Known Paintings in the World*, trans. Paul G. Bahn (New York: Harry N. Abrams, Inc., 1996), 51.

51. Gerstein, *First Drawing*, Author's Note, n.p.

52. Chauvet, et. al. discuss the dating of the cave in *Dawn of Art*, 118–126.

53. See David Lewis-Williams, *The Mind in the Cave: Consciousness and the Origins of Art* (London: Thames & Hudson, 2002), 29–31.

54. Frederick Starr, *Some First Steps in Human Progress* (Cleveland, OH: Chatauqua Assembly, 1901); and Minnie J. Reynolds, *How Man Conquered Nature*, 1914 (New York: The Macmillan Company, 1917).

55. Lewis-Williams, *The Mind in the Cave*, 31.

56. Chauvet et al., *Dawn of Art*, 126.

Bibliography

Primary sources

Aiken, J., and Mrs. Barbauld, *Evenings at Home; or, The Juvenile Budget Opened: Consisting of a Variety of Miscellaneous Pieces for the Instruction and Amusement of Young Persons*, 6 vols., 1793, 11th ed. (London: Baldwin, Cradock, and Joy, 1816).

Arnold, Matthew, *Culture and Anarchy: An Essay in Political and Social Criticism* (London: Smith, Elder and Company, 1869).

Essays in Criticism, Second Series: Contributions to 'The Pall Mall Gazette' and Discourses in America (London: Macmillan and Company, Ltd., 1903), 317–348.

Reports on Elementary Schools, 1852–1882 (London and New York: Macmillan and Company, 1889).

Baden-Powell, Robert, *Scouting for Boys*, 1908 (Oxford: Oxford University Press, 2004).

(as Lord Baden-Powell) *The Wolf-Cub's Handbook*, 1916, 9th ed. (London: C. Arthur Pearson, Ltd., 1938).

Barnard, Henry, *Object Teaching and Oral Lessons on Social Science and Common Things* (New York: F. C. Brownell, 1860).

Barrie, J. M., *The Little White Bird* (London: Hodder and Stroughton, 1902).

Peter Pan: Peter and Wendy and *Peter Pan in Kensington Gardens* (London: Penguin Books, 2004).

Bartley, George C. T., *The Schools for the People Containing the History, Development, and Present Working of Each Description of English Schools for the Industrial and Poorer Classes* (London: Bell and Daldy, 1871).

Bialik, Mayim, *Beyond the Sling: A Real-Life Guide to Raising Confident, Loving Children the Attachment Parenting Way* (New York: Touchstone, 2012).

Biber, Edward, *Henry Pestalozzi and His Plan of Education; Being an Account of His Life and Writings* (London: John Souter, 1831).

Blackwell, Antoinette Louisa Brown, *The Sexes Throughout Nature* (New York: G. P. Putnam's Sons, 1875).

Board of Education, *Suggestions for the Consideration of Teachers and Others Concerned in the Work of Public Elementary Schools* (London: His Majesty's Stationery Office, 1905).

Suggestions for the Consideration of Teachers and Others Concerned in the Work of Public Elementary Schools, Reprinted with revision of the parts relating to English, Arithmetic, Geography, History and Singing (London: His Majesty's Stationery Office, 1912).

Bolton, Henry Carrington, *The Counting-Out Rhymes of Children: Their Antiquity, Origin, and Wide Distribution* (New York: D. Appleton and Company, 1888).

Bosch, Pseudonymous, *The Secret Series Complete Collection* (New York: Little, Brown Books, 2012).

Buckland, Francis T., *Curiosities of Natural History* (New York: Follett, Foster and Company, 1864).

Buckland, William, *Geology and Mineralogy Considered with Reference to Natural Theology*, 2 vols., 1836 (Piladelphia: Carey, Lea, and Blanchard, 1837).

Buckley, Arabella, *Life and Her Children: Glimpses of Animal Life from the Amœba to the Insects*, 1880 (New York: D. Appleton and Company, 1882).

   The Winners in Life's Race; or The Great Backboned Family (New York: D. Appleton and Company, 1883).

Buckman, S. S., "Babies and Monkeys," *The Popular Science Monthly*, 46 (January 1895), 371–388.

Burnett, Frances Hodgson, *In the Garden* (Boston, MA: The Medici Society of America, 1925).

   A Little Princess, 1905 (New York: Penguin Books, 2002).

   My Robin (New York: Frederick A. Stokes, 1912).

   Sara Crewe; or, What Happened at Miss Minchin's (New York: Charles Scribner's Sons, 1888).

   The Secret Garden, 1911, ed. Gretchen Holbrook Gerzina (New York: W. W. Norton and Company, 2006).

Burroughs, Edgar Rice, *Tarzan of the Apes*, 1914 (London: Penguin Books, 1990).

Campbell, Mrs. C. C., *Natural History for Young Folks* (London: T. Nelson and Sons, 1884).

Cantlie, John, *Degeneration Amongst Londoners* (London: Field and Tuer, 1885).

Carnegie, Andrew, *The Gospel of Wealth, and Other Timely Essays* (New York: The Century Company, 1901).

Carpenter, William, *Principles of General and Comparative Physiology*, 1839, 3rd ed. (Philadelphia, PA: Blanchard & Lea, 1851).

Carroll, Lewis, *Alice in Wonderland*, ed. Donald J. Gray, 1971, 2nd ed. (New York: W. W. Norton and Company, 1992).

   Alice's Adventures in Wonderland, illus. John Tenniel, 1865 (London: Macmillan and Company, 1866).

   Alice's Adventures in Wonderland and Through the Looking-Glass, illus. John Tenniel, ed. Hugh Haughton (London: Penguin Books, 1998).

   Alice's Adventures under Ground: A Facsimile of the Original Lewis Carroll Manuscript, 1864 (Ann Arbor, MI: University Microfilms, Inc., 1964).

   (as Charles L. Dodgson) *Curiosa Mathematica: Part I, A New Theory of Parallels*, 1888 (London: Macmillan and Company, 1890).

Diversions & Digressions of Lewis Carroll, ed. Stuart Dodgson Collingwood (New York: Dover Publications, Inc., 1961).

Through the Looking-Glass, and What Alice Found There, illus. John Tenniel (London: Macmillan and Company, 1872).

Chamberlain, Alexander Francis, *The Child: A Study in the Evolution of Man*, 1900 (New York: Charles Scribner's Sons, 1903).

Chambers, Robert, *Vestiges of the Natural History of Creation*, 1844 (New York: Leicester University Press, 1969).

Clapperton, Jane Hume, *A Vision of the Future: Based on the Application of Ethical Principles* (London: Swan Sonnenscien and Company, Ltd, 1904), https://babel.hathitrust.org/cgi/pt?id=nyp.33433081957072;view=1up;seq=7.

Clodd, Edward, *The Childhood of the World: A Simple Account of Man in Early Times*, 1872 (London: Macmillan and Company, 1873).

Collins, Wilkie, *Woman in White*, 1860 (Oxford: Oxford World's Classics, 2008).

Cope, Edward Drinker, *The Primary Factors of Organic Evolution* (Chicago, IL: The Open Court Publishing Company, 1896).

Craik, Dinah Maria, *Our Year: A Child's Book in Prose and Verse*, illus. Clarence Dobell (Cambridge: Macmillan, 1860).

Dahl, Roald, *Revolting Rhymes* (London: Puffin Classics, 1982).

Darwin, Charles, "Autobiography," in Frances Darwin (ed.), *The Autobiography of Charles Darwin and Selected Letters*, 1892 (New York: Dover Publications, Inc., 1958), 5–58.

"A Biographical Sketch of an Infant," *Mind: A Quarterly Review of Psychology and Philosophy*, 2 (1877), 285–294.

Charles Darwin's Notebooks, 1836–1844: Geology, Transmutation of Species, Metaphysical Enquiries, ed. Paul H. Barrett, Peter J. Gautrey, Sandra Herbert, David Kohn, and Sydney Smith (Ithaca, NY: Cornell University Press, 1987).

The Descent of Man, and Selection in Relation to Sex, 1871 (Princeton, NJ: Princeton University Press, 1981).

On the Origin of Species: A Facsimile of the First Edition (1859), 1964(Cambridge, MA: Harvard University Press, 2000).

Darwin, Frances (ed.), *The Autobiography of Charles Darwin and Selected Letters* (New York: Dover Publications, Inc., 1958.

Defoe, Daniel, *Robinson Crusoe*, 1791, Norton Critical ed., 2nd ed., ed. Michael Shinagel (New York: W. W. Norton and Company, 1994).

DeJarnette, Joseph, MD, "Mendel's Law: A Plea for a Better Race of Men" (New York: Cold Spring Harbor, 1921). Reprinted by University of Virginia's Claude Moore Health Services Library at www.hsl.virginia.edu/historical/eugenics/exhibit4-3.cfm.

De Morgan, Augustus, *Remarks on Elementary Education in Science: An Introductory Lecture* (London: John Taylor, 1830).

Dewey, John, *The School and Society: Being Three Lectures*, 1899, 2nd ed. (Chicago, IL: University of Chicago Press and New York: McClure, Phillips and Company, 1900).

Dickens, Charles, *Great Expectations*, 1861 (London: Penguin Books, 2002).
Hard Times (London: Penguin Books, 2003).
Dickens, Charles and Eliza Boyce Kirk, *The Story of Oliver Twist, by Charles Dickens, Condensed for Home and School Reading* (New York: D. Appleton and Company, 1897).
Eastman, Charles Alexander, *Indian Boyhood*, 1902 (Garden City, NJ: Doubleday, Page and Company, 1915).
Eddy, Mary Baker, *Science and Health, with Key to the Scriptures*, 1875, 40th ed. (Boston, MA: Mary Baker Eddy, 1889).
Edwards, A. S., *The Psychology of Elementary Education* (Boston, MA: Houghton Mifflin Company, 1925).
Edwards, Henry, *Elementary Education: The Importance of Its Extension in Our Own Country* (London: Longman and Company, 1844), https://books.google.com/books?id=tjYiAQAAMAAJ&printsec=frontcover&dq=elementary+education+edwards&hl=en&sa=X&ved=0ahUKEwiahvPd_73JAhVJ6GMKHRlRAFoQ6AEIMTAC#v=onepage&q=elementary%20education%20edwards&f=false.
Ewing, Juliana Horatia, "Amelia and the Dwarfs" in Margaret Gatty (ed.), *Aunt Judy's Christmas Volume for Young People* (London: Bell and Daldy, 1870), 259–275, http://babel.hathitrust.org/cgi/pt?id=nyp.33433082288402;view=1up;seq=271.
Farrow, G. E., *The Wallypug of Why*, 1895, in Carolyn Sigler (ed.), *Alternative Alices: Visions and Revisions of Lewis Carroll's Alice Books* (Lexington, KY: University of Kentucky Press, 1997), 243–267.
Forbush, William Byron, *The Boy Problem: A Study in Social Pedagogy* (Boston, MA: The Pilgrim Press, 1901).
Forster, William E., "Speech by Mr. W. E. Forster, Vice President of the Council, Introducing the Elementary Education Bill, in the House of Commons – Feb. 17th, 1870," in J. Stuart Maclure (ed.), *Educational Documents: England and Wales 1816–1968*, 1969 (Oxford: Routledge, 1972), 98–105.
Freud, Sigmund, *Civilization and Its Discontents*, 1929, trans. and ed. James Strachey (New York: W. W. Norton and Company, 1961).
The Interpretation of Dreams, 1900, trans. and ed. James Strachey (New York: Avon Books, 1965).
The Origins of Religion: The Penguin Freud Library, Vol. XIII, ed. James Strachey and Albert Dickenson, trans, James Strachey (London: Penguin Books, 1990).
Three Essays on the Theory of Sexuality, 1905, trans. James Strachey (Mansfield Centre, CT: Martino Publishing, 2011).
Froebel, Friedrich, *The Education of Man*, 1826, trans. W. N. Hailmann, 1887 (New York: D. Appleton and Company, 1895), http://babel.hathitrust.org/cgi/pt?id=uc1.$b249450;view=1up;seq=3.
Galton, Francis, *Inquiries into the Human Faculty and Its Development* (London: Macmillan and Company, 1883).
Gamble, Eliza Burt, *The Evolution of Woman: An Inquiry into the Dogma of Her Inferiority to Man*, 1893 (New York: G. P. Putnam's Sons, 1894).

Gatty, Margaret, *Aunt Judy's Christmas Volume for Young People*, 8 (London: Bell and Daldy, 1870), http://babel.hathitrust.org/cgi/pt?id=nyp.33433082288402; view=1up;seq=271

    Parables from Nature, First and Second Series, With a Memoir by Her Daughter, Juliana Horatia Ewing, illus. P. H. Calderon, W. Holman Hunt, E. Burne Jones, Otto Speckter, G. H. Thomas, John Tenniel, M. E. Edwards, Lorenz Fröhlich, Harrison Weir, J. Wolf, et al., 2 vols. (London: George Bell and Sons, 1885 and 1886).

    Parables from Nature, with Notes on the Natural History, illus. P. H. Calderon, W. Holman Hunt, Otto Speckter, Lorenz Frolich, E. Burne Jones, Harrison Weir, J. Tenniel, J. Wolf, et al. (London: George Bell and Sons, 1888).

George, Jean Craighead, *Julie of the Wolves* (New York: Harper Collins, 2003).

Gerstein, Mordicai, *The First Drawing* (New York: Little, Brown and Company, 2013).

Gilman, Charlotte Perkins Stetson, *Women and Economics: A Study of the Economic Relation Between Men and Women as a Factor in Social Evolution* (Boston, MA: Small, Maynard and Company, 1898).

Goodrich, Samuel, *The Wonders of Geology, by the Author of Peter Parley's Tales* (Philadelphia, PA: Thomas Copperthwaite and Company, 1846).

"The Gorilla's Dilemma," *Punch* (October 1862), in Jerold Savory and Patricia Marks (eds.), *The Smiling Muse: Victoriana in the Comic Press* (Cranbury, NJ: Associated University Press, 1985), 60.

Gosse, Philip Henry, *Romance of Natural History*, 2 vols., 1860–1861, 4th ed. (London: James Nisbet and Company, 1861).

Gresswell, Albert and George Gresswell, *The Wonderland of Evolution* (London: Field & Tuer, 1884).

Groos, Karl, *The Play of Animals*, trans. Elizabeth Baldwin (New York: D. Appleton and Company, 1898).

    The Play of Man, 1901, trans. Elizabeth Baldwin (New York: D. Appleton and Company, 1912).

Gurian, Michael, *The Wonder of Boys: What Parents, Mentors and Educators Can Do to Shape Boys into Exceptional Men* (New York: Penguin Books, 1996).

Hack, Maria, *Harry Beaufoy; or, The Pupil of Nature*, 1821 (Philadelphia, PA: Thomas Kite, 1828), http://babel.hathitrust.org/cgi/pt?id=njp.32101063604183;view=1up;seq=3.

Haeckel, Ernst, *The Evolution of Man: A Popular Exposition of the Principal Points of Human Ontogeny and Phylogeny*, 1874 (New York: D. Appleton and Company, 1897).

Haggard, H. Rider, *She: A History of Adventure*, 1887 (New York: Random House, 2011).

Hall, G. Stanley, *Adolescence: Its Psychology and Its Relations to Physiology, Anthropology, Sociology, Sex, Crime, Religion and Education*, 2 vols., 1904 (New York: D. Appleton and Company, 1920).

"The Ideal School as Based on Child Study," in *National Education Association Journal of Addresses and Proceedings*, Washington D.C. (1901), 475–482 and 488.

Hardy, Thomas, *Tess of the D'Urbervilles*, 1892 (London: Penguin Books, 2009).

Harris, W. T., "Introduction to the Home Reading Book Series by the Editor," in Eliza Boyce Kirk (ed.), *The Story of Oliver Twist, by Charles Dickens, Condensed for Home and School Reading* (New York: D. Appleton and Company, 1897), V–X.

Hone, William, *The Year Book of Daily Recreation and Information*, 1832 (London: Ward, Lock, Bowden and Company, 1892).

Hood, Tom, *From Nowhere to the North Pole: A Noah's Ark-Æological Narrative* (London: Chatto and Windus, 1875).

Hooker, Worthington, MD, *The Child's Book of Nature, for the Use of Families and Schools, in Three Parts*, 1874, Rev. ed. (New York: Harper & Brothers, 1886).

Hughes, Thomas, *Tom Brown's Schooldays*, 1857 (Oxford: Oxford University Press, 1989).

Huxley, Thomas H., "The Brain of Man and Apes," *Medical Times and Gazette* (October 1862), 449.

Collected Essays, 9 vols. (New York: Greenwood Press, 1968).

Evolution and Ethics, and Other Essays (New York: D. Appleton and Company, 1899).

"Man and the Apes," *Athenaeum*, No. 1744 (March 30, 1861), 43.

Man's Place in Nature, and Other Anthropological Essays, 1863 (New York: D. Appleton and Company, 1919).

On the Educational Value of the Natural History Sciences (London: John van Voorst, 1854).

Science and Education, 1898 (New York: P. F. Collier & Son, 1905).

Jacobs, Joseph, *The Fables of Æsop, Selected, Told Anew and Their History Traced*, illus. Richard Heighway, 1889 (London: Macmillan and Company, 1894).

Johnson, Samuel and John Walker (ed.), *A Dictionary of the English Language*, 1755 (London: John Williamson ad Company, 1839).

Johonnot, James, *Friends in Feathers and Fur, and Other Neighbors, for Young Folks*, 1884 (New York: D. Appleton and Company, 1888).

Karp, Harvey, MD, *The Happiest Toddler on the Block: The New Way to Stop the Daily Battle of Wills and Raise a Secure and Well-Behaved One- to Four-Year-Old* (New York: Bantam Dell, 2004).

Keene, Carolyn, *The Secret of the Old Clock* (New York: Grosset & Dunlap, 1930).

Kingsley, Charles, *Alton Locke: Tailor and Poet*, 1850 (London: Cassell and Company, Ltd., 1967).

Glaucus; or, The Wonders of the Shore, 3rd ed. (Cambridge: Macmillan and Company, 1855).

Health and Education, 1874 (New York: D. Appleton and Company, 1893).

The Heroes; or, Greek Fairy Tales for My Children, 1855 (London and New York: Macmillan and Company, 1885).

Letter, Charles Kingsley to Charles Darwin (January 31, 1862), reprinted by the Darwin Correspondence Project. www.darwinproject.ac.uk/entry-3426.

Madame How and Lady Why; or, First Lessons in Earth Lore for Children, 1869, 3rd ed. (London: Strathan and Company, 1873).

The Water-Babies: A Fairy Tale for a Land-Baby (London: Macmillan, 1863).

The Water-Babies; A Fairy Tale for a Land-Baby, 1863, 4th ed., illus. Linley Sambourne (London: Macmillan and Company, 1890).

The Water-Babies: A Fairy Tale for a Land-Baby, illus. W. Heath Robinson (Boston, MA and New York: Houghton Mifflin, 1915).

The Water-Babies: A Fairy-Tale for a Land-Baby, Adapted for Use in Schools, Bell's Literature Readers, illus. Eva Roos (London: George Bell & Sons, 1908).

Westward Ho! (Chicago and New York: Rand, McNally and Company, 1855).

"Workmen of England," Placard, 1848. Reprinted in Frances Eliza Grenfell Kingsley (ed.), *Charles Kingsley, His Letters, and Memories of His Life*, 2 vols., 1877 (New York: Charles Scribner's Sons, 1889), 1: 95–96.

The Works of Charles Kingsley, 28 vols. (London: Macmillan and Company, 1880).

Kingsley, Charles and Winifred Howard, *The Water Babies, Adapted and Re-Told with Copious Natural History Notes and a Scheme of Correlated Lessons and Handwork*, illus. Margaret Ashworth (London: Sir Isaac Pitman, Ltd., 1913).

Kingsley, Charles and Coral Woodward, *Kingsley's Water-Babies, Arranged for Youngest Readers*, (Boston, MA: Educational Publishing Company, 1898).

Kingsley, Frances Eliza Grenfell (ed.), *Charles Kingsley, His Letters, ad Memories of His Life*, 2 vols. (New York: Charles Scribner's Sons, 1889).

Kipling, Rudyard, *The Jungle Books*, 1894 and 1895, ed. Daniel Karlin (London: Penguin Books, 1987).

The Jungle Play, ed. Thomas Pinney (London: The Penguin Press, 2000).

Just So Stories, 1902 (New York: Everyman's Library, 1992).

Kim, 1901 (New York: Everyman's Library, 1995).

Land and Sea Tales for Scouts and Scout Masters (Garden City, NJ: Doubleday, Page and Company, 1923).

Many Inventions, 1893 (New York: Doubleday, Page, and Company, 1914).

Something of Myself, and Other Autobiographical Writings, ed. Thomas Pinney (Cambridge: Cambridge University Press, 1990).

Stalky & Co., ed. Isabel Quigley, The Complete Stalky & Co. (Oxford: Oxford University Press, 1987).

Konigsburg, E. L., *From the Mixed-Up Files of Mrs. Basil E. Frankweiler* (New York: Simon & Schuster, 1967).

Konner, Melvin, *The Evolution of Childhood: Relationships, Emotion, Mind* (Cambridge, MA: The Belknap Press of Harvard University Press, 2010).

Kropotkin, Peter, *Mutual Aid: A Factor in Evolution*, 1902 (New York: McClure Phillips and Company, 1903).

Lamarck, Jean-Baptiste, *Zoological Philosophy: An Exposition with Regard to the Natural History of Animals*, 1809, trans. Hugh Elliot (London: Macmillan and Company, Ltd., 1914).

Lang, Andrew (ed.), *The Violet Fairy Book*, 1901 (New York: Dover Publications, 1966).

Lankester, E. Ray, *Degeneration: A Chapter in Darwinism* (London: Macmillan and Company, 1880).

Lear, Edward. *Nonsense Botany*, 1888 (Hyattsville, MD: Rebecca Press, 1983).

Lewis, C. S., *The Chronicles of Narnia*, 1950–1956 (New York: Harper Collins, 2004).

Locke, John, *An Essay Concerning Human Understanding*, 1689 (Oxford: Clarendon Press, 1975).

Some Thoughts Concerning Education, 1693 (Oxford: Clarendon Press, 1989).

London, Jack, *Before Adam*, 1907 (Lincoln, NE: University of Nebraska Press, 2000).

Loudon, Mrs. (Jane), *The Entertaining Naturalist; Being Popular Descriptions, Tales, and Anecdotes of More than Five Hundred Animals, Comprehending All the Quadrupeds, Birds, Fishes, Reptiles, Insects, &c. of Which a Knowledge is Indispensible to Polite Education*, 1849 (London: Henry G. Bohn, 1850).

Louv, Richard, *Last Child in the Woods: Saving Our Children from Nature-Deficit Disorder* (Chapel Hill, NC: Algonquin Books of Chapel Hill, 2006).

Low, Juliette, *How Girls Can Help Their Country, Adapted from Agnes Baden-Powell and Sir Robert Baden-Powell's Handbook* (Savannah, GA: M. S. & D. A. Byck, 1917).

Lyell, Charles, *Principles of Geology: Being an Attempt to Explain the Former Changes of the Earth's Surface, By Reference to Causes Now in Operation*, 3 vols., 1830–1833 (London: Penguin, 1997).

Mackarness, Mrs. Henry (ed.), *The Young Lady's Book: A Manual of Amusements, Exercises, Studies, and Pursuits* (London: George Routledge and Sons, 1876).

Maclure, J. Stuart (ed.), *Educational Documents: England & Wales 1816–1968*, 1969 (London: Methuen and Company, Ltd., 1972).

Mantell, Gideon, *The Wonders of Geology*, 2 vols. (London: Relfe and Fletcher, 1838).

Mason, Otis Tufton, *Woman's Share in Primitive Culture*, 1895 (New York: D. Appleton and Company, 1897).

Miller, Hugh, *The Foot-Prints of the Creator; or, The Asterolepis of Stromness*, 1849, 15th ed. (Boston, MA: Guild and Lincoln, 1873).

Nordau, Max, *Degeneration*, 1892 (Lincoln, NE: University of Nebraska Press, 1968).

O'Dell, Scott, *The Island of the Blue Dolphins* (Boston, MA: Houghton Mifflin Harcourt, 2010).

Owen, Richard, "The Gorilla and the Negro," *Athenaeum*, No. 1743 (March 23, 1861), 395–397.

"On the Characters, Principles of Division, and Primary Groups of the Class Mammalia," *Journal of the Proceedings of the Linnean Society of London*, 2:5 (June 1857), 1–37.

"On the Zoological Significance of the Brain and Limb Characteristics of the Gorilla, as Contrasted with Those of Man," *Medical Times and Gazette* (October 1862), 373–374.

Paley, William, *Natural Theology; or, Evidence of the Existence of Attributes of the Deity, Collected from the Appearances of Nature*, 1802 (Oxford: Oxford University Press, 2006).

Pullman, Philip, *His Dark Materials Trilogy: The Golden Compass, The Subtle Knife, and The Amber Spyglass*, 1995–2000 (New York: Laurel Leaf, 2003).

Reynolds, Minnie J., *How Man Conquered Nature*, 1914 (New York: The Macmillan Company, 1917).

Robinson, Louis, M.D., "Darwinism in the Nursery," *Eclectic Magazine of Foreign Literature, Science, and Art*, 54:6 (December 1891), 846–854.

Rossetti, Christina, *Speaking Likenesses* (London: Macmillan and Company, 1874).

Rousseau, Jean-Jacques, *Émile; or, On Education*, 1762 (London: Everyman, 1995).

Saleeby, Caleb Williams, *Parenthood and Race Culture: An Outline of Eugenics*, 1909 (New York: Moffat, Yard and Company, 1911),

Scieszka, Jon, *The Stinky Cheese Man, and Other Fairly Stupid Tales* (New York: Viking Juvenile, 1992).

Sendak, Maurice, *Where the Wild Things Are* (New York: Harper Collins, 1963).

Seton, Ernest Thompson, *The Gospel of the Redman: An Indian Bible*, 1936 (San Diego, CA: Book Tree, 2006).

Two Little Savages: Being the Adventures of Two Boys Who Lived as Indians and What They Learned, 1903 (New York: Grosset & Dunlap, 1911).

Wild Animals I Have Known (New York: Grosset & Dunlap, 1898).

Shinn, Milicent Washburn, *The Biography of a Baby* (Boston, MA: Houghton, Mifflin and Company, 1900).

Smith, Charlotte, *Conversations, Introducing Poetry: Chiefly on Subjects of Natural History for the Use of Children and Young Persons*, 1804 (London: T. Nelson & Sons, 1863), http://babel.hathitrust.org/cgi/pt?id=nyp.33433009360391; view=1up;seq=13.

Spencer, Herbert, *An Autobiography*, 2 vols. (London: Williams and Norgate, 1904).

Education: Intellectual, Moral, and Physical, 1860 (New York: D. Appleton and Company, 1896).

Illustrations of Universal Progress; A Series of Discussions, 1864 (New York: D. Appleton and Company, 1865).

"Psychology of the Sexes," *Popular Science Monthly*, 4 (1873): 30–38.

Spock, Benjamin and Michael B. Rothenberg, *Dr. Spock's Baby and Childcare*, 1946 (New York: Pocket Books, 1985).

Spurzheim, Johann Gaspar, *Education: Its Elementary Principles, Founded on the Nature of Man*, 12th American ed. (New York: Fowlers and Wells, 1847).

Starr, Frederick, *Some First Steps in Human Progress* (Cleveland, OH: Chatauqua Assembly, 1901).

Sully, James, *Studies of Childhood* (New York: D. Appleton, 1896).

Swiney, Frances, *The Awakening of Women; or, Woman's Part in Evolution* (London: George Redway, 1899).

Tatham, Julia Campbell, *The Secret of the Old Mansion* (Racine, WI: Western Publishing Company, 1948).

Torday, Piers, *The Last Wild* (New York: Viking Juvenile, 2013).

Trimmer, Sarah, *An Easy Introduction to the Knowledge of Nature, and Reading the Holy Scriptures. Adapted to the Capacities of Children*, 1780, 10th ed. (London: T. Longman and O. Rees, G.G. and J. Robinson, 1799).

Tylor, Edward Burnett, *Primitive Culture: Researches into the Development of Mythology, Philosophy, Religion, Art and Custom*, 2 vols. (London: John Murray, 1871).

Umphelby, Fanny, *The Child's Guide to Knowledge, Being a Collection of Useful and Familiar Questions and Answers on Every-Day Subjects, Adapted for Young Persons, and Arranged in the Most Simple and Easy Language. By a Lady*, 1825, 55th ed. (London: Simpkin Marshall, 1884).

U. S. Department of Education website: www.ed.gov/stem.

Wakefield, Priscilla, *Mental Improvement: or, The Beauties and Wonders of Nature and Art, Conveyed in a Series of Instructive Conversations*, 1794–1797 (East Lansing, MI: Colleagues Press, 1995).

Watts, Isaac, *Divine and Moral Songs for the Use of Children*, 1715 (London: John Van Vorst, 1848).

The Improvement of the Mind, 1837 (New York: Cosimo, Inc., 2007).

Webster, Jean, *Dear Enemy* (New York: Grosset & Dunlap, 1915).

Weismann, August, *Essays upon Heredity and Kindred Biological Problems*, 2 vols., 1889 (Oxford: Clarendon Press, 1892).

Weisner, David, *The Three Little Pigs* (New York: Clarion Books, 2001).

Westell, W. Percival, *Every Boy's Book of British Natural History*, with contributions by Sidney Newman Sedgwick and Sir John Lubbock (London: Royal Tract Society, 1906).

Wood, J. G., *The Boy's Own Book of Natural History*, 1861 (London: George Routledge and Sons, 1897).

Wordsworth, William, *William Wordsworth: The Major Works*, ed. Stephen Gill (Oxford: Oxford University Press, 1984).

The Prelude; or, The Growth of a Poet's Mind, 1805 (New York: D. Appleton and Company, 1850).

Secondary sources

Allen, Ann Taylor, "Children Between Public and Private Worlds: The Kindergarten and Public Policy in Germany, 1840-Present," in Roberta Wollons (ed.), *Kindergartens and Cultures: The Global Diffusion of an Idea* (New Haven, CT: Yale University Press, 2000), 16–41.

Armstrong, Nancy, *Desire and Domestic Fiction: A Political History of the Novel* (Oxford: Oxford University Press, 1987).

Avery, Gillian, "'Fairy Tales with a Purpose" and "Fairy Tales for Pleasure",' in Donald J. Gray (ed.), *Alice in Wonderland*, 1971, 2nd ed. (New York: W. W. Norton and Company, 1992).

Beatty, Barbara, "'The Letter Killeth': Americanization and Multicultural Education in Kindergartens in the United States, 1856–1920," in

Roberta Wollons (ed.), *Kindergartens and Cultures: The Global Diffusion of an Idea* (New Haven, CT: Yale University Press, 2000), 42–58.

Beckett, Sandra, "Parodic Play with Paintings in Picture Books," *Children's Literature*, 29 (2001), 175–195.

Bederman, Gail, *Manliness & Civilization: A Cultural History of Gender and Race in the United States, 1880–1917* (Chicago, IL: University of Chicago Press, 1995).

Beer, Gillian, *Darwin's Plots: Evolutionary Narrative in Darwin, George Eliot and Nineteenth-Century Fiction*, 1983 (Cambridge: Cambridge University Press, 2000).

Behlmer, George K., *Child Abuse and Moral Reform in England, 1870–1908* (Stanford, CA: Stanford University Press, 1982).

Bender, Bert, *Evolution and "the Sex Problem": American Narratives During the Eclipse of Darwinism* (Kent, OH: The Kent State University Press, 2004).

Benson, Stephen, "Kipling's Singing Voice: Setting the *Jungle Books*," *Critical Survey*, 13:3 (2001), 40–60.

Birchenough, Charles, *History of Elementary Education in England and Wales from 1800 to the Present Day*, 1914 (London: University Tutorial Press, 1938).

Birkin, Andrew, *J. M. Barrie & The Lost Boys: The Love Story that Gave Birth to Peter Pan* (New York: Clarkson N. Potter, Inc., 1979).

Bixler, Phyllis, "Gardens, Houses, and Nurturant Power in *The Secret Garden*," in James Holt McGavran (ed.), *Romanticism and Children's Literature in Nineteenth-Century England* (Athens, GA:University of Georgia Press, 1991), 208–224.

Black, Edwin, *War Against the Weak: Eugenics and America's Campaign to Create a Master Race* (New York: Four Walls Eight Windows, 2003).

Boas, George. *The Cult of Childhood* (Dallas, TX: Spring Publications, Inc., 1966).

Bowler, Peter J., *Biology and Social Thought: 1850–1914* (Berkeley, CA: Office for History of Science and Technology, University of California at Berkeley, 1993).

Evolution: The History of an Idea, 1983, 25th Anniversary ed. (Berkeley, CA: University of California Press, 2009).

Brock, William H., *Science for All: Studies in the History of Victorian Science and Education* (Aldershot: Ashgate Publishing Company, 1996).

Brognan, Hugh, *Mowgli's Sons: Kipling and Baden-Powell's Scouts* (London: Jonathan Cape, 1987).

Brooke, John and Geoffrey Cantor, *Reconstructing Nature: The Engagement of Science and Religion* (Oxford: Oxford University Press, 1998).

Brooke, John Hedley, *Science and Religion: Some Historical Perspectives* (Cambridge: Cambridge University Press, 1991).

Caesar, Terry, "I Quite Forget What – Say a Daffodily: Victorian Parody," *ELH*, 51:4 (1984), 795–818.

Cantor, Geoffrey, Gowan Dawson, Graeme Gooday, Richard Noakes, Sally Shuttleworth, and Jonathan R. Topham (eds.), *Science in the Nineteenth-Century Periodical: Reading the Magazine of Nature* (Cambridge: Cambridge University Press, 2004).

Carpenter, Humphrey, *Secret Gardens: The Golden Age of Children's Literature from Alice's Adventures in Wonderland to Winnie-the-Pooh* (Boston, MA: Houghton Mifflin Company, 1985).

Carrington, Charles, *Rudyard Kipling: His Life and His Work* (London: Macmillan, 1955).

Chamberlain, Edward J., and Sander Gilman (eds.), *Degeneration: The Dark Side of Progress* (New York: Columbia University Press, 1985).

Chauvet, Jean-Marie, Eliette Brunel Deschamps, and Christian Hillaire, *Dawn of Art: The Chauvet Cave, the Oldest Known Paintings in the World*, trans. Paul G. Bahn (New York: Harry N. Abrams, Inc., 1996).

Christ, Carol T., "The Victorian University and Our Own," *Journal of Victorian Culture*, 12:3 (2008): 287–294.

Cocks, Neil, "Hunting the Animal Boy," *The Yearbook of English Studies*, 32 (2002), 177–185.

Cohen, Morton N., *Lewis Carroll: A Biography* (New York: Alfred A. Knopf, 1995).

Cosslett, Tess, "Child's Place in Nature: Talking Animals in Victorian Children's Fiction," *Nineteenth-Century Contexts* 23:4 (2002), 475–495.

Talking Animals in British Children's Fiction, 1786–1914 (Aldershot: Ashgate, 2006).

Cuddy, Lois A. and Claire M. Roche (eds.), *Evolution and Eugenics in American Literature and Culture, 1880–1940: Essays on Ideological Conflict and Complicity* (Lewisburg, PA: Bucknell University Press, 2003).

Culler, A. Dwight, "The Darwinian Revolution and Literary Form," in George Levine and William Madden (eds.), *The Art of Victorian Prose* (Oxford: Oxford University Press, 1968), 224–246.

Cullingford, Benita, *British Chimney Sweeps: Five Centuries of Sweeping* (Chicago, IL: New Amsterdam, 2000).

Dane, Joseph A., *Parody: Critical Concepts Versus Literary Practices, Aristophanes to Stern* (Norman, OK: University of Oklahoma Press, 1988).

Darcy, Jane, "The Edwardian Child in the Garden: Childhood in the Fiction of Frances Hodgson Burnett," in Adrienne E. Gavin and Andrew Humphries (eds.), *Childhood and Edwardian Fiction: Worlds Enough and Time* (New York: Palgrave, 2009), 75–88.

Davidson, Cathy N., Paula Barker Duffy, and Martha Wagner Weinberg, "Why STEM Is Not Enough (and We Still Need the Humanities)," on Valerie Strauss, *The Answer Sheet* on *The Washington Post* (March 5, 2012): www .washingtonpost.com/blogs/answer-sheet/post/why-stem-is-not-enough-and-we-still-need-the-humanities/2012/03/04/gIQAniScr_blog.html.

Davies, Máire Messenger, "'A Bit of Earth': Sexuality and the Representation of Childhood in Text and Screen Versions of *The Secret Garden*," *The Velvet Light Trap*, 48 (2001): 48–58.

Dawson, Gowan, *Darwin, Literature and Victorian Respectability* (Cambridge: Cambridge University Press, 2007).

Desmond, Adrian, *Archetypes and Ancestors: Paleontology in Victorian London, 1850–1875* (Chicago, IL: University of Chicago Press, 1982).

The Politics of Evolution: Morphology, Medicine, and Reform in Radical London (Chicago, IL: University of Chicago Press, 1989).

Dewitt, Anne, *Moral Authority, Men of Science, and the Victorian Novel* (Cambridge: Cambridge University Press, 2013).

Dobrin, Sidney I. and Kenneth B. Kidd (eds.), *Wild Things: Children's Culture and Ecocriticism* (Detroit, MI: Wayne State University Press, 2004).

Eliot, T. S., *A Choice of Kipling's Verse*, 1941 (London: Faber & Faber, 1963).

Empson, William, *Some Versions of Pastoral* (New York: New Directions, 1935).

Foote, George A., "*The Place of Science in the British Reform Movement, 1830–1850*," *Isis*, 42 (1951), 92–208.

Francis, Daniel, *The Imaginary Indian: The Image of the Indian in Canadian Culture* (Vancouver: Arsenal Pulp Press, 1992).

Frew, Lee, "Settler Nationalism and the Foreign," *University of Toronto Quarterly*, 82:2 (January 2013), 278–297.

Fyfe, Aileen and Bernard Lightman (eds.), *Science in the Marketplace: Nineteenth-Century Sites and Experiences* (Chicago, IL: University of Chicago Press, 2007).

Gates, Barbara T., *Kindred Nature: Victorian and Edwardian Women Embrace the Living World* (Chicago, IL: University of Chicago Press, 1998).

Gates, Barbara T. and Anne Shteir (eds.), *Natural Eloquence: Women Reinscribe Science* (Madison, WI: University of Wisconsin Press, 1997).

Gavin, Adrienne E. and Andrew Humphries (eds.), *Childhood and Edwardian Fiction: Worlds Enough and Time* (New York: Palgrave, 2009).

Gerzina, Gretchen, *Frances Hodgson Burnett: The Unexpected Life of the Author of The Secret Garden* (New Brunswick, NJ: Rutgers University Press, 2004).

Gloriosus, Miles, Review of "Charles Kingsley: *The Water-Babies*," *School and Home Education*, 36:3 (November 1916), 78.

Goldthwaite, John, *The Natural History of Make-Believe: A Guide to the Principal Works of Britain, Europe, and America* (New York: Oxford University Press, 1996).

Gosden, P. H. J. H., *How They Were Taught: An Anthology of Contemporary Accounts of Learning and Teaching in England, 1800–1950* (Oxford: Basil Blackwell, 1969).

Gould, Stephen J., *Ontogeny and Phylogeny* (Cambridge, MA: The Belknap Press of Harvard University Press, 1977).

Green, Roger Lancelyn, *Kipling and the Children* (London: Elek Books Ltd., 1965).

Gubar, Marah, *Artful Dodgers: Reconceiving the Golden Age of Children's Literature* (Oxford: Oxford University Press, 2009).

Haley, Bruce, *The Healthy Body and Victorian Culture* (Cambridge, MA: Harvard University Press, 1977).

Hines, Maude, "'He Made *Us* Very Much Like the Flowers': Human/Nature in Nineteenth-Century Anglo-American Children's Literature," in Sidney I. Dobrin and Kenneth B. Kidd (eds.), *Wild Things: Children's Culture and Ecocriticism* (Detroit, MI: Wayne State University Press, 2004), 16–30.

History of Education Society (ed.), *Studies in the Government and Control of Education since 1860* (London: Methuen, 1970).

Hollinger, David A., "The Wedge Driving Academe's Two Families Apart: Can STEM and the Human Sciences Get Along?," *The Chronicle of Higher Education* (October 14, 2013): http://chronicle.com/article/Why-Cant-the-Sciencesthe/142239/.

Hopkins, Lisa, "Jack London's Evolutionary Hierarchies: Dogs, Wolves, and Men," in Lois A. Cuddy and Claire M. Roche (eds.), *Evolution and Eugenics in American Literature and Culture, 1880–1940: Essays on Ideological Conflict and Complicity* (Lewisburg, PA: Bucknell University Press, 2003), 89–101.

Hotchkiss, Jane, "The Jungle Eden: Kipling, Wolf Boys, and the Colonial Imagination," *Victorian Literature and Culture*, 29:2 (2001), 435–449.

Howsam, Leslie, Christopher Stray, Alice Jenkins, James A. Secord, and Anna Vaniskaya, "What Victorians Learned: Perspectives on Victorian Schoolbooks," *Journal of Victorian Culture*, 12:2 (Autumn 2007), 262–285.

Hubbard, Ruth, *The Politics of Women's Biology*, 1990 (New Brunswick, NJ: Rutgers University Press, 1997).

Hurt, J. S., *Elementary Schooling and the Working Classes, 1860–1918* (London: Routledge & Kegan Paul, 1979).

Hutcheon, Linda, *A Theory of Parody: The Teaching of Twentieth-Century Art Forms* (New York: Methuen, 1985).

Jack, R. D. S., "*Peter Pan* as Darwinian Creation Myth," *Literature and Theology*, 8:2 (June 1994), 157–173.

Jann, Rosemary, "Revising the Descent of Woman: Eliza Burt Gamble," in Barbara T. Gates and Anne B. Shteir (eds.), *Natural Eloquence: Woman Reinscribe Science* (Madison, WI: University of Wisconsin Press, 1997), 147–163.

Jenkins, Ruth Y., "Frances Hodgson Burnett's *The Secret Garden*: Engendering Abjection's Sublime," *Children's Literature Association Quarterly*, 36:4 (Winter 2011), 426–444.

Jones, Donald K., *The Making of the Education System, 1851–81* (London: Routledge & Keegan Paul, 1977).

Katz, Wendy, *The Emblems of Margaret Gatty* (New York: AMS Press, 1993).

Kearney, Anthony, "Matthew Arnold and Herbert Spencer: A Neglected Connection in the Victorian Debate About Scientific and Literary Education," *Nineteenth-Century Prose* (March 22, 2001); reprinted and available via *The Free Library* www.thefreelibrary.com/Matthew+Arnold+and+Herbert+Spencer%3a+a+neglected+connection+in+the. . .-a0188997974.

Keating, Peter, *Kipling, the Poet* (London: Secker and Warburg, 1994).

Kidd, Kenneth B., *Making American Boys: Boyology and the Feral Tale* (Minneapolis, MN: University of Minnesota Press, 2004).

Kincaid, James R., *Child-Loving: The Erotic Child and Victorian Culture* (New York: Routledge, 1992).

King, Amy M., *Bloom: The Botanical Vernacular in the English Novel* (Oxford: Oxford University Press, 2007).

Knoepflmacher, U. C., "The Balancing of Child and Adult: An Approach to Victorian Fantasies for Children," *Nineteenth-Century Fiction*, 37:4 (1983), 497–530.

Ventures into Childland: Victorians, Fairy Tales, and Femininity (Chicago, IL: University of Chicago Press, 1998).

Knoepflmacher, U. C. and G. B. Tennyson (eds.), *Nature and the Victorian Imagination*, (Berkeley, CA: University of California Press, 1977).

LaCapra, Dominick (ed.), *The Bounds of Race: Perspectives on Hegemony and Resistance* (Ithaca, NY: Cornell University Press, 1991).

Larson, Edward J., *Evolution: The Remarkable History of a Scientific Theory* (New York: Modern Library, 2004).

Layton, David, *Science for the People: The Origins of the School Science Curriculum in England* (New York: George Allen & Unwin Ltd., 1973).

Leavis, Q. D., "*The Water Babies*," *Children's Literature in Education*, 23 (1976), 155–163.

Lerer, Seth, *Children's Literature: A Reader's History from Aesop to Harry Potter* (Chicago, IL: University of Chicago Press, 2009).

Levine, George and William Madden (eds.), *The Art of Victorian Prose* (Oxford: Oxford University Press, 1968).

Darwin and the Novelists: Patterns of Science in Victorian Fiction (Cambridge, MA: Harvard University Press, 1988).

Lewis-Williams, David, *The Mind in the Cave: Consciousness and the Origins of Art* (London: Thames & Hudson, 2002).

Lightman, Bernard, *Victorian Popularizers of Science: Designing Nature for New Audiences* (Chicago, IL: University of Chicago Press, 2007).

"'The Voices of Nature': Popularizing Victorian Science," in Bernard Lightman (ed.), *Victorian Science in Context* (Chicago, IL: University of Chicago Press, 1997), 187–211.

Lightman, Bernard (ed.), *Victorian Science in Context* (Chicago, IL: University of Chicago Press, 1997).

Lightman, Bernard and Bennett Zon (eds.), *Evolution and Victorian Culture* (Cambridge: Cambridge University Press, 2014).

Lovell-Smith, Rose, "The Animals of Wonderland: Tenniel as Carroll's Reader," *Criticism*, 45:4 (2003), 383–415.

"Eggs and Serpents: Natural History Reference in Lewis Carroll's Scene of Alice and the Pigeon," *Children's Literature*, 35 (2007), 27–53.

"'The Walrus and the Carpenter': Lewis Carroll. Margaret Gatty, and Natural History for Children," *Australasian Victorian Studies Journal*, 10 (2004), 43–69.

MacDonald, Robert H., *Sons of the Empire: The Frontier and the Boy Scout Movement, 1890–1918* (Toronto: University of Toronto Press, 1993).

MacDuffie, Allen, "*The Jungle Books*: Rudyard Kipling's Lamarckian Fantasy," *PMLA*, 129:1 (2014), 18–34.

Maier, Thomas, *Dr. Spock: An American Life* (New York: Basic Books, 2003).

Martin, Jane, *Women and the Politics of Schooling in Victorian and Edwardian England* (London: Leicester University Press, 1999).

Martindell, E. W., *A Bibliography of the Works of Rudyard Kipling* (London: The Bookman's Journal, 1922).

Maxwell, Christabel, *Mrs. Gatty and Mrs. Ewing* (London: Constable, 1949).

McGavran, James Holt (ed.), *Romanticism and Children's Literature in Nineteenth-Century England* (Athens, GA: University of Georgia Press, 1991).

Miller, Susan, *Growing Girls: The Natural Origins of Girls' Organizations in America* (New Brunswick, NJ: Rutgers University Press, 2007).

Mitchell, Sally, *The New Girl: Girls' Culture in England, 1880–1915* (New York: Columbia University Press, 1995).

Mohanty, Satya P., "Drawing the Color Line: Kipling and the Culture of Colonial Rule," in Dominick LaCapra (ed.), *The Bounds of Race: Perspectives on Hegemony and Resistance* (Ithaca, NY: Cornell University Press, 1991), 311–343.

Morgan, Monique, *Narrative Means, Lyric Ends: Temporality in the Nineteenth-Century British Long Poem* (Columbus, OH: The Ohio State University Press, 2009).

Morris, Norman, "State Paternalism and Laissez-Faire in the 1860s," in The History of Education Society (ed.), *Studies in the Government and Control of Education since 1860* (London: Methuen, 1970), 13–26.

Morse, Deborah Denenholz and Martin A. Danahay (eds.), *Victorian Animals Dreams: Representations of Animals in Victorian Literature and Culture* (Surrey: Ashgate Publishing Limited, 2007).

Myers, Greg, "Science for Women and Children: The Dialogue of Popular Science in the Nineteenth Century" in John Christie and Sally Shuttleworth (eds.), *Nature Transfigured: Literature and Science, 1700–1900* (Manchester: Manchester University Press, 1989), 171–200.

Nelson, Claudia, *Boys Will Be Girls: The Feminine Ethic and British Children's Fiction, 1857–1917* (New Brunswick, NJ: Rutgers University Press, 1991).

Olby, R. C., G. N. Cantor, J. R. R. Christie, and M. J. S. Hodge, *Companion to the History of Modern Science* (London: Routledge, 1990), 946–959. Excerpted in William H. Brock, *Science for All: Studies in the History of Victorian Science and Education* (Aldershot: Ashgate Publishing Company, 1996), X.

Ospovat, Dov, *The Development of Darwin's Theory: Natural History, Natural Theology, and Natural Selection, 1838–1859* (Cambridge: Cambridge University Press, 1981).

Padley, Jonathan, "Marginal(ized) Demarcator: (Mis)Reading *The Water-Babies*," *Children's Literature Association Quarterly*, 34:1 (Spring 2009), 51–64.

Paris, Leslie, *Children's Nature: The Rise of the American Summer Camp* (New York: New York University Press, 2008).

Patterson, William, *Robert Heinlein: In Dialogue with His Century*, 2 vols. (New York: Tor Books, 2010).

Phillips, Jerry, "The Mem, Sahib, the Worthy, the Rajah, and His Minions: Some Reflections on the Class Politics of *The Secret Garden*," *The Lion and the Unicorn*, 17 (1993), 168–194.

Pick, Daniel, *Faces of Degeneration: A European Disorder, 1848–1918* (Cambridge: Cambridge University Press, 1989).

Polhemus, Robert, *Comic Faith: The Great Tradition from Austen to Joyce* (Chicago, IL: University of Chicago Press, 1980).

Price, Danielle E., "Cultivating Mary: The Victorian Secret Garden," *Children's Literature Association Quarterly*, 26:1 (2001), 4–14.

Rackin, Donald, *Alice's Adventures in Wonderland and Through the Looking-Glass: Nonsense, Sense, and Meaning* (New York: Twayne Publishers, 1991).

Randall, Don, *Kipling's Imperial Boy: Adolescence and Cultural Hybridity* (New York: Palgrave, 2000).

Rauch, Alan, "Parables and Parodies: Margaret Gatty's Audiences in the *Parables from Nature*," *Children's Literature*, 25 (1997), 137–152.

"The Sins of Sloths: The Moral Status of Fossil Megatheria in Victorian Culture," in Deborah Denenholz Morse and Martin A. Danahay (eds.), *Victorian Animals Dreams: Representations of Animals in Victorian Literature and Culture* (Surrey: Ashgate Publishing Limited, 2007), 215–228.

Useful Knowledge: The Victorians, Morality, and the March of Intellect (Durham, NC: Duke University Press, 2001).

Richards, Grace, "Oh, the Humanities! Why Stem Shouldn't Take Precedence over the Humanities," 2014, Arizona State University Project Humanities website: https://humanities.asu.edu/oh-humanities-why-stem-shouldnt-take-precedence-over-arts.

Richards, Robert J., *The Meaning of Evolution: The Morphological Construction and Ideological Reconstruction of Darwin's Theory* (Chicago, IL: University of Chicago Press, 1992).

Richardson, Alan, *Literature, Education, and Romanticism: Reading as Social Practice 1780–1832* (Cambridge: Cambridge University Press, 1994).

Richardson, Angelique, *Love and Eugenics in the Late Nineteenth Century* (Oxford: Oxford University Press, 2003).

Ritvo, Harriet, *The Animal Estate: The English and Other Creatures in the Victorian Age* (Cambridge, MA: Harvard University Press, 1987).

Ritvo, Lucille, *Darwin's Influence on Freud: A Tale of Two Sciences* (New Haven, CT: Yale University Press, 1990).

Romero, Lora, *Home Fronts: Domesticity and Its Critics in the Antebellum United States* (Durham, NC: Duke University Press, 1997).

Rose, Jacqueline, *The Case of Peter Pan; or, The Impossibility of Children's Fiction*, 1984 (Philadelphia, PA: University of Pennsylvania Press, 1993).

Rothbard, Murray N., *Education: Free and Compulsory* (Auburn, AL: The Ludwig von Mises Institute, 1999).

Rudwick, Martin J. S. *Georges Cuvier, Fossil Bones, and Geological Catastrophes: New Translations & Interpretations of the Primary Texts* (Chicago, IL: University of Chicago Press, 2008).

Ruse, Michael, *Monad to Man: The Concept of Progress in Evolutionary Biology* (Cambridge, MA: Harvard University Press, 1996).

Savory, Jerold and Patricia Marks (eds.), *The Smiling Muse: Victoriana in the Comic Press* (Cranbury, NJ: Associated University Press, 1985).

Schmitt, Cannon, *Darwin and the Memory of the Human* (Cambridge: Cambridge University Press, 2009).

"Evolution and Victorian Fiction," in Bernard Lightman and Bennett Zon (eds.), *Evolution and Victorian Culture* (Cambridge: Cambridge University Press, 2014), 17–38.

Schwartz, Nancy Lacey, "The Dodo and the Caucus Race," *Jabberwocky*, 6:1 (Winter 1977): 3–15.

Secord, James A., *Victorian Sensation: The Extraordinary Publication, Reception, and Secret Authorship of Vestiges of the Natural History of Creation* (Chicago, IL: University of Chicago Press, 2000).

Seeley, Levi, *Elementary Pedagogy* (New York: Hinds, Noble & Eldredge, 1906).

Seitler, Dana, *Atavistic Tendencies: The Culture of Science in American Modernity* (Minneapolis, MN: University of Minnesota Press, 2008).

Sheffield, Suzanne Le-May, *Revealing New Worlds: Three Victorian Women Naturalists* (London: Routledge, 2001).

Shuttleworth, Sally, *The Mind of the Child: Child Development in Literature, Science, and Medicine, 1840–1900* (Oxford: Oxford University Press, 2010).

Sigler, Carolyn (ed.), *Alternative Alices: Visions and Revisions of Lewis Carroll's Alice Books* (Lexington, KY: University of Kentucky Press, 1997).

Smelser, Neil J., *Social Change and Social Paralysis: British Working-Class Education in the Nineteenth Century* (Berkeley, CA: University of California Press, 1991).

Smith, Paul, "Move Over, Stem: Why the World Needs Humanities Graduates," *The Guardian* (March 19, 2014): www.theguardian.com/higher-education-network/blog/2014/mar/19/humanities-universities-global-stem.

Stanley, Arthur Penryn, *The Life and Correspondence of Thomas Arnold, D.D.*, 2 vols. (London: B. Fellowes, 1844).

Stewart, Susan, *nonsense: Aspects of Intertextuality in Folklore and Literature* (Baltimore, MD: The Johns Hopkins University Press, 1979).

Stockton, Kathryn Bond, *The Queer Child; or Growing Sideways in the Twentieth Century* (Durham, NC: Duke University Press, 2009).

Straley, Jessica, "Of Beasts and Boys: Kingsley, Spencer, and the Theory of Recapitulation," *Victorian Studies*, 49:4 (Summer 2007), 583–609.

Sullivan, Zohreh T., *Narratives of Empire: The Fictions of Rudyard Kipling* (Cambridge: Cambridge University Press, 1993).

Sulloway, Frank, *Freud: Biologist of the Mind* (New York: Basic Books, 1983).

Sumpter, Caroline, *The Victorian Press and the Fairy Tale* (Basingstoke: Palgrave, 2008).

Super, R. H., "The Humanist at Bay: The Arnold-Huxley Debate," in U. C. Knoepflmacher and G. B. Tennyson (eds.), *Nature and the Victorian Imagination* (Berkeley, CA: University of California Press, 1977), 231–245.

Thwaite, Ann, *Waiting for the Party: The Life of Frances Hodgson Burnett, 1849–1924* (London: Faber, 1994).

Tigges, Wim (ed.), *Explorations in the Field of Nonsense* (Amsterdam: Rodopi, 1987).

Walker, Nancy E., Catherine M. Brooks, and Lawrence S. Wrightsman, *Children's Rights in the United States: In Search of a National Policy* (Thousand Oaks, CA: Sage Publications, Inc., 1999).

Walsh, Sue, *Kipling's Children's Literature: Language, Identity, and Constructions of Childhood* (Aldershot: Ashgate, 2010).

Wollons, Roberta (ed.), *Kindergartens and Cultures: The Global Diffusion of an Idea* (New Haven, CT: Yale University Press, 2000).

Wood, Naomi, "A (Sea) Green Victorian: Charles Kingsley and *The Water-Babies*," *The Lion and the Unicorn*, 19:2 (December 1995), 233–252.

Zon, Bennett, "The 'Non-Darwinian' Revolution and the Great Chain of Musical Being," in Bernard Lightman and Bennett Zon (eds.), *Evolution and Victorian Culture* (Cambridge: Cambridge University Press, 2014), 196–226.

Index

CAMBRIDGE STUDIES IN NINETEENTH-CENTURY
LITERATURE AND CULTURE

GENERAL EDITOR: Gillian Beer, *University of Cambridge*

Titles published

CPSIA information can be obtained
at www.ICGtesting.com
Printed in the USA
LVHW031110170320
650297LV00009B/279